PERFORMING FILIAL PIETY
IN NORTHERN SONG CHINA

PERFORMING FILIAL PIETY IN NORTHERN SONG CHINA

Family, State, and Native Place

Cong Ellen Zhang

University of Hawai'i Press
Honolulu

25   24   23   22   21   20   6   5   4   3   2   1

Library of Congress Cataloging-in-Publication Data

Names: Zhang, Cong, author.
Title: Performing filial piety in Northern Song China : family, state, and
   native place / Cong Ellen Zhang.
Description: Honolulu : University of Hawai'i Press, 2020. | Includes
   bibliographical references and index.
Identifiers: LCCN 2020022814 | ISBN 9780824882754 (cloth) | ISBN
   9780824884406 (pdf) | ISBN 9780824884413 (epub) | ISBN 9780824884420
   (kindle edition)
Subjects: LCSH: Filial piety—China—History—To 1500. |
   Intellectuals—China—History—To 1500. | China—Intellectual
   life—960-1644.
Classification: LCC BJ1533.F5 Z4345 2020 | DDC 299.5/114—dc23
LC record available at https://lccn.loc.gov/2020022814

Cover art: Houma Tomb No. 1 (tomb of Dong Qijian, dated 1210), Houma, Shanxi Province. Photograph by Jeehee Hong.

Contents

ACKNOWLEDGMENTS

While writing and conducting research for my first book on Song (960–1279) travel culture, several large questions lingered in the back of my mind. If the Song literati traveled so extensively and frequently, how did they maintain meaningful connections with their parents, wives, and children at a time when transportation and communication were slow and not always reliable? In what ways did these men's lengthy absences from their homes and native regions affect their abilities to manage crucial familial duties and routine household matters? Did the tension between these men's public pursuits and domestic obligations lead to new ideals about family life and people-place relationships? There are obviously different ways to approach these questions. This study of the changing rhetoric and performance of filial piety in the Northern Song period (960–1127) represents one attempt.

Over the course of this monograph's ten-year evolution, many individuals helped shape it into its current form. Patricia Ebrey, Beverly Bossler, Jim Hargett, and Ari Levine read the entire manuscript at its different stages. All of them responded with many pages of extremely insightful and constructive feedback and guided me to think more broadly and critically, sharpen my arguments, and write more clearly. I am profoundly grateful for their numerous queries, observations, and suggestions, which have helped improve the quality of this book.

In the past several years, I have presented the material in this book on many occasions and would like to express my genuine appreciation of the valuable comments and questions from the discussants, fellow panelists, and those in the audiences, whose names are too many to be included here. I especially would like to thank Valerie Hansen at Yale University, Zhang Ying at Ohio State University, and Liu Chen at the National University of Singapore for giving me the opportunity to present my work on their campuses and have fruitful exchanges with them and their colleagues and students. The contributors at the two workshops that I (co-)organized, at Peking University (PKU, 2011) and the University of Virginia (2013) respectively, likewise engaged in robust discussion about the various aspects of filial piety in imperial China, providing a rich context for this study. As the notes and bibliography of the book show, I am indebted to all of them and those who were not at the workshops but have written on the topic.

Many friends have continued to offer emotional support that remains crucial to the long journey of writing a book. I especially would like to thank Anne Kinney, Lu Weijing, Helen Schneider, Kim Wishart, and Yao Ping for bearing with me during many long hours of conversation on my struggles with the project. Kim has been my most reliable editor and has helped make this book more readable than I alone ever could.

This project was also made possible by generous financial support from the University of Virginia (UVA) in the form of summer research support, travel subsidies, publication grants, and workshop sponsorship. For these important contributions, I thank the Provost Office, the College and Graduate School of Arts and Sciences, and the East Asia Center. The Hong Kong University of Science and Technology and the Buckner W. Clay Awards in the Humanities at UVA deserve special thanks for allocating funds for the PKU and UVA workshops on filial piety.

I am indebted to my editor, Stephanie Chun, and her team at the University of Hawai'i Press, for being most helpful in guiding me every step of the way in turning the manuscript into a book. My copy editor, Bojana Ristich, has done a meticulous job. Her comments, suggestions, and corrections were indispensable in polishing the manuscript and bringing it to press. Jeehee Hong of McGill University generously gave me permission to use a photograph of hers as the cover image for the book. Thank you very much, Jeehee!

Over the past several years, what began as a personal research interest grew into a family project. I thank my husband, Baowen, and son, Max, not only for their willingness to listen to all the filial piety–related stories but also their genuine interest in any progress that I made. Researching and writing this book coincided with my parents and in-laws' advancing age. Living far away from them and only being able to visit once or twice a year, we as a family have pondered the meanings and proper performance of filial piety countless times. Most important, our absence from our parents' sides has made us increasingly appreciative of our sisters and brothers-in-law, the devoted parental caregivers. This book is dedicated to them.

NOTES ON CONVENTIONS

Romanization

I have adopted *pinyin* romanization of Chinese terms throughout the book. For the sake of consistency, I have modified direct quotations from English-language sources whose authors used the Wade-Giles system into the *pinyin* system.

Place Names

I use Song place names in the text, with their modern equivalents provided in parentheses. When a place's Northern Song and modern names remain the same, I include in the parenthesis only the name of the province, as in Kaifeng (in Henan).

Title of Offices

As a rule, I use the translations of office titles given in Charles Hucker, *A Dictionary of Official Titles in Imperial China* (1985).

Measures

1 *li* = 1,800 *chi* = 0.56 kilometer = 0.35 mile

Northern Song Emperors and Their Reign Titles

Taizu 太祖, r. 960–976

Jianlong 建隆	960–963
Qiande 乾德	963–968
Kaibao 開寶	968–976

Taizong 太宗, r. 976–997

Taiping xingguo 太平興國	976–984
Yongxi 雍熙	984–987
Duangong 端拱	988–989
Chunhua 淳化	990–994
Zhidao 至道	995–997

Zhenzong 真宗, r. 997–1022

Xianping 咸平	998–1003
Jingde 景德	1004–1007
Dazhong xiangfu 大中祥符	1008–1016
Tianxi 天禧	1017–1021
Qianxing 乾興	1022

Renzong 仁宗, r. 1022–1063

Tiansheng 天聖	1023–1032
Mingdao 明道	1032–1033
Jingyou 景佑	1034–1038
Baoyuan 寶元	1038–1040
Kangding 康定	1040–1041
Qingli 慶歷	1041–1048
Huangyou 皇祐	1049–1054

| Zhihe 至和 | 1054–1056 |
| Jiayou 嘉祐 | 1056–1063 |

Yingzong 英宗, r. 1063–1067

| Zhiping 治平 | 1064–1067 |

Shenzong 神宗, r. 1067–1085

| Xining 熙寧 | 1068–1077 |
| Yuanfeng 元豐 | 1078–1085 |

Zhezong 哲宗, r. 1085–1100

Yuanyou 元祐	1086–1094
Shaosheng 紹聖	1094–1098
Yuanfu 元符	1098–1100

Huizong 徽宗, r. 1100–1025

Jianzhong jingguo 建中靖國	1101–1101
Chongning 崇寧	1102–1106
Daguan 大觀	1107–1110
Zhenghe 政和	1111–1118
Chonghe 重和	1118–1119
Xuanhe 宣和	1119–1125

Qinzong 欽宗, r. 1125–1127

| Jingkang 靖康 | 1126–1127 |

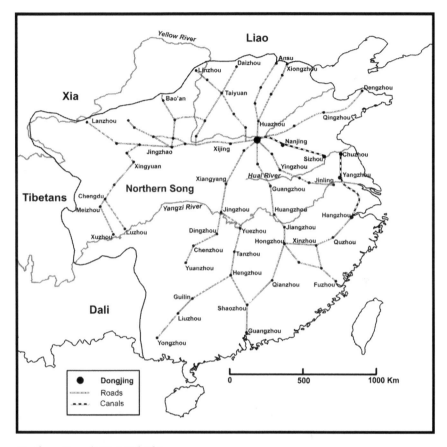

Northern Song (960–1127) China

Introduction

Wang Yi (994–1039), father of the renowned Northern Song (960–1127) scholar and statesman Wang Anshi (1021–1086), earned the *jinshi* degree in 1016 and served multiple official positions in five modern provinces.[1] When relocating to these posts, he would bring his parents along in order to practice reverent care (*xiaoyang*).[2] There was one exception to this common practice: Wang's parents did not join him at Xinfan (in Sichuan) due to a government policy that prohibited family members from accompanying civil servants to remote destinations. Living apart from his parents took a heavy emotional toll on Wang. While in Xinfan, he missed his parents so much that he often wept despondently and rarely partied with colleagues.

Wang Yi mourned the loss of his father in the mid-1030s before assuming his last position in Jiangning (Nanjing, Jiangsu), where he died in 1039. His wife, Miss Wu (998–1063), and their seven sons diligently observed the three-year mourning rites.[3] All became emaciated from nonstop wailing, coarse food, and longing for their loved one. In a long poem, "Remembering the Past," Wang Anshi recollected:

> One day, Heaven sent down a disaster,
> With my father dead, on whom would I rely?
> My spirit wandered aimlessly; my body was distressed,
> With a face covered in bloody tears, I sighed nonstop.
> Mother and older brothers wailed loudly while keeping each other's
>   company.
> After three years, we grew tired of eating common vetch at Zhongshan.[4]

After completing their mourning duties, Wang Anshi and his brothers concentrated on preparing for the civil service examinations. Wang Yi's burial was subsequently put on hold. When he was finally laid to rest in 1048, nine years after his death, Wang Yi was entombed in Jiangning, not in the family's ancestral graveyard in their native place of Linchuan (in Jiangxi).

This new burial ground established Jiangning as the Wangs' new home base, where Miss Wu lived and her sons returned to visit. Sometime in the 1050s, Wang Anshi moved his mother to the capital city in Dongjing (Kaifeng, Henan), where he was posted. When Miss Wu passed away in 1063, Wang Anshi immediately had her body transported back to Jiangning for burial. Thorough arrangements had apparently been made well in advance. Despite the long-distance travel from Kaifeng to Jiangning (about 1,200 *li* or 400 miles), Miss Wu was laid to rest within two months of her death, unusually speedy by contemporary standards and a large contrast to the way Wang Yi's posthumous affairs had been handled.

Wang Anshi continued to wear mourning in Jiangning after his mother's burial. An anecdote related that due to bereavement and his sleeping on straw for a lengthy period, he became so feeble and skinny that his bones stood out. This, in combination with the sackcloth garments that he wore, made him look like an old servant.[5] Wang Anshi's two remaining brothers exhibited similar filial sentiments. Wang Anli (1034–1095) especially stood out for practicing *lumu*, living in a thatched hut, next to Miss Wu's tomb, and praying for his mother's spirit by copying Buddhist sutras using his own blood.[6]

The above account, brief as it is, offers an alternative chronicle of the life of two generations of the Wang family. Instead of elaborating on their official careers, scholarly achievements, and social and cultural activities, this narrative concentrates on the way the Wang men fulfilled their most sacred domestic duties: filial obligations to parents.[7] For performing parental care with dedication, mourning the loss of their parents with sincerity, and managing their posthumous affairs according to ritual stipulations, both Wang Yi and his sons were labeled filial by their funerary biographers and other contemporary sources.

In becoming the filial children that they were, the Wang men had to juggle their family obligations and career pursuits. In order to perform reverent care, Wang Yi subjected his parents to long journeys and extended absences from the comfort of their own home. Similarly, Wang Anshi's and his brothers' scholarly and bureaucratic interests were directly responsible for, among other things, the long delay in Wang Yi's entombment. In fact, it was due only to imperial generosity that Wang Anshi was granted a short leave to manage his father's burial. After Wang Yi was interred, Wang Anshi passed by Jiangning occasionally and was posted there twice, but between 1042, when he earned the *jinshi* degree, and the mid-1050s, when he relocated his mother to the capital, he was mainly preoccupied with his official responsibilities and was unable to perform any substantial parental care for Miss Wu.

The tension between public service and domestic duties impacted the Wangs in other ways as well. After mourning his father, Wang Yi left his widowed mother, Miss Xie (964–1053), in Linchuan when assuming his appointment in Jiangning. Even though such a decision might very well have been Miss Xie's wish, it meant that Wang Yi was not involved in the care of his mother in the last years of his life before his sudden death far away from her. The same can be said about Wang Yi's wife. Despite being praised for "acting extremely filial toward her parents-in-law throughout her life," Miss Wu was absent from her mother-in-law's side for many years, nor did she attend Miss Xie's funeral. Both were serious unfilial acts. For Wang Anshi and his brothers, Wang Yi's early death meant that their mother became the sole object of their filial devotion. As far as we can tell, Miss Wu lived in Jiangning for at least a decade and a half as a widow, presumably being cared for by her non-office-holding sons, before being relocated to the capital. While Wang Anshi and his brothers were praised for satisfying Miss Wu's material needs and devoting themselves to her happiness, this arrangement makes us wonder about the actual allocation of filial duties among the Wang men. Seen from a different perspective, with multiple sons actively pursuing civil service careers and living apart from each other, Miss Wu was separated from most of them no matter where and with whom she lived.

The complexities in fulfilling one's familial obligations also had significant consequences for the Wang family in geographical terms. When Wang Yi died in his office, the family might very well have considered transporting his body back to Linchuan. In the end, his sons' preoccupation with government service, their lack of close connections with their native place, and Jiangning's prime location made a new graveyard there a more expedient and attractive choice. This decision complicated the meaning and performance of filial piety for the Wangs in two important ways. First, Wang Yi married twice and had two sons with his first wife, Miss Xu, who died young and was most likely entombed in Linchuan. The family's perennial absenteeism from Linchuan means that Miss Xu's sons, raised by Miss Wu, never performed any graveside sacrifices to their biological mother. Second, Wang Yi's burial in Jiangning marked a permanent segmentation of his branch from the Wangs' home region and ancestral graveyard, signifying the extent to which physical mobility shaped the lives of the Wang men and women, in both life and death. Throughout his adult life, Wang Anshi visited Linchuan only twice. Both trips were undertaken early in his career as detours from official assignments to the southeast. It was to more conveniently located Jiangning that he grew attached. Wang Anshi spent the last years of his life in Jiangning and was buried there.

Did Wang Anshi and his brothers ever consider their settlement in Jiangning an unfilial act? How clean was their "break" from the ancestral home? Evidence shows that despite their physical absence, the Wang men continued to identify themselves as natives of Linchuan and maintained connections with it through personal correspondence and friendship with clan members and Jiangxi natives. Wang Anshi, for example, became known as Wang Linchuan during his lifetime, and his collected work was entitled *Linchuan ji* (the Collected Works of [Wang] Linchuan). He, his brother, Wang Anguo (1028–1074), and son, Wang Pang (1044–1076), were labeled the "Three Wangs of Linchuan." Most important, because of the prestige that Wang Anshi had brought his clan and native place, he and his descendants remained distinguished members of the Linchuan Wangs in the Song and onward. In this sense, who was to say that Wang Anshi was not the family's *most* filial son?

This book will show that the Wangs' experience was far from rare among their fellow scholar-officials. All grappled with fulfilling their domestic duties to parents and family while meeting the demands of their scholarly and political careers. As a result, the Northern Song witnessed unprecedented state involvement and literati activism in bolstering ancient filial ideals as well as promoting new "standard" practices. In addition to shedding light on a major shift in the state-literati relationship, this development allows for an examination of long-term social and cultural changes from the tenth to the twelfth centuries. Another emphasis of this research is the relationship between people and places. As the Wangs' story has shown, extensive geographical mobility greatly shaped mourning and reverent care performance, as well as patterns of burial and commemoration.[8] Among the consequences of large-scale elite migration was the growing importance of "new" places, in both life and death, for office-holding men and their families. Above all, by putting human faces to a seemingly generic, universal idea and practice, this study highlights that there was never one neat model of filial expression. In real-life scenarios, a combination of factors conditioned both expectations and practices. The result was the transformation of filial piety into a more gender- and status-based virtue in the Northern Song.

Filial Piety in Chinese History

Few ideas and ideals are more permeating and socially, politically, and culturally unifying than *xiao*, filial piety, in Chinese history.[9] Ancient in its origin, the concept grew out of the early Chinese understanding of the mutual dependence between the dead and the living. This belief gave rise to ancestral worship as a practical concern as well as a religious obligation.[10] The gradual elevation of *xiao* as a symbol of Chinese cultural identity went hand in hand with the evolution of the Confucian School as a system of family ethics. Whereas *xiao* was most often associated with providing the dead (lineage ancestors in particular) with sacrificial food in the Shang (1500s–1040s BCE) and Zhou (1040s–256 BCE) periods, Confucian classics increasingly linked filial devotion to sons' profound respect toward living parents in the patriarchal household. The propagation of *xiao* as a paramount, even defining, value in Chinese culture was achieved especially through the Confucian exaltation of the importance of ritual performance and ritualized behavior. Pre-Han and Han (202 BCE–220 CE) texts not only included meticulous guidelines for ideal daily conduct, mourning and burial protocols, and ancestral ceremonies, but they also elevated the proper expression of filial sentiments as part of the cosmic order necessary for maintaining family harmony and hierarchy.[11]

The influence of the Confucian discourse on *xiao* can be readily observed in the responses of the school's main opponents. In his writing, Mozi (fifth century BCE) famously advocated for "impartial caring (*jian'ai*)" and condemned extended mourning, lavish funerals, and other ritual performances as excessive and wasteful. The Legalist thinker Han Feizi (?–233 BCE) similarly argued against filial piety, especially in terms of the inherent conflict between private interest and public duty. To Han Feizi, there was no doubt that one's political loyalty to the king and state should be placed higher than one's concerns for and attachment to parents and family. Moreover, political and social order was established through the systematic implementation of clearly worded state policies, not by relying on sons' devotion and submission to their parents.[12]

The founding of a unified empire and establishment of Confucianism as the imperial ideology in the Han resulted in the cult of *xiao*. This development was evidenced in a Confucian classic of the same name (*Xiaojing* [the Classic of Filial Piety]), which pinpoints filial piety as the root of all virtues and the source of all teachings.[13] In the political realm, the dynasty institutionalized the recruitment of *xiaolian* (the filial and honest) into government and the promotion of filial exemplars in local societies.[14] More important, the Han witnessed the extension of the father-son relationship to political realms. Han imperial pronouncements, and those from later dynasties, routinely equated the relationship between emperor and official with that of father and son. Intended to lessen the tension between duty to family and allegiance to the state, the juxtaposition of the two relationships effectively elevated *xiao* to a political virtue.[15]

Recognizing the utility of *xiao* in maintaining harmony at the social and political levels, all successive dynasties continued the Han rhetoric that they "rule[d] All-Under-Heaven with filial piety [*xiao zhi tianxia*]."[16] In addition to a large number of imperial edicts idolizing the power of *xiao*, government officials were specifically charged with promoting harmonious family relationships among local subjects through a reward system. Unfilial behavior had already become punishable by law in the Han.[17] By the Tang (618–907), it was formally categorized as one of the Ten Abominations.[18] The *Great Tang Code* (*Da Tanglü*) and later legal texts specified a variety of unfilial deeds, including (among the most heinous crimes) suing, cursing, or neglecting one's parents and grandparents; improper mourning behavior; and the division of family property while parents were still alive.[19] That filial piety occupied a central place in the crime and punishment system of imperial times can also be seen from how sons and daughters were sentenced for avenging parents. From the Han to the Qing dynasties (1644–1911), children involved in "filially motivated homicide" routinely received leniency.[20]

Political and legal measures to endorse filial piety were matched by vigorous efforts on the part of scholar-intellectuals. These efforts are evident in the extensive commentaries on the *Classic of Filial Piety*, the compilation of the *Classics of Filial Piety for Women* (*Nü xiaojing*), abundant exposition of the meanings and moral power of *xiao* in reforming the general populace, and the exaltation of "the filial and the righteous [*xiaoyi*]" in dynastic histories.[21] The propagation of ritual and philosophical discourses on *xiao* was accompanied by the active promotion of proper ritual behavior in schools and daily life. A major focus of children's education in the Confucian curriculum was to inculcate such virtues as filial piety, respect for elders, and the learning of ritualized conduct and life-cycle ceremonies.[22] Starting from the Han, a variety of filial tales celebrated outstanding role models who denied themselves comfort and pleasure for the sake of satisfying parents' needs and wishes. The same material especially portrayed sons staying in perpetual mourning, compromising their health through excessive emaciation, or dying of grief following a parent's death. The wholehearted dedication of these filial children was believed to move heaven and the spirits, which subsequently manifested their approval of the extraordinary conduct with auspicious signs and miracles.[23] In more than one way, these tales were instrumental in the creation of the key filial motifs and performative language associated with them.

The penetration of the value of filial piety into every layer of Chinese society was especially aided by liturgical writing in the Tang and Song periods. The new literati elite of the Song took pains to reinterpret classical ancestral rites to bring them into conformity with society.[24] This effort culminated in Zhu Xi's (1130–1200) *Family Rituals* (*Jiali*) and the establishment of a standard ritual structure across regions and class divisions in the late imperial times.[25] The family and death rituals popularized by Zhu's writing not only exerted a large influence on the daily life of all members of society, but also helped form a unified Chinese identity.

Many other genres of writing, including family instructions, community covenants, and guidance for social life, stressed the value of filial piety, respect for elders, and ancestral rites in private and public life.[26] A flourishing printing industry and the development of vernacular literature contributed to the wide circulation of ballads, plays, illustrated texts, and short stories on filial piety from the Song onward.[27] The period also saw the emergence of unfilial tales as a staple component in anecdotal writing (*biji*), featuring sons and daughters-in-law neglecting, abusing, and even murdering their parents. Even though the wrongdoers were not always caught or punished by the local authorities, they rarely escaped the wrath of natural and supernatural powers.[28]

One place to observe the centrality of filial piety in elite as well as ordinary life is in the material culture of life and death. Large-scale underground structures, commemorative buildings, and abundant funeral arts and tomb goods had ancient roots and were common practices throughout Chinese history.[29] The fifth century saw the popularity of entombed funerary inscriptions (*muzhiming*) as a permanent record of the deceased's virtues and a powerful tool of ancestral commemoration.[30] Depictions of filial children and theatrical performances of and for the dead remained a prominent feature in tombs for the affluent.[31] To ensure ancestors' good fortune in the afterlife, families also buried with the deceased a variety of contracts as evidence of land-holding and business transactions.[32] The time and resources invested in death rites often alarmed social observers, leading to recurrent debates on "opulent (*houzang*) vs. simple (*bozang*)" burials in Chinese history.[33] The Song period witnessed a parallel development in sons' filial performance directed to living parents. "In a *jia* [house] various structures, such as pavilions, ponds, and yards, were constructed or made the most of to make parents happy. Entertaining mothers with multiple house structures is likely to have been a popular practice favored by filial sons during the Song period."[34]

Xiao has remained a key political, social, religious, and cultural virtue largely because of its ability to accommodate the needs of the imperial state, diverse belief systems, and men and women of different familial roles and social statuses. Tension and conflicts nonetheless remain. In many ways, the history of filial piety is also one of negotiation, appropriation, and competition. A few examples: within Confucianism, the meaning and place of *xiao* has been interpreted differently in relation to other key Confucian virtues, such as *ren* (humaneness) and *zhong* (loyalty).[35] The tension between *xiao* and *zhong* and rites and law especially put individuals in difficult positions when the state prioritized its political needs over its officials' private interests;[36] even though Confucian orthodoxy insisted that filial piety, learned and internalized in early childhood, naturally translated into faithful service to one's lord, political relationships were not seamless extensions of the father-son relationship.[37] The mother-son bond gained prominence when Eastern Han (25–220) elites used extended mourning for mothers to highlight their personal obligations over court service;[38] other familial and political situations, such as property disputes and the filial duties of emperors and daughters-in-law, also complicated the understanding and performance of *xiao*.[39]

As closely as *xiao* was associated with Confucianism, the continuing appeal of filial piety as a social and cultural value owed much to the spread of other beliefs and practices.[40] The Buddhist notion of "merit" gave rise to new filial expressions in the form of sutra copying, merit-cloisters, public construction projects, and donations to monasteries as gestures of devotion to parents.[41] Representation of filial piety grew to be a special focus of Chinese Buddhist art and literature.[42] The religion especially contributed to the popularization of filial piety by stressing the suffering that parents, especially mothers, endured in raising a child.[43] Blood writing, using one's blood to copy scriptures, and filial slicing (*gegu*), cutting a slice of one's flesh to cure a parent, both partly derived from Buddhism, remained standard filial tropes in mid- and late imperial times.[44] By the Song era, cremation was practiced by all classes in all regions.[45] The desire for religious salvation, a seemingly selfish pursuit, came to be seen as the most filial act as devotees contributed to the salvation of their parents.[46] Subsequently, Daoist and Buddhist funerary rituals became a necessary staple of filial expression.[47]

Filial Piety and the Elite in the Northern Song

Like its predecessors, the Song dynasty claimed that it "rule[d] all under Heaven with filial piety."[48] In its legal codes, imperial decrees, and court cases, the government routinely upheld the value of filial piety in establishing harmony and order within the family and society. Unfilial behavior was clearly forbidden and punishable by flogging, banishment, or even death.[49] Charged with reforming the minds and hearts of their subjects, local administrators undertook numerous initiatives that aimed to correct unfilial conduct and establish proper family hierarchies. These efforts were accompanied by state promulgation of multiple versions of ritual codes that regulated the mourning duties, funeral and burial protocols, and ancestral rites for commoners as well as ranking officials.[50]

In their capacity as scholars, writers, and court officials, Song educated men eagerly promoted filial piety. Their efforts can be observed in the multiple commentaries on and wide transmission of the *Classic of Filial Piety*.[51] Equally significant were the numerous philosophical treatises that expounded on the power of filial piety and the large number of funerary biographies that made it a centerpiece of the genre.[52] Ritual and genealogical writing, two closely related developments that involved many leading Neo-Confucians of the time, also gained prominence in the Song.[53] These trends were accompanied by frequent debates among leading statesmen and intellectuals, making death rituals an arena of political confrontation.[54]

Rather than focus on the aforementioned political, ritual, and intellectual discourses on *xiao*, this book will examine elite filial practice in the large context of the social and cultural changes in the Northern Song. To put this another way, a distinguishing feature of this study will be its attention to the ways scholar-officials from diverse family circumstances understood and performed their parental care, mourning and burial rite, and ancestral commemoration responsibilities. This approach is made possible by the use of over two thousand *muzhiming* (epitaphs, funerary biographies, funerary inscriptions) in *Quan Song wen* (The Complete Prose of the Song Period) and many other sorts of evidence, ranging from poetry and letters to government documents and from anecdotal writing to archeological findings.[55] By illustrating the complexities and diversities of elite men's filial performance, this study aims to deepen scholarly understanding of literati identity, family and social life, and people-place relationships.

FILIAL PIETY, THE STATE, AND LITERATI IDENTITY

Both traditional and modern scholars have viewed the Song period as an era of change. Among the most significant transformations of the time was the rise of a new national elite, the scholar-official class. Collectively, the men in this group were known as *shi* (or *shiren*, gentlemen), the social-cultural elite of the country. Those who served in the government identified themselves as *shidafu* (scholar-officials), the bureaucratic elite. In reality, the two terms were used interchangeably in court debates, literary works, and private correspondence, indicating the extent to which learning and examination success, culture, and government service coalesced to shape the outlook and self-identity of Song educated men.[56] For this reason, throughout the book, I use the terms "national elite," "literati," "educated men," "social and cultural elite," "scholar-officials," and "political or bureaucratic elite" to refer to this group of examination candidates and degree holders, government officials, and scholar-gentlemen.

The nature and growing influence of the literati and their evolution in the Tang-Song transition have been the focus of many scholarly works.[57] To chart this development in the simplest terms, compared to their aristocratic counterparts of earlier times, Song educated and bureaucratic elites were larger in number and more diverse in their familial and geographic origins.[58] Above all, these men pursued examination success and official service with unprecedented enthusiasm.[59] This attraction to officialdom and political influence can also be observed in the intellectual thinking, literary and aesthetic criticism, and kinship and marriage practices of the time.[60] As the size of this group expanded, competition for the limited number of examination degrees and government positions intensified. Song scholar-officials subsequently developed a variety of social and cultural mechanisms to mark their statuses.[61] Prevalent factionalism during both the Northern and the Southern Song (1127–1279) further complicated the situation, making court service an especially hazardous and unpredictable career choice.[62] As a result, Song political and social elites multiplied their approaches to status. Southern Song educated men turned more attention to local affairs, utilizing a wide range of methods, such as marriage alliances, kinship organizations, school building, and relief and religious initiatives, to strengthen their leadership role in local societies.[63]

This study will show that the above shifts in elite orientations in politics, culture, and society coincided with a reconfiguration of its members' most sacred domestic obligations, resulting in the establishment of new filial discourses and practices. The Northern Song witnessed a vigorous effort on the part of the central government to establish, modify, and institutionalize policies and procedures that aimed to regulate its civil servants' reverent care, mourning, and burial-related duties. This systematic intrusion into the domestic lives of the bureaucrats resulted in the popularity of a new, alternative filial ideal: *luyang* (to support and honor one's parents using the *lu* [official emoluments] that one earned). In combining two interconnected filial models—reverent care (*yang* or *gongyang*, to provide and care for) and distinguishing one's parents by establishing oneself (*rongyang* or *xian fumu*)—the *luyang* model fused the literati's official pursuits and domestic obligations.

In more than one way, the new ideal redefined elite male filiality. By categorizing office holding and the benefits and privileges that came with it as the most desirable form of filial expression, the *luyang* rhetoric transformed the political and social elites into the most filial of sons but also made them more dependent on the state and the emoluments that it granted. This change was enthusiastically embraced by the scholar-official class. Song writers produced large quantities of poetry, anecdotal accounts, and funerary biographies to enhance the image and reputation of the *lu*-earning practitioners and new filial tropes. These ranged from official sons practicing parental care at their local offices to their obtaining honorary titles for parents and other ancestors to elevating their family and clan through epitaph writing. The ideal office-holding man was also frequently featured as wailing uncontrollably while traveling a long distance to rush to parents' bodies. As a result, not only did the mourner emerge from the narrative a moral exemplar, but his tears were also depicted as a powerful tool to reform the minds and hearts of his audience. Filial devotion was subsequently made central to Song scholar-officials' collective identity as the country's sociopolitical elite, as well as their masculine self-conceptions as virtuous men and dutiful sons.[64]

FILIAL PIETY AND ELITE FAMILY

Recent scholarship on the family in China's imperial times has concentrated on several key areas.[65] There is, for example, a large literature on women and marriage.[66] Family property issues have similarly drawn much interest.[67] A major focus of Song historians has been on the various elite strategies aiming to perpetuate and advance family status.[68] Many scholars have also written about active elite efforts in formulating family rituals and cementing kinship solidarity, two large trends that lasted into the late imperial times.[69]

This study approaches family life through an examination of the parent-child relationship in elite households.[70] It will show that while the elevation of *luyang* as the most significant filial performance was not met with strong resistance from members of the scholar-official class, the reconfiguration of elite male filial obligations had a large impact on family life and dynamics. More specifically, this study will attempt to address the following questions: with office-holding sons being automatically identified as filial offspring in official rhetoric and funerary biographical writings, how much "control" could parents have over their successful descendants? How did the official sons react to and rationalize their unavailability for domestic duties? Were there detectable patterns in terms of making up for this deficiency? Seen from a different perspective, how might some parents feel about the *luyang* model? What did they do to differentiate their expectations of their official and "stay-at-home" sons? Most important, in what concrete ways did the *luyang* rhetoric affect family life and relationships, especially those between parents and their official and non-official sons and daughters-in-law?

A focused discussion of these issues will shed light on elite family dynamics from three aspects. First, the rise of the *luyang* ideal led to the articulation of a system of divided filial duties. While office-holding men concentrated on obtaining for their parents honor and privileges bestowed by the state and made possible by their bureaucratic careers and social and cultural achievements, their reverent care duties were relegated to their wives and non-office-holding brothers. By distinguishing the *lu* earners from and placing them above the non–*lu* earners, the *luyang* standard redefined family roles in a way that had large consequences not only on the allocation of familial responsibilities, but also on the way the entire family operated.

Second, the *luyang* ideal, while legitimizing political and scholarly ambition as major contributions to the family, did not rid Song scholar-officials of the psychological burden for slighting their domestic duties. For failing to practice parental care and proper mourning and for postponing parents' burials, elite men confessed a strong sense of pain, shame, guilt, and anxiety. Drawing on classical tropes as well as new motifs, their self-reflections offer invaluable insight into the emotional worlds of the members of this privileged segment of society. The same texts also serve as strong evidence for the persistent tension in office holding and filial practice, as well as the unsustainability of the *luyang* model.

Third, while highlighting the significant impact of the *luyang* model on elite families, this research will demonstrate that not all *xiao*-related decisions were the result of careful deliberations. Diverse familial circumstances proved powerful factors in shaping the way filial duties were carried out. Many parents died young, relieving children of reverent care duties early in their lives. Others outlived all sons, even grandsons, and ended up depending on other family members. The number of sons a couple had also made a large difference. Since women often lived longer than men, caring for and mourning widowed mothers is highly visible in extant records, as is filial piety to concubine mothers. Adoption and remarriage likewise complicated filial performance and family relationships.[71] It is through a consideration of these varied situations and the people who coped with specific challenges and crises that we learn about filial piety in real-life scenarios.

Filial Piety, Home, and Native Place

Variations in family circumstances aside, a common challenge that all office-holding men dealt with in fulfilling their filial duties was geographic distance. In committing to their scholarly and political careers, Song scholar-officials all became frequent travelers. Such an experience offered unprecedented opportunities for political influence and social and cultural engagement, but it was also responsible for the lengthy separation of office-holding men from their parents, families, and native places.[72] In poetry, letters, and epitaphs, Song scholar-officials routinely referred to fathers, sons, and brothers moving about the country, losing track of each other's whereabouts, receiving news belatedly of deaths in the family, and failing to attend to loved ones' dying wishes. Many parents were left at home; others ended up accompanying their sons on official trips and died far from their native place. Subsequently, official sons mourning the loss of parents on the road or at their official posts gained great visibility in Song writing. Similar occurrences included long delays in burials and the negligence and desertion of ancestral graveyards for new, more conveniently located complexes.

This large-scale elite geographic mobility, in both life and death, calls for an examination of the meanings of *jia* (home) and *xiang* (*lüli* or *xiangli*, home or native region). How problematic was it when one maintained little physical connection with one's home and native region? Was it filial for a son to insist on having his parents buried in the ancestral graveyard when he knew that he would be unable to regularly visit and perform ancestral sacrifices? How did one deal with having more than one family graveyard? This study will show that despite the continual utility of standard tropes on missing and dreaming of "home" and the fear of dying and being buried far from one's native place, *jia* and *xiang* became increasingly fluid in connotation in the Northern Song. In their stead were *new* places of significance, including those where one had been posted, owned property, fell in love with, or hoped to eventually retire and be buried.

This fluidity in turn generated interest in and innovations to strengthen family and kinship solidarity and local identity. The result was growing elite attention to ancestral rite performance, family instruction and genealogy writing, lineage organization building, native place–based social and cultural activities, and a diverse range of local projects. Partly originated as individual initiatives to sustain connections with home and native place, these developments ran parallel to and eventually coalesced with the Neo-Confucian articulation of ideal moral, familial, and social order. Seen from a different perspective, a rethinking of filial practice for elite men helped lay a solid foundation for the success of Neo-Confucianism in the Song and later times.[73]

Organization

The book is divided into four chapters, each focusing on one key filial performance. Chapter 1, "The Triumph of a New Filial Ideal: Supporting Parents with Official Emoluments," documents the close relationship between the centrality of court service in the lives of the Northern Song elite and the growing importance of a discourse on filial piety. *Luyang*, the support of parents with official remunerations one obtained from office holding, became the most celebrated form of elite filial performance. For Northern Song office-holding men, being filial increasingly meant bringing parents honor through success in the examinations and officialdom, practicing reverent care at close-to-home appointments, or bringing parents to one's official posts. To a certain extent, daughters-in-law and non-office-holding sons, through their devotion to parents' physical welfare, became the filial surrogates of their official siblings.

The second chapter, "Mourning and Filial Piety: Policies and Practices," examines the way that the Northern Song state determined if, where, and for how long an elite man mourned his parents. This was especially true in the first half of the dynasty, when practically no one was allowed to take full mourning leaves. Even though centuries-old ritual language continued to be used in the portrayal of a grieving son, the period witnessed a growing trend for sons to mourn a parent while remaining in office far from the parent's body, the family graveyard, and the home region. In the meantime, new mourning motifs, especially sons' public displays of grief while in transit, became established literary tropes in Song writing. This chapter also documents a major change in filial performance: the growing prominence and acceptance of mourning concubine mothers.

Chapter 3, "When and Where? Burial and Filial Piety," explores the various factors that were responsible for the long delays in entombment and frequent graveyard movements in the Northern Song. These large changes in burial practices subsequently gave rise to new filial ideals, popularized by funerary biographers. Office-holding sons became routinely commended for following parents' instructions in the selection of burial sites, for continuing to renovate or even relocate damaged graves, and for demonstrating extraordinary commitment in laying parents to rest. The chapter also discusses three common yet controversial burial practices: graveyard negligence, cremation, and divination.

The last chapter, "Remembering and Commemorating," illustrates the establishment of epitaph writing as a prominent form of filial expression. The first part of the chapter concentrates on the conspicuous place that sons, the epitaph-obtaining sons in particular, occupied in their parents' epitaphs and the epitaph writer's eagerness to promote filial piety through honoring the sons' wishes. This development confirms that office-holding men's filial duties were increasingly defined and fulfilled through means made possible by their official careers, as well as literary and social connections. The discussion of the problems of commemoration in the second half of the chapter highlights the various challenges that sons faced in epitaph requests and the lengths to which they went in securing their filial reputation in their parents' funerary biographies.

CHAPTER 1

The Triumph of a New Filial Ideal
Supporting Parents with Official Emoluments

Li Yin (?–1001), a native of Jian'an (in Fujian), lived in the early Northern Song and served in multiple official positions far from his native region. When relocating from one post to another, he never brought his mother along with him due to the difficulties of long-distance travel. Instead, he entrusted her well-being to his wife and sons in Jian'an. Li Yin later petitioned for and was granted early retirement at sixty, even though the official retirement age was seventy, on the basis of his mother's advanced age. From that time forward, he remained dedicated to her care. For demonstrating unusual devotion to his mother, Li Yin was lauded as a filial son by his biographer.[1]

Li Yin's two sons, Li Xuji (active 960s–1030s) and Li Xuzhou (971–1059), continued the family's filial tradition. When Xuji's official rank qualified his parents and wife for honorary titles, he insisted that his wife's honor be given to his grandmother, a request that the court happily obliged. The emperor Taizong (r. 976–997) also rewarded Xuji with a substantial cash prize to recognize his commitment to elevating his grandmother. Later in his career, Xuji requested an appointment near his hometown so that he could regularly visit his father and grandmother. When the court rejected his appeal and assigned him to Hongzhou (Nanchang, Jiangxi), Xuji, instead of leaving the care of the two seniors to other family members, as his father had done, brought them both to Jiangxi. The move proved felicitous. His father loved the local conditions in Hongzhou so much that he wished to spend the rest of his life there. Xuji subsequently arranged for the family to settle in Hongzhou permanently.

Li Yin's second son, Xuzhou, entered court service through the protection (*yin*) privilege.[2] When his career ended abruptly due to a negligence accusation, Xuzhou returned to Hongzhou to care for his father and was praised for going beyond traditional mourning rites following Li Yin's death. "Living in a thatched hut next to the grave (*lumu*), he personally managed his father's burial and planted many trees at the family graveyard. In the morning and at dusk, he would weep and shed bloodstained tears."[3]

Of the third generation Lis, we know only of Xuzhou's two sons, Li Kuan and Li Ding. Both were devoted to their father's welfare. Li Kuan once served in a neighboring prefecture of Hongzhou. Since his father refused to relocate, Kuan regularly visited home. Later, when he was assigned to another circuit, Kuan memorialized the court five times to be transferred to a location near Hongzhou but to no avail. Xuzhou eventually convinced his son to assume the position, but Li Kuan kept petitioning while in transit to the new office and was later reassigned to Hongzhou, where he could perform parental care with greater ease. Li Ding was also portrayed as a filial son. He once willingly accepted a lower-ranked office closer to home so that he could see his father more often. Because of their perseverance, we learn, both Li Kuan and Li Ding were posted in or around Hongzhou for over a decade.

The above account reveals that in three generations, the Li family of Fujian had the good fortune of producing at least five government officials. Variations in their rank and accomplishments aside, all had faced a similar challenge: their official careers kept taking them far away from their parents and home, making reverent care (*yang*, *xiaoyang*, or *gongyang*), a son's utmost obligation to parents, a nearly impossible task. In seeking to balance their official and domestic responsibilities, none of the Li men found perfect solutions, only compromises and temporary accommodations. These included procuring honorary titles for parents and grandparents, performing reverent care through obtaining close-to-home assignments, and bringing senior family members to local appointments.

The above efforts, while earning filial reputations for the caretakers, greatly complicated the meaning and practice of filial piety. In Li Yin's case, having concluded that it was impractical to bring his mother to his official posts, Li designated his wife and sons as his "surrogates," an arrangement that caused the long-term separation not only of Li Yin and his mother, but also that of Li and his wife and sons. Li's absence from his mother's side might very well have changed his approach to parental care when it was his turn to be the recipient of filial devotion. Li Yin's move to Hongzhou with Xuji therefore makes us wonder whether he genuinely liked the place or had only said so to lessen his son's burden. From Xuji's perspective, bringing his father to Hongzhou must have appeared to be the right decision at the time, even though neither father nor son could have anticipated its long-term implications. Of the two brothers, Xuzhou was said to have contributed more than Xuji to Li Yin's physical well-being. This was made possible, however, by a setback in Xuzhou's career, not due to his personal initiative. In the third generation, even if Xuzhou's sons, Li Kuan and Li Ding, served in or around Hongzhou for over a decade, they would still have been posted away from their father for lengthy periods of time and faced the same dilemma that had frustrated Li Yin and Li Xuzhou.

This chapter will show that the Lis' experience, in terms of both their family circumstances and the choices that they made, was anything but unique. In the Northern Song, the ability of office-holding men to practice reverent care, or their inability to do so, was greatly conditioned by their official careers and the personnel policies that meant to separate them from their home prefectures. Such a restriction in and of itself was not a new phenomenon. What distinguished the period from earlier times in Chinese history was the growing number of men aspiring to office, as well as the prominent place that reverent care occupied in both policymaking and literati writing. That parental care became a major concern of both the state and members of the literati can be seen especially clearly in the abundant references to and poignant stories about the way individuals and families juggled court service and domestic obligations.

This perennial challenge caused neither the withdrawal of scholarly men from officialdom nor the marginalization of filial piety in elite self-identification. What did take place was the elevation of *luyang* or *rongyang* as *the* most celebrated mode of filial expression in the Northern Song. Often used interchangeably, both terms portrayed sons supporting (*yang*) parents through attaining a variety of emoluments (*lu* or *rong*), such as examination degrees, official ranks and salaries, and honorary titles. Less tangible yet equally celebrated were the benefits and privileges included in bringing parents to official posts or obtaining close-to-home appointments for the purpose of parental care. In other words, at a time when civil service became ever more attractive to aspiring individuals and families, a son's success in officialdom was singled out as a special form of *yang* to parents.

The elevation of *luyang* by office-holding men and their families was supported by government policies. By labeling a son's ability to obtain *lu* through his government career as the most conspicuous filial act, the *luyang* ideal and the forms of performance that it sanctioned transformed elite male filiality, making it less about practicing reverent care at parents' sides. Rather, official sons were labeled filial for successfully obtaining *lu*-related recognitions for parents. Reverent care performance became feasible only if parents moved with office-holding sons when the locations and lengths of a son's assignment allowed for such an arrangement.

This change in the rhetoric on and practice of filial piety had significant implications for family life in elite households. The *luyang* model, by singling out the official son's success in government as especially desirable, transformed parental care into a more role-based and gender-specific virtue in the Northern Song. With the constant absence of *lu*-earning sons from home and native region, many of the filial duties in elite households were relegated to daughters-in-law and non-office-holding sons. This divide in domestic obligations was anything but straightforward. A variety of circumstances, including the location of an official's native region in relation to his post, the number of office-holding and non-office-holding sons a couple had, widowhood and remarriages, and a family's fortune in producing officials across generations, affected how individuals and families understood and allocated filial duties.

From Reverent Care (*yang*) to Honoring Parents with Official Emoluments

An understanding of the emergence of *luyang* as the dominant discourse on elite male filiality in the Northern Song necessitates a brief review of the meaning and place of *yang* in earlier history. In pre-Han and Han Confucian classics, caring for parents' physical and emotional well-being was depicted as a son's most significant filial duty. When articulating the meaning of *yang*, Confucius famously stated, "[Nowadays filial piety] is taken to mean just seeing that one's parents get enough to eat, but we do that much for dogs or horses as well. If there is no reverence, how is it any different?"[4] During another conversation, the Master said, "The difficult part is the facial expression," making clear the importance of sincerity in sons' dealings with parents.[5] Mencius similarly highlighted that one's "most important duty" is "one's duty towards one's parents" and that "the content of benevolence is the serving of one's parents." In serving parents, sons should aim to "please" them.[6] The importance of reverent care was further propagated in other Confucian texts, which required sons to personally tend to the needs and pleasures of parents. The *Book of Rites* (*Liji*) is emphatic that when a parent reaches eighty, at least one son should stay by his or her side. If a parent is over ninety, all the sons should quit their official positions in order to care for them.[7] The *Classic of Filial Piety* gives more detail about a son's tasks: "In serving his parents, a filial son renders utmost reverence to them while at home. In supporting them, he maximizes their pleasure. When they are sick, he takes every care."[8]

Yang (*xiaoyang* or *gongyang*) became a ubiquitous term for parental devotion during the Eastern Han (25–220) and the Period of Disunity (220–589). A standard trope of contemporary filial tales was the "connectedness" between parents and sons and sons' genuine concern for parents' needs and happiness. To realize this goal, protagonists demonstrated extraordinary dedication through such simple acts as sucking puss from parents' wounds, cleaning parents' chamber

pots, or satisfying parents' cravings for a non-seasonal food item.⁹ Similar filial tales continued to circulate in the Tang, as seen in extant Buddhist transformation texts (*bianwen*).¹⁰ Not only did *yang* remain a central motif in Tang
filial stories, but another, more extreme form of reverent care, *gegu*, also made
its first appearance in this period. A practice closely related to the flourishing
of Buddhism, *gegu* typically dictated that a son, but occasionally a daughter or
daughter-in-law, slice off a piece of his or her own flesh or an organ to cure a
parent's illness.¹¹ The deeds of these filial exemplars would become prominent
reverent care themes in later times.

Two major factors contributed to the rise of the *luyang* ideal in the Northern
Song: the changing nature of the political and social elite from the late Tang to
the Song and the growing importance of office holding and its benefits in the self-
identification of the scholar-officials. To put this in the simplest terms, a major
difference between Song political and social elites and their predecessors was
their diversity in geographical and social backgrounds. Without impeccable ped-
igrees to boast of or powerful local bases to rely on, Song scholar-officials came to
see examination success and government service as the most significant channels
to distinction. This shift in elite orientation coincided with institutional changes
that promoted the value of civil rule following the tumultuous times from the
late Tang to the early Song. As a result, hard-earned compensations and privileges from office holding became a significant status marker, as well as powerful
expressions of filial devotion. In other words, as *lu* became the highest honor a
son could bring his parents, *yang* and *luyang* converged to carry the same con-
notations for office-holding men and their families.

The second half of the Tang already saw references to sons demonstrating
filial devotion through fulfilling parents' wishes for the sons' success in offi-
cialdom.¹² It was not until several decades into the Northern Song, however,
that a variety of *lu*-earning-related terms emerged as standard vocabulary in
both official documents and literati writing. Imperial bestowals of honorary
titles on officials' parents routinely praised civil servants for achieving the goal
of *xianqin*, distinguishing one's parents or other ancestors, through the acquisition of high ranks.¹³ Leading scholar-officials similarly upheld the *luyang* ideal.
In a petition for a close-to-home position, Zhang Yong (946–1015) of the early
Northern Song claimed, "It is the common way for filial sons to support parents
with *lu*. And sagacious rulers manifest their magnanimity by allowing sons to
realize their wish."¹⁴ Ouyang Xiu (1007–1072) voiced his strong support of this
trend several decades later: "A filial son should stop at nothing to distinguish
his parents. While they are alive, he supports them with *lu*. After their death,
he elevates their fame."¹⁵ *Luyang* was widely used by funerary biographers in

their portrayal of ideal conduct, indicating that earning *lu* had become one of the most respectable elite male virtues. A man surnamed Zhang claimed that he had entered officialdom because of the pressure to support his parents with *lu*.[16] A contemporary, Shi, was said to show no interest in family estate management, relying only on his *lu* to support his parents.[17] Another man put his lifetime aspiration in the most straightforward manner: "to gain and use *lu* to glorify my parents."[18] There was so much pressure for achieving *luyang* that Mr. Ju considered himself unfilial for having failed to earn *lu* to support his parents while they were alive.[19]

The centrality of the *luyang* ideal in Northern Song elite men's conception of filial conduct is best illustrated in the propagation of three additional groups of standard terminologies. All extended the meanings of *luyang*. These included (1) *shiyang* or *shiqin* (to wait on and care for parents, most often at a son's official post); (2) *qi bianjun* (or *qi jinjun*), *bianyang*, and *jiuyang* (to request a convenient or close-to-home prefecture to perform reverent care); and (3) *qushi jiuyang* (to leave office in order to perform reverent care). Of these seven expressions, the last five explicitly marked a son's official status and his attempts or capacity to perform parental care while serving in officialdom. All were measures that the Li men, discussed above, adopted and for which they were labeled filial. The remaining two terms, *shiyang* and *shiqin*, did not specify a son's official status. However, as our discussion will demonstrate, in both official documents and literati writing, when a son was portrayed as performing *shiyang* or *shiqin*, the care was normally given at his official post rather than the parents' home.

The Four Types of *Luyang*

Under the general premise of *luyang*, the varieties of filial performance can be divided into four categories, all of which involved office-holding men spreading the remuneration, prestige, and benefits that they received from the state to their parents and family. The following sections will discuss these filial expressions.

Realizing *Luyang* through Examination Success

The first type of *luyang* involved sons elevating their parents and families through earning the highly competitive examination degree. This form of filial performance was most conspicuously promoted in Northern Song poetry and funerary biographies.

Compared to poetry from earlier times, Song works featured the filial deeds of elite men in more prominent ways.[20] This is seen most clearly in the poetic glorification of successful examination candidates as *lu*-earning sons. One of the earliest Northern Song poems, by Xu Xuan (916–991), portrays a newly minted degree holder in this way:

> You are now well known [i.e., the subject of the poem just passed the
>   examination],
> There is no need to be embarrassed anymore [i.e., he had failed before].
> You have earned *lu* to extend its benefits to your beloved parents.[21]

As brief as it is, this stanza conveys three messages: first, a young man had just passed the examination after years of preparation; second, the degree made him eligible to earn *lu*; third, this accomplishment confirmed his ability to support and honor his parents, even though the poem stops short of calling the young man a filial son.

The famous poet Mei Xun (964–1041) was more straightforward in equating examination success as evidence of filial devotion. When bidding farewell to a newly minted degree holder, Mei wrote the following:

> Now that you have realized both wishes
> Of getting the degree and fulfilling your filial sentiments,
> Do not feel miserable when passing through the Jian Passages [on your
>   way to Sichuan].[22]

If the successful candidate in Xu Xuan's poem still appeared overwhelmed by his success in the examination, Mei Xun's subject had already received his first appointment. The thought of traveling to a remote region had generated much anxiety, which Mei tried to mitigate. The gist of the poem, however, is to affirm the ideal of *lu* as a form of filial devotion.

A third poem, by Li Zhiyi (1038–1117), further expounded on the desirability of *luyang* in the elite imagination of filial performance:

> A son of the Chens just passed the examination.
> Donning the newly bestowed official garments, he has come home to see
>   his parents;
> I want to tell people on the road to wipe their eyes [so they can see
>   clearly].
> Who would not be envious of parents who have a son like him?[23]

Using vivid language, here the poet depicts the return of a successful candidate as a public event. The good news itself, indicated by the official robe that the son is wearing and the crowd that has gathered for this occasion, puts the Chens in the spotlight. Although the parents are not in plain view here, the poet calls attention to the one thought on the minds of all the spectators: "How lucky the Chens are! I wish this was my son!" For bringing such a high honor to his parents and family, Chen was immediately transformed into a filial son.

In epitaphs, as in poetry, Northern Song writers equated degree earning with filial performance. In fact, not only did they praise their subjects for bringing *lu* to their parents through examination success, but the biographers also singled out the deceased's filial sentiments as the driving force for their scholarly and official pursuits. Mr. Sun, for example, attributed his good fortune in the examination to his father. Sun was determined to succeed in the examination after hearing his father say, "If I could have one son who enters officialdom before I die, I would be satisfied."[24] Another man recollected that since his father had passed away when he was young, it was his mother who pushed him to study hard and stay on track in his scholarly commitment.[25] A third person remembered his mother's words: "The important responsibility of a son is to establish himself. This way, his parents would not need to worry either in life or death. You work hard, and I hope that by the time I am old, you will have received *lu* to fulfill my expectations."[26]

Song men especially credited their mothers, often widows, with their educational and scholarly accomplishments. As Beverly Bossler has pointed out, this "virtuous widow and talented son" trope reveals changing notions of ideal female virtue from the Tang to the Northern Song, when women were increasingly praised for contributing to their children's education, caring for in-laws, and managing household affairs.[27] A close reading of Northern Song epitaphs shows another side of this cultural stereotype: sons working against great odds to honor their mothers' wishes. In other words, examination success became an important way for a son to affirm his worthiness, as well as his love and appreciation for his mother's sacrifices. In old age, Su Xianxi (961–1035) related to his sons and grandsons, "I lost my father when I was young and had no other means but to study hard, hoping that I could earn *lu* to serve my mother. Not only did she receive that in the end, but I was also able to feed and clothe my sons and grandsons with *lu*. [Because of this achievement] I am proud of myself."[28] It is interesting to note that having lost his father early in life, Su identified the earning of *lu*, and not personally tending to his widowed mother's physical well-being, as the most significant form of service that he had performed. Subsequently, it was the realization of *luyang* that brought Su a strong sense of pride.

Earning *lu* while parents were still alive was considered so important a life goal that some felt justified to seek shortcuts. Bian Rihua (961–1012) remembered deliberating to himself:

> My mother already has gray hair and is dependent on me for support. How could I want to [spend many years to] learn extensively and be selfish about getting a reputation for being knowledgeable? I should instead focus on mastering the skills that would guarantee me a quick success, hoping that, in this way, I can earn *lu* [as soon as possible] to make my mother proud.[29]

Having determined his priority, Bian proceeded to focus on one classic, the *Spring and Autumn Annals*, and obtained his degree the next year. Here Bian implied that had he not rushed to take the examination, he would and could have become a more erudite scholar and earned the more prestigious *jinshi* degree. Yet he had no regrets but considered himself lucky for achieving *luyang* while his mother was alive.[30]

Becoming a Filial Son through Earning Honorary Titles for One's Parents

For Bian Rihua and his fellow scholar-officials, an equally, if not more attractive, filial expression was the acquisition of honorary titles for parents. Compared to the Tang and earlier periods, the Song state was extremely accommodating in this respect. Most titles were bestowed under two circumstances.[31] First, officials ranked five and above became automatically eligible to make requests on behalf of their parents, grandparents, wives, and other more remote ancestors.[32] The higher an official's rank, the greater the generations of ancestors he was qualified to honor and the more illustrious the titles would be. Dozens of the highest-ranked officials earned honors for three generations of their ancestors in the Northern Song.[33] Many more earned titles for both parents or multiple parents and grandparents.[34] Moreover, individual officials routinely received honorary ranks for ancestors based on their outstanding service. Han Qi (1008–1075), for example, earned titles for several of his ancestors, including his concubine mother, due to his key role in dealing with the Song-Tangut relationship in the 1040s.[35]

Second, officials of all ranks were allowed, although not necessarily encouraged, to exchange their own merit and promotion opportunities for honorary titles for aging parents. Numerous such requests have survived from the Northern Song.[36] In 1031, a man named Duan Shaolian petitioned to exchange his rank for an honorary title for his father.[37] Fan Zhongyan (989–1052) memorialized to present a title he had earned to his stepfather.[38] Another official, Zhao, asked that a promotion given to him be transferred to his mother. In response to the request, the grand councilor opined that since Zhao was already an academician, it would not be long before his mother would be granted a title. To that Zhao replied, "My mother is eighty-two. I would like to earn her the honor from the emperor sooner rather than later," implying his worry that his mother might die without a title.[39]

Normally very short, title-granting pronouncements were largely formulaic in style and replete with archaic language and classical allusions. Broadly speaking, these decrees usually included three messages to elevate the *luyang* ideal: first, to extol the "greatness of filial piety" and a son's "wish to glorify his parents"; second, to reward the filial son for his devotion and inspire others to act accordingly; third, to encourage and celebrate the filial son "to extend his loyalty to the king."[40] The following is a relatively wordy edict granting a title to the stepmother of two official-brothers.

> To have sons serving at court and white-haired parents of kind countenance being cared for in a large hall, the glory of a family does not exceed this! The mother of the officials is tender, pure, and dignified and has demonstrated capabilities in managing the household. Now that her two sons enjoy prominence due to their talents, the official emoluments they have been granted should be equally extended [to their mother]. Previously Zhongyou [Zilu, 542–480 BCE] was able to please his parents by feeding them rice he carried home [from a long distance]. Would not using the *lu* of a secretarial court gentleman and an assistant minister of the Court of Imperial Sacrifices bring even more joy to the parent than Zhongyou did?[41]

The above decree reveals several things: first, the family has produced two office holders; second, the two brothers were very likely brought up by their stepmother; third, it was considered natural that whatever *lu* the two sons had earned should be extended to the mother; above all, the imperial pronouncement compared the two *lu*-earning sons to Zhongyou. A famous disciple of Confucius and a filial exemplar, Zhongyou was best known for feeding his parents white rice that he had personally carried home by walking a long distance when he himself consumed low-quality food. In alluding to Zhongyou, the author of the edict made the official sons in question his equals. In fact, the edict explicitly compared Zhongyou's filial performance with that of the office-holding sons, asserting the superiority of *luyang* as a form of filial expression over reverent care. In the most straightforward manner, the imperial edict acknowledged that bringing *lu* to parents in the form of honorary titles, official rank, and lavish residence would bring parents more joy than Zhongyou's simple gesture of saving the fine rice for his parents. Consequently, honorary titles for parents not only represented the court's recognition of its officials' talents and dedication, but also became vehicles through which elite men translated their political success into exemplary filial performance. Seen from a different perspective, given that Zhongyou served the court of the Chu state only after the death of his parents, the fact that the two officials in question were able to bring glory to their mother in her lifetime made them more outstanding and "successful" filial sons. In this way, *luyang* emerged as a higher category of filial expression than a son's attentiveness to parents' basic needs.

At first glance, this practice was not a new development. After all, parents and grandparents of court officials had routinely received official bestowals in earlier dynasties. What distinguished the Northern Song from previous eras was the state's willingness and active promotion of granting titles to the parents of its civil servants, seen clearly through the *xiao*-related language used in the decrees, the promulgation of protocols for various occasions, and the large number of titles given. Of equal importance were the voluminous official memorials that aimed to acquire titles for parents and grandparents.[42] The availability of such opportunities created so much pressure that those who had failed to obtain such titles would confess shame and frustration. In one instance, a man surnamed Huang succeeded in the examination; however, because he was not promoted fast enough to qualify his parents for honorary titles while they were alive, he later "often lamented that the *lu* he had earned did not reach his parents."[43] Another man went so far as to call himself unfilial because he had not earned titles for his parents until long after he had entered government service. According to his biographer, when he was finally eligible for this privilege, "he felt much better about himself."[44]

A distinctive characteristic in the granting of titles for parents was that more mothers than fathers received such awards. Of the many edicts drafted by Lü Tao (1028–1104), six were for fathers and nineteen for mothers, including one concubine mother and multiple stepmothers.[45] Zheng Xie (1022–1072) authored decrees that granted titles to nine mothers alone.[46] These decrees routinely promoted the idea that mothers could gain rank based on their sons' merit (*mu yi zi gui*).[47] Others went even further, singling out the sons' duty to elevate their mothers. Cai Xiang (1012–1067), for example, wrote rhetorically, "If a son has distinguished himself [*rong*], yet he does not obtain a high rank for his mother, how could he be considered filial?"[48]

Why did more mothers receive titles than fathers? One explanation is that many officials came from office-holding families, so their fathers and grandfathers had already earned titles for themselves. Two additional factors played a role. First, women, especially successor wives, lived much longer to enjoy the benefits of their (step) sons' advancing careers.[49] Second, a fair number of Northern Song elite men had more than one mother and grandmother. Based on the rhetoric of the imperial edict cited above, the two officials' deceased biological mother had been granted a title; hence the reference to official emoluments being "equally extended" to the stepmother. Subsequently, the two unnamed officials earned honorary titles for at least two mothers. Some of their colleagues did so for as many as three or four mothers, including legal, step-, and concubine mothers.[50] Gao Ruone's (997–1055) two great-grandmothers, two grandmothers, and two mothers were among the many women that received imperial generosity.[51] So did Wen Yanbo's (1006–1097) two grandmothers and mother.[52]

It should be noted that in both legal and ritual stipulations, biological mothers and stepmothers were treated equally for the purpose of receiving titles. This means, in theory, that adoption and remarriage would not complicate a son's filial duties. One imperial order especially emphasized that "natural and stepmother[s] should share the same [glory]."[53] In reality, Song educated men were acutely aware that remarriage and concubinage could cause much trouble in the family.[54] Sima Guang (1019–1086) famously said that successor wives and concubines often ruined the family because when brothers did not get along, it was likely because they had different mothers.[55] This generalization was corroborated by epitaph writers' eagerness to praise second wives for treating their stepchildren just like their own, a strong indication that such impartiality was not always practiced.

Considerations for concubine mothers were even more complicated. The earliest court deliberation of the issue occurred in 1017. In the memorial, the ritual official Chao Jiong (951–1034), after summarizing some regulations from the earlier periods, proposed that officials ranked five and above be eligible for requesting honorary titles for concubine mothers if their legal and stepmothers had passed away.[56] It is not clear if Chao's initiative came into effect immediately. We are certain that Han Qi's (1008–1075) mother, Miss Hu (968–1030), was the recipient of three honorary titles in the 1030s and 1040s.[57] Filial performance to concubine mothers will be discussed in a separate section in this chapter below and in the next chapter.

REQUESTING CLOSE OR CONVENIENTLY
LOCATED POSTS FOR PARENTAL CARE

Compared to obtaining examination degrees and honorary titles, the third type of filial performance, requesting close or conveniently located posts, best underscored the utility of the *luyang* ideal in reconciling the inherent conflicts between civil service, which necessitated that office holders stay away from their homes and native regions, and reverent care, which required sons' physical presence at their parents' sides. In official discourse and literary work, office-holding men were often said to have petitioned for a close-to-home or conveniently located prefecture in order to practice reverent care either by regularly visiting parents at home or relocating parents to sons' local posts.

The long-term separation of parents and sons due to the latter's public duties was by no means a new phenomenon. Many official sons in early history were celebrated for their genuine expression of devotion to parents when circumstances prevented them from performing reverent care. The *Zuo Tradition (Zuozhuan)*, China's earliest work of history, recorded that when Zhao Xuanzi (Dun, ?–601 BCE) was on an official mission, he consumed only half of the food prepared for him. When asked why, Zhao explained that he had been away from home for a long time and did not even know if his mother was still alive. "I am now close to home. I ask for permission to give [the other half of the food] to my mother."[58] By regularly depriving himself half of each meal, Zhao demonstrated that even when he was traveling, he never forgot his mother's welfare.

One remedy to prevent the separation between parents and their office-holding sons was for the senior couple to relocate with their sons.[59] One of the earliest known precedents was a trip taken by the Han scholar Ban Zhao (45–117), with her son, Cao Cheng (n.d.). Dated in 113, the journey from Luoyang (in Henan) to Chenliu (in Henan) was made well known because of Ban's "Rhapsody on an Eastward Journey [Dongzheng fu]." Ban's writing did not touch on the rationale behind this long-distance trip. Based on the strong feelings that she voiced for leaving the capital, this might not have been her preference. However, since she was both widowed and elderly, Ban Zhao might have wanted to stay by the side of her only son and Cao Cheng, his mother. Since Cao had been posted five hundred *li* away from the capital, the mother and son would have had no other option if Cao intended to perform even the minimum amount of reverent care.[60]

Historical records about official sons fulfilling their filial duties while being absent from home were scarce until the second half of the Tang dynasty, as were government policies addressing the relationship between elite men's public and private responsibilities.[61] It was not until the early eleventh century that attention to this issue gained momentum. From the perspectives of both the central government and individual officials, there was an urgent need to address and balance civil servants' official and domestic obligations. The result was an increasingly standard, state-sanctioned practice: official sons could perform reverent care by bringing parents to their posts. If Li Yin, introduced at the beginning of this chapter, decided to leave his mother in the family's native place of Fujian due to concerns about the hardships of long-distance journeys, by the eleventh century, when the empire was enjoying long-term peace and water and land travel had improved significantly, it was nothing out of the ordinary for parents to relocate to their sons' local positions.

One way to confirm the demand for and popularity of this practice was its institutionalization. The Northern Song was the first dynasty in Chinese history that issued systematic policies in this regard to accommodate civil servants' reverent care needs.[62] This serves as strong evidence of the court's acknowledgement of its officials' domestic duties, as well as its willingness to uphold the *luyang* ideal. The earliest decree, dated 1001, stipulated that officials whose parents were over seventy and who did not have a brother performing parental care at home were eligible for appointments at their home or a close-to-home prefecture. Those who did have adult brothers, however, were not qualified for this benefit.[63] Another policy, issued twenty years later, specified that civil servants with parents over eighty were entitled to be posted at their home or neighboring prefectures. Under this policy, whether the official had a stay-at-home brother or not ceased to be an issue.[64] A 1023 pronouncement made newly minted degree holders with parents aged seventy and over eligible for the same benefit.[65] In 1040, officials serving in most regions in Sichuan were allowed to be relocated to a close-to-home position if they had sick or old parents.[66] At least three more decrees, issued between 1040 and 1054, reiterated the above policies.[67] In some cases, officials were even allowed to "swap posts [*duiyi*]" so that they could move closer to where their parents lived.[68]

By allowing officials with aging parents to serve close to home, the government went beyond paying mere lip service to "ruling with filial piety." Procedurally and logistically, this was no easy task. Any requests for special consideration in (re)appointments went against the spirit of the Song personnel management system, which centralized the selection, rotation, and assessment of its civil servants. The Principle of Avoidance (*huibi*) in particular was designed to keep the civil servants away from their home regions to prevent nepotism and potential conflicts of interest. Even if the central government intended to be generous, being overly accommodating would create a bureaucratic nightmare.[69] Moreover, the diverse geographical backgrounds of the civil servants meant that ideal local posts varied greatly for different individuals and families, with some keen on posts close to home and others favoring transportation hubs for more convenient travel. Families with multiple office holders would have even more factors to consider. For the central government to meet its administrative needs and satisfy its civil servants' preferences required quite a balancing act. Seen from another perspective, the promulgation of this series of personnel management policies underscored the state's expectation that officials prioritize court service over their familial obligations. With parents' age thresholds being set so high, only a small percentage of the civil-service class would stand to benefit from these policies. The majority of officials, as long as their parents were healthy and cared for, were expected to focus on their careers and, by extension, remain far from home.

Northern Song civil servants nonetheless took advantage of the above policies. Hundreds of requests have survived in extant court memorials, funerary inscriptions, and personal correspondence in which officials petitioned to be posted at a place of their choice due to parents' illness, advancing age, or particular family circumstances.[70] Many received positive results.[71] For example, after several times expressing a wish to retire in order to care for his parents, a man surnamed Sun was granted a close-to-home position.[72] Another, Zhou, firmly declined a remote appointment based on his parents' old age and was subsequently assigned to a neighboring prefecture.[73] After being appointed to Quanzhou (in Fujian) near his native place, Cai Xiang expressed his gratitude in a memorial: "Passing by one's family ancestral graveyard was the most glorious thing in ancient times. Serving in one's native prefecture to care for one's parents is a son's highest fortune."[74] A few years after finishing his tenure there, Cai recollected that the joy he had shared with families and relatives was enough to comfort his mother's heart. "If it were not for the vastness of [Your Majesty's] filial rule, how could there be such good fortune from Heaven?"[75]

Abundant evidence suggests that with the policies in place, Northern Song officials deliberately tested the boundaries even when their parents were not sick or had not reached an age that prompted a greater level of care. In the epitaph for Cheng Jun (1001–1082), a native of Meizhou (in Sichuan), we learn that Cheng

> requested to be assigned to a convenient post because his parents were old. The court showed exceptional kindness and granted his request. Cheng was later appointed the controller-general of Jiazhou (Leshan, Sichuan) [despite government policies that prohibited officials from serving in their

native prefectures]. His colleagues and friends all considered him filial and fellow-natives felt honored by his return. [While serving in Sichuan,] he either brought his parents to his post or came home to visit when [leaves of absence were] permitted by the court. This lasted for more than ten years. His parents were happy [with the arrangement], and he fulfilled his filial duties as a son.[76]

We learn from Cheng's funerary biography that for over a decade, he was appointed to three positions in Sichuan and able to perform reverent care through either bringing his parents to his posts or visiting them at home. This extraordinary show of imperial generosity was the result of multiple appeals. "According to government policies, Sichuan natives were not allowed to serve in nearby places for more than two terms. . . . The court had showed exceptional kindness in responding positively to his petitions."[77] Cheng's dedication to his filial duty not only pleased his parents, but also won him praise from colleagues and fellow-natives. For successfully balancing his career and his familial obligations, Cheng realized the *luyang* ideal.

It is impossible to pinpoint the exact number of officials who had the good fortune of serving near their hometowns for the simple reason that most of the epitaphs, when praising a son for achieving *luyang*, did not normally specify the location of such performance or whether the official had requested a close-to-home appointment. Nor were rejections always recorded. In the pages that follow, I introduce three cases from the early, mid-, and late Northern Song respectively. Each offers a different angle through which we can assess a variety of attempts of office holders to secure a desirable post in the name of practicing *luyang*.

The first case involves the famous statesman Bi Shi'an (938–1005) of the early Northern Song. When he was appointed to Shaanxi, Bi, known for his filial piety, worried that his stepmother might not be able to deal with the hardships of a long-distance journey. He therefore requested and was granted a nearby post in Henan.[78] Bi's petition did not survive, but it might not be unreasonable for us to imagine how he had convinced the court. Orphaned at a young age, Bi was brought up by his stepmother and credited his success to her finding him outstanding mentors and schools in the capital region. Upon entering officialdom, he would have every reason to want to repay her love and dedication by keeping her away from any adversity in old age. Bi's petition went through but at the expense of his career, as the new position was lower-ranked than the one previously offered. By sparing his stepmother from living in a remote and strange place, Bi was labeled a filial son.

My survey of Northern Song epitaphs shows that in the first half of the dynasty, the court was rather generous in granting petitions of this nature. One support for this observation is that very often little detail other than the positive result of a petition would be given in an epitaph—for example, "He petitioned for a close-to-home post based on his parent's age and was given such an appointment." Sometimes even the positive result was not overtly stated but only implied. This gives the impression that requests of this nature were more of a formality than a negotiation between the petitioners and the Department of Personnel. Starting from the mid-Northern Song, as redundant officials became a serious problem, requests for special treatment seemed to take more time and met with declining success rates, as seen in our second case, which involves Zhang Chu (1015–1080), a native of Henan.

According to Zhang's epitaph, when he was appointed to Yuezhou (Guiji, Zhejiang), worrying that it would be too far for his stepmother to travel with him, Zhang petitioned for a close-to-home post. He was subsequently dispatched to Mizhou (in Shandong) but was quickly transferred to Cangzhou (in Hebei), a prefecture close to the Song-Liao borders. It is unclear if Zhang attempted a transfer request. We do know that he assumed the position without his stepmother, and while in Cangzhou, he often lamented being separated from her. Zhang's biographer recorded that Zhang even feared for his life in the military zone: should he die, no one would be able to care for his stepmother. It took Zhang a few more years to get a post in Chenzhou (in Henan), to which he brought his stepmother. She felt immediately at home and was reluctant to leave by the end of Zhang's tenure. Zhang therefore decided to settle there permanently and conveyed to the court his wish to retire. The court, however, did not grant his request. As an alternative, he pleaded to be posted close to Chenzhou so that his stepmother could continue to live there. Just like Bi Shi'an, Zhang expressed his willingness to accept a lower-ranked position if it meant he would be able to fulfill his familial obligations.[79]

It is unclear whether or not Zhang's wish was satisfied. His case nevertheless illustrates the unpredictability of imperial generosity. It took Zhang years to obtain a local post that could afford his stepmother a comfortable life. His petitions for early retirement and nearby posts might not have gone through, once again putting Zhang in the position of having to choose between leaving his stepmother behind and bringing her to an unfamiliar place. Zhang's story reminds us of Li Xuji, who (as noted at the beginning of this chapter) brought Li Yin to Hongzhou from Fujian. Although the Lis moved there permanently, Xuji's career continued to take him away from their new home.

The above examples occurred during the early and mid-Northern Song and involved two northerners. Our third case concerns a southerner, Shi Jiong (n.d.), a native of Changzhou (in Jiangsu) who lived in the late Northern Song. When assigned a post in Hebei, Shi Jiong petitioned that he be reappointed to a close-to-home position out of concern for his parents' advanced age. He was subsequently relocated to the Huaidong Circuit (part of modern Jiangsu and Anhui) and brought his father to live with him. When he was relocated to Poyang (in Jiangxi) a few years later, knowing that "the road is hard to travel and Poyang is a faraway place," Shi Jiong sent in a memorial for reappointment. This time his request was rejected. In the end, Shi moved his father to the more conveniently located Jinling (Nanjing, Jiangsu) so that he could visit him from time to time.[80]

What do the above stories reveal about Northern Song men's *luyang* experience? First, the court, if not as supportive of its officials' reverent care duties as they wished, was responsive to many individual requests. This generosity should not be taken lightly. After all, in any given year, hundreds, if not thousands, of civil servants would have to be evaluated and reappointed.[81] To accommodate even a fraction of the requests for relocation considerations would have created a heavy workload for the various government offices under the guidance of detailed personnel management policies. More important, even if the court had been willing to be more flexible, given that requests had to be managed on a case-by-case basis at a time when communication was slow and not always reliable, it would have been difficult to process all of them in the time allowed for incumbent officials to ready themselves for new posts. That officials had to petition for relocation and often did so multiple times to no avail also indicates that throughout the North Song, close-to-home and conveniently located assignments were meant to symbolize the compassion of the court and therefore were not accommodations to be taken for granted.[82]

Second, our sources do not point to a noticeable trend among civil servants wishing to be dispatched to the same, most selective, destinations. Few, for example, pleaded to be placed in Kaifeng. This observation must be taken with caution, however, since an official would have submitted a memorial only when he was appointed to a place deemed undesirable or inconvenient. In the cases discussed above, Shaanxi, Cangzhou, and Poyang made the list precisely because all were seen as remote and inhospitable. Few would have asked to be transferred away from the capital region, the key political and cultural centers along the Grand Canal, or the middle and lower reaches of the Yangzi River. The officials' geographic origins also played a large role in whether they petitioned for reassignment. Continuing to serve in Sichuan was seen by Cheng Jun as worthy of such a petition, but Bi Shi'an and Zhang Chu would not have considered it feasible to bring their parents there. In the end, the diversity in the office holders' geographic origins determined the large differences in their needs.

Performing *Shiyang*: Serving Parents at Local Posts

In addition to requesting close-to-home posts for reverent care purposes, many official sons achieved *luyang* at its highest level, *shiyang*. Numerous examples of this form of filial practice are available. The mother of Mr. Zhu was said to have moved with her son to several local positions over a period of thirteen years.[83] Similarly, for fifteen years, another official had his mother travel with him to five different destinations.[84] The epitaph for Miss Tian did not give any specific information in this regard. Instead, her eulogist simply remarked that Miss Tian had traveled with her son to far reaches in every direction of the country.[85] Mr. Cao confessed to Huang Tingjian (1045–1105) in multiple letters that he had enjoyed performing *shiyang* since the county he had been serving "is isolated and does not have much official business." Huang responded, "Holding office not far from your native place, which has enabled you to either visit your mother regularly or have her stay with you. . . . Is there any other joy that matches this?"[86]

It should be noted that, just as in the formation of policies that enabled the appointment of officials to close-to-home prefectures, it took the government several decades to allow civil servants to perform *shiyang* at local posts. As late as 1019, state regulations still prohibited civil servants from bringing families to Hedong (modern Shanxi).[87] It was not until 1034 that officials stationed in Sichuan and Shaanxi were permitted to travel with family.[88] Citing safety concerns and the hardships of long-distance travel, these regulations effectively caused lengthy separations between civil servants and their families. Wang Yi and Li Yin, whose *shiyang* deeds or lack thereof are discussed in the introduction and at the beginning of this chapter, fell into this category.

Shiyang practice gained visibility from the mid-eleventh century, a trend that can be readily observed in epitaph writing. In the funerary biographies they authored, Northern Song writers employed the same reverent-care tropes found in earlier filial tales, commending their fellow scholar-officials for being extraordinarily attentive to their parents' most basic needs, including food, lodging, and emotional well-being. Miss Zhao's epitaph recounts that after her son, Mr. Liu, brought her to the capital, he and his wife would wait on her day and night, satisfying her every need. Moreover, Miss Zhao received an honorary title because of her son's merit.[89] A man named Ye was said to have brought his father from Jinling (Nanjing, Jiangsu) to Kaifeng. Every day, Ye would prepare delicious food and strive to please his father.[90] In a particularly detailed account, an official, Zhao, had a Hall of Pleasing Parents (Yuelao Tang) built while serving in Rongzhou (in Sichuan). Since administrative affairs in the prefecture were in order, Zhao was able to spend abundant time with his parents and considered caring for them the "highest pleasure under Heaven." His deeds became so well known that local gentry and scholar-officials extolled him in songs and poems. His fellow-natives and clan members similarly took pride in his outstanding deeds.[91]

In two rather extreme cases, we learn that parents in their eighties relocated with their office-holding sons. An official, Zhao, brought his mother to his post in Suzhou (in Jiangsu) when she was eighty-two. In fact, Zhao specifically asked to be assigned there because his mother would crave bamboo shoots in the early spring, and Suzhou had them in abundance.[92] At eighty-four, Miss Lin moved to live with her official son, Xu, in a neighboring prefecture. Before her arrival, Xu "completely furnished the residence and equipped it with all the necessary utensils. He also prepared everything that could possibly entertain his mother before going home to fetch her."[93]

How do we understand this construction of the ideal family life, in which sons were depicted as parents' devoted caregivers at their local posts? On the one hand, there is no reason for us to question the authenticity of these depictions. After all, we are dealing with the most fundamental familial relationship: that of parents and children. As this study will continue to show, many men confessed the deepest attachment to their parents, took pains to please them, and suffered from shame and guilt when they failed to do so. That many would request hospitable destinations, take parents on official missions, and make their stay comfortable should not come as a surprise. Satisfying parents' cravings for certain foods, providing them with the best furnishings, and preventing boredom with a variety of entertainments would have been the most natural things to do.

On the other hand, given the tendency of funerary biographies to aggrandize the deceased's virtuous conduct, we should treat depictions of such filial deeds with caution, especially when it comes to descriptions of local officials spending a great deal of time with their parents and allusions to sons personally preparing fine food and waiting on their parents. These portrayals were surely hyperbolic because at the same time that they were applauded for dedicating themselves to their parents' welfare, the very same officials were represented as diligent, committed local administrators, another standard trope in Northern Song epitaph writing. When we consider their official responsibilities as well as their social and literary activities, even when office-holding men brought parents with them, most of the mundane tasks were probably performed by their wives, other family members, and maids and servants. This explains why Mr. Zhao's eulogist, mentioned above, highlighted that Zhao was able to concentrate on pleasing his parents because "administrative affairs were in order."

Even though it is impossible to gauge the percentage of official sons who had their parents relocate with them, the practice seems to have become rather common from the mid-eleventh century. One way to confirm this trend is that failing to practice *shiyang* could lead to one's being labeled unfilial. In 1080, Wang Bohu (n.d.) was accused of having left his parents in Fujian for almost a decade while his wife and children were living with him in Kaifeng. Wang was then ordered to move and care for the senior couple in the capital.[94] Similarly, two brothers surnamed Qi got in trouble for leaving their aging parents at home. One was subsequently dismissed so that he could return home to perform his filial duties; the other was allowed to continue his career, but "scholar-officials despised him."[95] In 1108, an official, Zheng, was reevaluated by the Department of Personnel because both his parents were over seventy, yet they had been left at home and had never been brought to Zheng's official post.[96] In 1110, another official was demoted in part because he had neither visited his father (who was over eighty) at home nor brought the father to his place of office for *shiyang*.[97]

Records of this nature appeared only sporadically in the second half of the eleventh century. When they did, it was often in the context of office-holding men having caught the attention of the central government for grossly neglecting their parents' welfare. All the cases above involved a son not visiting his parents for a lengthy period, not to mention failing to care for them. That all were punished to some extent confirms the court's expectation that office-holding men would practice *shiyang*, at least during parts of their careers. In other words, since civil service remained scholar-officials' top career choice, for one to be able to perform reverent care, especially if he was an only son, the only option was to relocate his parents to his local posts.

Responses to Unwilling Parents

For encouraging official sons to practice reverent care at their local appointments, the *shiyang* ideal best embodied the spirit of *luyang*, even though this meant that filial performance occurred away from the parents' home and was subject to official regulations. The idealization of *shiyang* and denunciation of those who failed to bring parents along make us wonder: What if parents were unwilling to travel to a son's local post? If parents were somewhat coerced to relocate, would this not discount the sincerity of the son's filial sentiments?

Abundant evidence reveals that under the façade of a filial son's endeavoring to care for and honor his parents, the *luyang* ideal was not universally accepted by parents with enthusiasm; many found it hard to leave the comfort of their own homes for a son's official destinations. In one instance, an official, Li, reported that it took him much patience to persuade his mother to come to his local post.[98] After having followed her son to different places, a woman broke down in the midst of a conversation about the family's ancestral graveyard. Weeping non-stop, she said to her son, "I would rather return home to sweep the ancestral tomb. What am I doing here staying at government inns?"[99] In a particularly detailed case, upon being appointed to Xiangzhou (Anyang, Henan), a coveted destination, Zhang Yong requested a position in Puzhou (Puyang, Henan) that was closer to his native region. Zhang reasoned:

> I live in a time when Your Majesty rules with filial piety, yet I blame myself for neglecting my parents. I am often reminded that for ten years when I attended school, I was away from home. This was followed by serving two terms in remote places, during which I did not bring my parents with me. Recently, I returned home on an official mission. Upon seeing me, my parents, old and weak, wept. I am not a piece of dead wood. How could I not feel sad? I did evoke the imperial kindness that I had received to console and encourage them. Yet they were not willing to relocate with me due to their attachment to the native place. [For this reason,] I worry day and night, and my mind is troubled."[100]

Citing the fact that "one could not get another pair of parents," Zhang said he was fortunate to have lived in the time of such a sagacious ruler. For this reason, he felt obligated to express his genuine thoughts to the emperor. We do not know if Zhang's request was granted. With his parents adamantly against leaving their native region, Zhang would have to continue to endure both the agony of living far away from them and the resultant guilt from his failure to tend to their needs and well-being.

That many aging parents might have relocated unwillingly can also be seen from the issuance of an imperial order. Dated 1048, the pronouncement condemned and demoted an official, Pang, for forcing his mother to relocate with him.[101] Another indication that some parents might not have been eager to leave their own homes is the emergence in Northern Song epitaphs of praise for parents, and especially mothers, for transferring with their sons. Through sharing the ordeals of long-distance travel, we are told, parents and children expressed deep feelings of love and tenderness for each other.[102]

What was an official son to do if his parents simply chose to stay home? Northern Song office-holding men responded to unwilling parents with one of two approaches. The first involved using their wives as filial surrogates. In the second, sons interrupted their careers to perform reverent care.

The rise of the *luyang* ideal as a new vision for elite male filiality affected women, as both wives and daughters-in-law, in important ways. A survey of Northern Song epitaphs reveals that many were routinely portrayed as the only ones in a household capable of pleasing their in-laws, mothers-in-law in particular, by meticulously caring for the in-laws' material comfort and nursing them back to health in the absence of their office-holding husbands. In this sense, these women became their husbands' filial substitutes when the latter were unavailable and incapable of performing reverent care. In the epitaph for Miss Chen, Fan Zhongyan recounted, Miss Chen's husband, Hu, was repeatedly appointed to remote places in the country:

> But his parents loved to live at home and socialize with families and relatives. Miss Chen was willing to wait on them at their side instead of traveling with her husband. For twenty years, she personally sewed her in-laws' clothes and prepared their meals. When her in-laws passed away, she mourned them for three years with her husband. Only then did she travel to her husband's official post. This was Miss Chen's greatest virtue.[103]

The arrangement at the Hu household reminds us of Li Yin's actions, recounted at the beginning of this chapter. When it was impractical to bring his mother to his official post, Li Yin left her to the care of his wife. The Hus adopted the same strategy. This arrangement ensured that even when the office-holding son was not present, the parents were not alone and were cared for. To further indicate how commonplace this practice was, Su Shunqin's (1008–1048) epitaph for his wife, Miss Zheng, recorded that when he was about to assume a position in Bozhou (in Anhui), Miss Zheng insisted that he leave with their sons and that she stay with his parents.[104] In another instance, as soon as Miss Gao married, her husband was appointed to a distant post and wanted Miss Gao to take care of his aging parents at home. Miss Gao served them diligently and proved her devotion, winning praise from her in-laws and other relatives.[105] Similarly, Miss Tan was specifically praised for staying at home with her mother-in-law, even though the latter urged her to accompany her husband.[106]

The above phenomenon had historical precedents. Daughters and daughters-in-law were expected to and had played an active role in parental care from ancient times. Pre-Han and Han writings from the *Book of Rites* to the *Instructions for Women (Nüjie)* detailed a daughter-in-law's filial duties. The compilation of the *Book of Filial Piety for Women* further established *xiao* as the supreme virtue for women of all social stations.[107] Filial exemplars in early and medieval China were nonetheless mostly men. When women were featured in contemporary accounts, they typically were described as having gone to greater extremes to express their filial devotion. This was so, argues Keith Knapp, because filial piety was considered a male virtue that females performed in the absence of male relatives. "In short, filial females were surrogate sons."[108]

Northern Song representations of female filiality continued to highlight women's care-giving duties as specified in the classics. This general continuity paralleled a major change in social and familial realities: scholarly and office-holding men routinely lived apart from their wives; hence the increasing visibility of the self-sacrificing and all-pleasing daughter-in-law in the absence of the *lu*-earning son. In their daily dealings with the in-laws, women ended up managing their own filial duties as well as those of their husbands. Indeed, Fan Zhongyan put his understanding of women's duties in the most straightforward manner when he wrote, "Nothing surpasses a woman's responsibilities toward her in-laws."[109] In this sense, the redefinition of ideal female virtue in the Northern Song was in part the result of major changes in social and cultural values, especially shifting ideals of male behavior. The *luyang* model, for example, allowed elite men to relegate much of the *yang* duties to their wives. In this context, we can better understand the development of courtesan and concubine culture and the domestication of concubines in the Song.[110] Facing the challenge of balancing their filial duties and official demands, office-holding men might have found a practical solution in apportioning the roles of their wives and concubines, with the latter traveling with them and attending to their needs while the wives stayed at home to care for parents and children. This new "responsibility system" mainly benefited office-holding men, but their wives might not necessarily have resented it due to the distance this arrangement established between themselves and the concubines and the variety of complications that were avoided if these women were not living together under the same roof.

We should not take it for granted, however, that this structure would have been universally favored by parents, especially given the parents' concern for a son's welfare. In the case of Su Shunqin's wife, Miss Zheng, we learn that although she offered to stay with her in-laws, Su's parents insisted that she go along with her husband, as "No officials should leave their wives and children at home."[111] This response from Su's parents reveals that from the perspective of the senior couple, husband and wife should stay together. In this context, women who "chose" to serve their in-laws in the absence of their husbands were considered all the more extraordinary.

Family circumstances could further complicate the way filial duties were understood and carried out by women. When Miss Duan was caught between her reverent care responsibilities to her mother-in-law and her son's wish to practice reverent care at his official position, her mother-in-law reasoned, "My grandson is young and has just entered officialdom, so you should go with him. This way, you can give him advice to prevent him from making and regretting any mistakes." To this Miss Duan responded: "My mother-in-law is old. How could I leave her for a single day?" Eventually convinced to accompany her son, Miss Duan reportedly died soon from missing her mother-in-law.[112] A possible exaggeration of Miss Duan's sense of duty to her mother-in-law aside, her case allows us to see a woman torn between fulfilling her filial obligations and "helping" her son realize his goal of achieving *shiyang*.

In addition to using their wives as filial substitutes, Northern Song scholar-officials found another way to lessen the tension between public service and domestic duties. In the midst of *luyang*'s gaining a prominent place in the representation of male filiality, some office-holding men gave up their careers, either temporarily or permanently, in order to perform reverent care. Among the earliest examples of this practice was a man named Sang, who retired and returned home to wait on his parents.[113] Two other officials, Liu and Du, were said to have resigned for the same reason.[114] Zhao Junci (active mid- to late eleventh century), an extremely filial son, was said to have taken meticulous care of his father. For years, he made sure his father's quilt and clothes were comfortable and warm enough. He personally tasted his father's medicine and food, clipped his nails, and combed his hair. Every night, he slept at his father's side. When he earned the *jinshi* degree, it dawned on him that he could not possibly leave his father behind. For this reason, it was not until his father's death that Zhao accepted an official appointment.[115]

These cases confirm that not all educated men and their families saw government service as the absolute priority and *luyang* as the most desirable filial ideal. The most renowned case we can use to substantiate this supposition is that of Bao Zheng (999–1062), a native of Luzhou (Hefei, Anhui) who chose to continue to practice reverent care over pursuing his official career.[116] Receiving the *jinshi* degree in 1027, Bao was appointed the magistrate of Jianchang (in Jiangxi).

[Bao] declined the appointment [due to its remote location] on the basis of his parents' old age. He was then reappointed to be the Storehouse Keeper in Hezhou [in Anhui, which was close to home]. But his parents simply did not want to leave their native place [i.e., to relocate with their son].

[Bao] Zheng then petitioned for temporary retirement and went home to care for his parents. When his parents died, he lived in a hut next to their graves and did not want to leave for government service even after he had completed mourning.[117]

The above summary appeared in all four biographies for Bao Zheng, for the simple reason that Bao had put his career on hold for almost a decade in order to fulfill his *yang* duties rather than focus on earning *lu*. In coping with his official and private responsibilities, Bao, unlike the majority of his fellow scholar-officials, did not use his wife as his surrogate, nor did he "force" his parents to relocate with him. Instead, he chose *yang* over *lu*. To put his decision in context, of the fifteen hundred or so Northern Song epitaphs for men that I have studied, Bao Zheng was one of only two men who were explicitly designated as having declined two consecutive appointments so that the parents would not have to be left alone or be relocated to an unfamiliar place. For this reason, Bao was given the posthumous title Xiaosu, "the filial and solemn."[118] The other filial exemplar in this category was Fan Chunren (1027–1101), the son of the famous statesman Fan Zhongyan. Fan's biography recorded that when Fan Zhongyan asked Chunren why he had declined a close-to-home post, Chunren said, "How could I consider *lu* to be so important if I had to leave my parents? Although the post is close, it would still be impossible for me to practice *yang* [on a daily basis]."[119]

As less-traveled a path as this was, Bao Zheng and Fan Chunren did have followers who simply could not "bear to leave their parents for distant places."[120] The case of Ge Shusi (1032–1104) is especially noteworthy. "Shusi had always been keen on supporting his parents with *lu*." After earning the examination degree and receiving his first official post, he "pleaded that his father move with him." When the senior Ge refused to do so, Shusi said to himself, "Zengzi (505–435 BCE, a disciple of Confucius) would not leave his mother for one day; how could I change my aspiration because of my pursuit of civil service?" Ge eventually decided to give up his appointment. For years, everyone in the family, including his father, tried to change his mind. Evoking the *luyang* ideal, they went so far as saying, "How could one's filial devotion for his parents be as great as one's being distinguished with glory and fame?" Shusi, however, remained unconvinced. When he was assigned another position ten years later, even though the father disliked traveling, he decided to relocate with Shusi because of his son's demonstrated devotion.[121]

As much as Bao Zheng's and Ge Shusi's deeds made them extraordinarily filial sons, their decade-long withdrawal from officialdom demonstrated to their fellow scholar-officials and their families the negative effects of choosing *yang* over *lu*. Given that Bao went on to have a very successful career, we can only imagine the difference an extra decade would have made. Bao's and Ge's experiences also beg consideration of the implications of *luyang* for parents. While the ideal promoted official ranks, salaries, and privileges as more desirable symbols of filial performance, parents who preferred otherwise might have been put under a great deal of pressure to comply. Bao's and Ge's cases ended differently: Bao Zheng's parents preferred that he stay out of officialdom as long as they lived; Ge Shusi's did not and eventually agreed to move with him.

In a third scenario concerning the choice between *lu* and *yang*, Xie Jikang (1027–1083) of the mid-Northern Song considered temporary retirement for the sake of his aging father, but his father was strongly against his decision. Unwilling to leave his father behind, Xie kept delaying the acceptance of his office. In the end, a friend convinced Xie to continue his career: "Although your father is old, he is unusually strong and healthy. You are from a poor clan. [To help make it prominent,] everyone in the family should work hard to pursue a career in government to satisfy their parents' wishes. How could you be content with receiving food and clothing from your parents while staying at home caring for them?"[122]

Evoking the *luyang* rhetoric, Xie's friend made a strong argument. By staying at home and contributing to his parents' well-being, Xie actually became dependent on his parents for food and clothing. Being from a "poor" family, Xie certainly should not act this way. More important, for the sake of his clan, Xie simply could not afford to lose his official rank and position. Xie's biographer would have us believe that Xie agreed to resume his career only because of strong pressure from his father and friend. In fact, Xie had pleased his father by leaving him behind. As far as his father was concerned, Xie's official career was what he and the family cherished more. Without a doubt, both by his willingness to put his career on hold and for eventually following his father's wishes, Xie demonstrated his filial devotion.

The above cases shed light on the diverse understandings of the relationship between earning *lu* and practicing *yang*. Bao Zheng stayed with his parents at home for a decade. Everyone else succumbed to pressure from parents, family members, and friends. In addition to illustrating the growing influence of the *luyang* ideal throughout the Northern Song, this discussion illustrates the dynamics of parent-son relationships in real-life scenarios. Since ancient times, legal and ritual prescriptions stipulated that children obey parents unconditionally. Ample evidence shows that everyday practice differed greatly from such prescriptions. Keith Knapp's study of medieval filial tales concludes that parental authority was conditional and far from overwhelming. Seniors often worried that adult sons would subvert their authority by disobeying them, make financial transactions behind their backs, or regard them as cumbersome burdens.[123] In fact, unfilial children in the Song were known to have acted outrageously, going so far as to mistreat, abuse, and even murder parents.[124] In the context of our current discussion, with the elevation of *lu* earning and the common practice of parents being relocated for *yang* purposes, parents (and widowed mothers in particular) often found themselves in a disadvantaged position. With sons giving up *lu* being seen as the least desirable option, none of the remaining choices, which included a parent's being left at home alone, living with a daughter-in-law, or traveling long distances with the office-holding son, presented an ideal situation.

The lack of a perfect solution aside, some families fared better than others. The next section features the Meis of Xuanzhou (in Anhui) and the way its members managed their filial duties.

A Divided System of Filial Performance: The Meis of Xuanzhou

In highlighting office-holding men's filial sentiments, Northern Song government documents and literati writings often portrayed these men as if they were their parents' only sons and sole caregivers. In reality, many had multiple siblings and shared parental care responsibilities with their wives, non-office-holding brothers, and other family members. This case study uses the Meis of Xuanzhou to illustrate the allocation of reverent care duties in a family across two generations. More important, it provides us with an opportunity to consider the filial performance of non-official sons and approach reverent care from the perspective of a father.

Some background about the family under discussion is in order. The Mei family of Xuanzhou saw its rise in the early Northern Song, with Mei Xun earning the *jinshi* degree in 989.[125] Xun went on to enjoy a long official career. He and his older brother, Mei Rang (959–1049), each had five sons. Of the ten junior Mei men, all of Xun's and three of Rang's sons held office, with Mei Yaochen (1002–1060), son of Mei Rang, being the most famous of that generation. Mei Yaochen was a prominent poet and close friend of Ouyang Xiu. As a result, Ouyang, one of the most outstanding political and literary figures and the most highly regarded epitaph writer in the Northern Song, authored the funerary biographies of Mei Xun, Mei Rang, and Mei Yaochen.[126] Mei Xun's and Mei Yaochen's biographies almost exclusively focus on their bureaucratic and scholarly achievements. Except for references to the honorary titles that the two earned for their parents, neither mentions any specific filial deed.[127] It is Mei Rang's epitaph that depicts a non-office-holding man and his role as the practitioner and recipient of filial devotion. Another important text for the study of the family is Yang Jie's (1022–1091) funerary biography for Mei Zhengchen (1004–1082), Yaochen's younger brother.[128]

Ouyang Xiu's funerary biography for Mei Rang begins with Mei's unique view about earning *lu*. Although a "learned man," Mei Rang was ambivalent about entering civil service. When his younger brother, Mei Xun, encouraged him to seek an official career, Mei Rang replied as follows:

> If a gentleman intends to serve the court, it is easy to acquire emolument. What is difficult to accomplish is for one to realize his aspirations but still be able to have a clear conscience [while remaining in officialdom]. How could I not wish to serve the court? I would rather not enter officialdom, however, if, as a result of becoming an official and receiving a salary, I cannot fulfill my aspirations or maintain a clear conscience. I now live in my parents' native region. I wait on my elders with respect, associate with friends I trust, guard my family graveyard with care, and lead a contented life amid my neighbors. I would have no regrets aging and dying this way. These are my true aspirations.[129]

Mei Rang made it clear that he and his brother had very different life goals and that in the early Northern Song examination success and civil service might not have thoroughly captivated the local elites. While Mei Xun pursued an official career that took him to distant places, Mei Rang was pleased to stay close to his family and ancestral graveyard. In the end, Xun obtained a sinecure position for Rang so that he could continue to live at home.[130]

Mei Rang's elaboration of his aspirations pointed to a vision of divided responsibilities between himself, the at-home care provider, and his younger brother, the *luyang* performer. Xun was expected to bring honor to his parents and the family through earning official emoluments, while Rang stayed home to manage household matters, including waiting on family elders, planning for their funerals and burials, and tending to the ancestral graveyard and sacrificial ceremonies. Short of calling himself filial, Mei Rang's summary of these obligations revealed his understanding of filial performance and the high value he saw in its fulfillment. Nowhere in Mei Xun's biography is it indicated that he had ever requested a close-to-home appointment or brought his parents to a local position. Indeed, because of Mei Rang's availability and willingness to take on the *yang* duties, Mei Xun never needed to worry about his parents' well-being.

For obtaining *lu* (Mei Xun) and practicing *yang* (Mei Rang), both men would have been considered filial sons. In addition to earning the brothers the much sought-after reputation and assuring the well-being of their parents, this model of divided filial duties had other significant implications. Mei Xun's appreciation of Mei Rang's commitment to parental care materialized in his protection of three of Rang's sons into civil service.[131] Xun's elevation of his nephews makes us wonder: Did he do so as compensation for the reverent care tasks that Rang had performed in his stead? Given Rang's role as the parents' principal caregiver, did the senior Meis ever suggest to Xun that he should return the favor to the best of his abilities? Extant sources do not provide us with definite answers. These questions nonetheless allow us to consider the dynamics of family life, especially the blurring boundaries between *xiao* and *ti* (brotherliness), which made filial performance as much a family strategy as an individual endeavor.

The Meis' system, in which the sons took on distinct filial duties, seems to have worked reasonably well. As a father, Mei Rang clearly expressed the desire to continue the same pattern. Ouyang Xiu wrote that three of Mei Rang's five adult sons held office. When Rang grew old, all were eager to seek temporary retirement and return home to care for their father. Mei Rang rejected their proposal firmly: "That would not be my wish." He then went on to elaborate:

> [Mei Rang] turned to the two sons [who were not officials] and said: "Make an effort day and night to assist me in my old age." He then turned to the three [office-holding] sons and said: "Work hard to earn honors to make me proud. Those of you who stay at home care for my body, and those who serve in officialdom help me realize my aspirations. This would be ideal."[132]

What makes Ouyang Xiu's epitaph for Mei Rang most interesting is its inclusion of a parent's perspective on filial performance and the relationship between seeking *lu* and practicing *yang*. Mei Rang acknowledged that he needed to be cared for, but he did not wish for or need all of his sons to take on the care-giving role. Instead, he recognized his good fortune in having been afforded the most desirable arrangement, with two sons by his side to wait on him and three others to bring him and the family honor and prestige.

We do have to ask whether Mei Rang actually said what Ouyang recorded or whether Mei Yaochen or Ouyang put those words in Mei Rang's mouth. It is certainly possible that Mei Rang had expressed similar ideas. After all, as a son, he had acted as the caretaker while his younger brother was away earning *lu* for the family. Having personally experienced the system's effectiveness, Mei Rang expected the same from his sons. There is also the possibility that Mei Yaochen, when providing Ouyang Xiu with information about his father, polished Rang's words to suit his own purposes. Being the oldest of five sons and constantly away from his parents and native place, Yaochen must have seen the resemblance in his situation and that of his uncle. If the division of filial responsibilities had worked for the Meis in the previous generation, there was no reason why the same structure should not continue in the current one.

The experience of Mei Zhengchen, son of Mei Rang and younger brother of Yaochen, further reveals the complexities of reverent performance in the family setting.[133] Yang Jie, Zhengchen's funerary biographer, recounted that Zhengchen, just like his father, was not genuinely interested in office holding and had prepared for the examination only at his father's request. He occupied at least six local positions in the southeast before being impeached and dismissed. Yang Jie continues:

> At the time, his mother was over seventy. After returning to their native place, she would see family members and relatives every day and was happier than when she lived in other prefectures [with Zhengchen]. Mr. Mei then told his friends, "Ever since entering officialdom, I have traveled often on imperial order so have not been able to be at my parents' side. I often feel that I have failed in caring for my parents. Now that my mother is old, how could I dare to concentrate on office holding?" He therefore renovated the family residence, built a pond, and planted bamboo and over one hundred varieties of plants and fruit trees. Every day, he would lead his sons and grandsons to wait on his mother. He enjoyed the time with his family so much that he lost interest in anything else. The year after he completed his mother's mourning, he had reached seventy so did not return to officialdom. Those who knew him applauded his actions.[134]

Mei Zhengchen's epitaph reveals several things that were missing from those of the other Mei men. First, Mei Rang married twice, first to a Miss Shu, then to a Miss Zhang. It is unclear which of the five sons each of the two women mothered individually. It is probably safe to assume that Miss Zhang was Zhengchen's birth mother and that she traveled with Zhengchen to multiple official posts, almost certainly after Mei Rang's death. Second, just like his two other office-holding brothers, Zhengchen did not perform much reverent care at his father's side but was said to have mourned Mei Rang with propriety. Third, after Mei Rang's death, Zhengchen took his mother to his official posts. This, in combination with the time that he spent at home after his dismissal, meant that Zhengchen played a significant role in caring for his mother.

For the purpose of this case study, Miss Zhang's departure from Xuanzhou with Zhengchen indicated that the ideal system that Mei Rang envisioned, with parents enjoying the honor earned by official sons while being cared for at home by a non–office holder, had ceased to work. Many factors might have contributed to this change. One explanation is that while Mei Rang did not want to leave his home, Miss Zhang was eventually convinced by Zhengchen to visit other places. Another possibility is that Zhengchen was his mother's favorite son or that Miss Zhang simply wanted to live with Zhengchen after the death of her husband. It is also conceivable that with Mei Rang's passing, Miss Zhang no longer received the level of care that she and her husband used to enjoy, now that the stay-at-home sons did not feel the pressure from an authoritative family head. Zhengchen might have taken his mother to his official posts because all or most of his brothers had died, leaving him with no other alternative. If Zhengchen took on parental care responsibilities "involuntarily," the setback in his career and the return of the mother and son to Xuanzhou afforded him the precious opportunity to focus on his mother's well-being in the last years of her life. Seen from a different perspective, even though Yang Jie praised Zhengchen's wholehearted dedication to his mother's well-being, it was not until his dismissal from officialdom that Zhengchen became the filial son that Yang Jie made him out to be.

This story about the Meis allows us to reconstruct how reverent care was performed in an elite household. Mei Rang proved the key figure in articulating a well-divided system, allowing all his sons to be deemed filial for fulfilling dramatically different duties. The system made it possible for the office-holding sons to continue their careers yet spared the senior Meis long-distance travel and a parting from their home, native region, and ancestral graveyard. Most important, the Meis' experience provides solid evidence regarding the popularity of the *luyang* ideal and the sort of changes that it triggered in filial practice for office-holding and non-office-holding sons. In addition to celebrating Mei Rang's life, Ouyang's epitaph for Mei Rang highlighted Mei Yaochen's *luyang* achievement. To portray his friend as a filial son, Ouyang described a time when Yaochen went home to visit his aging father. "Wearing a red official robe and carrying an official tablet [a symbol of official ranks], Yaochen stood at his father's side. Fellow villagers did not envy Yaochen but rather his father."[135]

The image of Yaochen standing next to his father reminds us of the poem on the successful candidate returning home and creating a scene in the village, cited above.[136] To Ouyang, for bringing official emoluments to his parents and conveying his willingness to seek temporary retirement to practice *yang*, Yaochen demonstrated his strong devotion to his parents. This perspective also explains the lack of filial reference in Mei Yaochen's epitaph. Long before he wrote Yaochen's epitaph, Ouyang Xiu had established Yaochen's *luyang* accomplishments in his father's funerary biography.[137] In focusing on Mei Yaochen, however, Ouyang Xiu slighted Yaochen's non-office-holding brothers and their wives. All ended up being voiceless.

Other factors further complicated Mei Rang's ideal system of divided filial duties. First of all, its continuation required that in each generation, a family produced multiple sons who lived to adulthood, with at least one succeeding in government service and one staying home. This would not have worked for families of other circumstances, such as that of Ouyang Xiu. Having lost his father as a boy, Ouyang was brought up by his mother, Miss Zheng. He was successful in practicing *luyang*, and out of necessity, Miss Zheng accompanied her only son on multiple official trips and died far away from the family's native region of Jiangxi. Given a choice, both mother and son might have preferred having a non-official member to share the responsibilities of parental care. The Meis' divided system also would not have worked for families that saw extraordinary success in examinations and civil service. Take Mei Yaochen's contemporary, Zeng Gong (1019–1083) of Nanfeng (in Jiangxi). With all the Zeng brothers in officialdom, their mother, Miss Zhu, was never in the position of choosing to live in their native region. Relocating with one of her sons became the norm and a necessity for Miss Zhu for the rest of her life.[138]

Despite its moderate success, Mei Rang's system did not solve the conflict between *lu* and *yang* for Yaochen and his official brothers. Even though they did not have to worry about their father's well-being, the father and sons had to live far apart from each other, and the office-holding sons had to live far from their native region and the family graveyard. Finally, Mei Rang's juxtaposition of the roles of his official and non-official sons aside, the reverent care deeds of the two non-official sons were effectively marginalized in extant records while the *lu*-earning sons emerged as outstanding filial exemplars.

Performing *Shiyang* to Concubine Mothers

Another factor complicated elite family life. As concubines "became fully integrated into elite households, by the late Northern Song, their widespread presence and the new social and household dynamics they created gave rise to two parallel discourses about them," one emphasizing the danger they posed, the other emphasizing the role of concubine mothers as the objects of filial devotion from their literati sons.[139] Sons by concubines subsequently gained increasing visibility in Northern Song portrayals of ideal *luyang* performance.

References to sons waiting on concubine mothers with diligence and sincerity appeared more than sporadically in *muzhiming* writing. In his epitaph for his concubine mother, Miss Hu, Han Qi highlighted his *luyang* and *shiyang* performance. Since he was too young when his father and legal mother, Miss Luo, died, Han wrote that he was able to practice filial piety only to Miss Hu. Han provided two pieces of evidence in this regard. First, when he and his older brother passed the examination in 1027, "We prostrated ourselves in front of *furen* [Miss Hu] in colorful clothes and congratulated her. This was considered a glorious event at the time."[140] Alluding to a legendary filial paragon pleasing his aging parents, Han Qi juxtaposed his and his brother's action with that of the exemplar, therefore establishing themselves as *luyang* models. In the next several decades, Han Qi would earn multiple honorary titles for Miss Hu.[141] She was listed in Han Qi's *xingzhuang* and epitaph. His *xingzhuang* author, Li Qingchen, even referred to Miss Hu as Han Qi's mother, completely ignoring her concubine status.[142]

Han Qi's devotion to Miss Hu did not stop with his bringing her unprecedented honor. His dedication can also be seen through his performing *shiyang*. As soon as he received his first official appointment, Han Qi brought Miss Hu with him and, along with his wife, "waited on her meals in the morning and evening. We tried to please her and practiced reverent care without any violation. When I was about to be transferred in the eighth year [of the Tiansheng reign, 1030], *furen*'s old illness attacked her again. I looked for folk prescriptions day and night, prepared medicine, and personally ground herbs without entrusting the matter to anyone else. I prayed to gods and looked for doctors, but nothing worked."[143]

We have no reason to doubt the close bond between the concubine mother and son. Another important factor further explained Han Qi's genuine attachment to Miss Hu. Han Qi was only four when he lost his father. His legal mother, Miss Luo, soon moved back to be with her natal family, where she died several years later. By the time Han Qi earned the *jinshi* degree, three of his five older brothers had also passed away. This means not only that Han Qi was practically brought up by Miss Hu alone, in the absence of Miss Luo, but also that Miss Hu had been in charge of the Han household, a fact that was confirmed by Han Qi's epitaph.[144] Thus Miss Hu's relocation with Han Qi to his local post did not result from any pressure from other family members.

To a large extent, Han Qi's reverent care duties were made simple because both his father and legal mother had died before he reached adulthood. What if

Miss Luo had stayed in the Han household and lived longer? How would Han Qi have dealt with caring for two mothers? While extant sources do not provide an answer to these hypothetical questions, the experience of two Northern Song officials, Zhang Yongde (928–1000) and Jia An (1022–1065), offer a rare look at sons fulfilling filial duties to both a legal and a concubine mother simultaneously.[145]

Zhang Yongde of the early Northern Song was best known for bringing his concubine mother, Miss Ma, back to the Zhang household after she had been expelled and remarried. Zhang made another extraordinary move when he was appointed to Dengzhou (in Henan): he took both his stepmother, Miss Liu, and Miss Ma with him in order to practice *shiyang*. More specifically, Zhang had two halls built, housing Miss Liu in one and Miss Ma in the other. Day in and day out, Zhang would care for and treat both mothers equally. After Miss Liu's death, Miss Ma was even allowed to attend imperial audiences with Emperor Taizong, a strong case of a mother gaining privilege through her son.[146]

There are many unanswered questions in Zhang's story. Did Miss Ma leave the Zhang household when Yongde was only a baby or an older boy? Who was the one that raised him, and to whom did he have the closest emotional attachment? How old were the two women when Miss Ma returned, and how did they feel about their son's two-hall arrangement? Given that Miss Liu went with Zhang Yongde to his official post, it is very possible that he was her only source of support. In this sense, by the time Miss Liu lost her husband, there was little she could have done to stop Zhang from bringing his birth mother back.

Zhang's reunion with his concubine mother and his *shiyang* practice represented the earliest references in the Northern Song on both counts. Zhang readily acknowledged that his stepmother deserved a more prominent place. Yet the fact that Miss Ma had her own quarters on the opposite side of the same complex indicates that Zhang designed a somewhat "separate but equal" system that meant to blur the status differences between Miss Liu and Miss Ma. Moreover, although the two buildings were said to have allowed Zhang to show special respect for Miss Liu, it was entirely possible that the arrangement came about because the two women did not get along. Last, note that Zhang's merit won his concubine mother an imperial audience at age eighty-one. Not only was Miss Ma given an honorary title, but Zhang's stepbrother by Miss Ma was even granted official rank.[147]

Jia An's experience paralleled that of Zhang Youde in more than one aspect. Jia's birth mother, Miss Chen, was a concubine and divorced by Jia's father. Jia An's *xingzhuang* (record of conduct) records that when Jia was young, he implored that Miss Chen be allowed to return to the Jia household. Jia's father responded that he would allow it when and if Jia An passed the examination.

When Jia An earned the degree, he realized his wish and welcomed Miss Chen home. Both Miss Chen and Jia's stepmother, Miss Shi, were later granted honorary titles due to Jia An's merit.[148] In the anecdotal version of the same story, Jia was specifically portrayed as performing reverent care to both mothers, even though his official biography specifically stated that "the two mothers did not get along."[149]

A discussion of filial performance toward concubine mothers would not be complete without reference to the case of Zhu Shouchang (n.d.), who, upon learning that his concubine mother was expelled from the family when he was three, vowed to locate her. Having succeeded in finding her fifty years later, in 1070, Zhu "supported and waited on her for three years before she died, when he was completely devastated."[150] Zhu's filial performance, most possibly dated after Jia An's, attracted tremendous political and literary attention. Multiple memorials and poems were composed in his honor.[151] His outstanding deed earned him a place in the official Song history.[152] Categorized as one of the illustrious "Twenty-Four Filial Exemplars," Zhu continued to inspire sons from later periods to emulate his behavior.[153]

Although small in number, the above cases reveal the close relationship between a son's success in officialdom and his filial performance toward concubine mothers. While most concubines received no recognition in their husbands' epitaphs, some benefited from their sons' success. Other factors were at work as well. For the four men discussed above, the reverent care experience with their birth mothers was possible owing to the lack of a father or strong legal mother in their lives. Miss Luo, Han Qi's legal mother, left the Han household and later died with her natal family. Miss Liu, Zhang Yongde's stepmother, and Miss Shi, Jia An's stepmother, were dependent on Zhang and Jia and therefore not in a position to challenge their sons' reunion with and devotion to their concubine mothers. Zhu Shouchang did not learn about his birth mother's identity until his fifties, presumably after having lost both his father and legal mother. In the end, it was not only the sons' wishes but also their circumstances that allowed for their expressions of devotion to the concubine mothers.

In the Northern Song, the self-identity of China's scholarly and social elite was more intricately linked to office-holding than ever before. As a result, an educated man's performance of the most sacred familial duty became inseparable from his fortunes in officialdom. The *luyang* ideal—by recognizing office-holding sons' ability to glorify and support parents through the honors and privileges they received from the state as legitimate and most desirable symbols of filial devotion—firmly established a *lu*-earning son as the new filial paragon. This major change in elite male filiality was promoted by literati writings, as well as by government policies that recognized and accommodated civil servants' domestic obligations. As recipients of examination degrees, official ranks and salaries, and honorary titles for parents and other ancestors, Northern Song office holders were portrayed as filial sons, even though most were rarely physically available for parents because of their demanding careers.

Clearly, the *luyang* ideal and the institutional measures that supported the rhetoric did not and were not meant to completely unravel the inherent conflict between filial piety and court service. As long as earning *lu* was seen as educated men's top career choice, they were required to embark on long-distance journeys. It was up to office-holding sons and their families to strike a balance between their public and private obligations. The rise of the *luyang* discourse had two additional ramifications. First, the promotion of *luyang* increasingly juxtaposed the filial performance of *lu*-earning sons and that of women and non-office-holding men. Having always been parental caretakers, the non-office-holding men and women took on larger shares of the same responsibilities due to the absence of the office-holding members of the family. Women often served in this capacity and acted as their husbands' substitutes. Given that our most important sources, official documents and epitaphs, were predominantly written by office-holding men for their fellow officials and wives, the role of non-official men remains especially marginalized. Suffice it to say that the uneven attention to the *yang* performances of men and women in elite households transformed filial piety into a more gendered and status-oriented virtue.

The propagation of the *luyang* ideal also had large implications for family life, characterized by the frequent and extensive geographical mobility of office-holding men, their parents, and other family members, as well as the lengthy separations between parents and sons and husbands and wives. Many died in transition, making mourning and burial, already emotional, expensive, and time-consuming tasks, even more overwhelming to manage. As the following chapters will show, this process not only complicated filial practices for both office- and non-office-holding family members, but it also led to changing views on and relationships with one's home and native region.

CHAPTER 2

Mourning and Filial Piety
Policies and Practices

The renowned statesman and literary giant Ouyang Xiu lost his father when he was four years old. As an only son, Ouyang brought his mother, Miss Zheng (981–1052), to multiple local appointments so that he could perform parental care. When Miss Zheng died in the Southern Capital (Shangqiu, Henan) in the third month of 1052, Ouyang immediately began to prepare for her funeral in Yingzhou (Fuyang, Anhui). Far from the family's native place of Jizhou (in Jiangxi), where his father was buried, Yingzhou had been chosen as Miss Zheng's final resting place years ago. For unknown reasons, Ouyang later changed his mind and moved Miss Zheng's coffin, along with the remains of his two wives, back to Jiangxi for entombment. As soon as the burials were complete, he returned to Yingzhou, where he continued mourning until mid-1054.[1]

Three aspects of Ouyang's mourning practice merit mention. First, Ouyang, just as his filial counterparts from earlier times, was said to have been devastated by his mother's passing; he was so grief-stricken that his hair turned completely white.[2] Second, Ouyang was able to complete the three-year rites from 1052 to 1054 only after he had secured the court's permission for a mourning leave and declined multiple orders recalling him back to office. Third, Miss Zheng died in the Southern Capital, far from where she was originally intended to be (Yingzhou) and eventually buried (Jizhou). This meant that Ouyang spent a large chunk of his mourning leave traveling among the three places.

This chapter delineates mourning as a filial expression for Northern Song scholar-officials. One common challenge in studying how Ouyang Xiu and his peers dealt with the loss of their parents is the paucity of personal narratives; Song elite men rarely recorded in detail the devastating experience of parental death. One explanation relates to protocol: ritual codes required that mourning sons discontinue their normal lives, remain in seclusion, and focus on grieving and managing parents' posthumous affairs. For the sake of decorum, writing was simply not supposed to be a preoccupation for even the most distinguished authors. The lack of self-representation vis-à-vis mourning also derived from practicality: a son might have been too emotionally overwhelmed and physically debilitated to write. A third factor was the universal acceptance of the vocabulary of mourning made available by the classics. As this chapter will show, despite the emergence of new practices in the Northern Song, the dominant terminologies employed to describe mourning and a grieving son were continuations from earlier times. This was true of most genres of elegiac writing. For these reasons, it is almost impossible to trace one person's mourning experience over a lengthy period of time.

This study therefore takes a different approach. The first half of the chapter will focus on evolving government policies on mourning leave for civil servants. It will show that compared to earlier dynasties, the Northern Song government implemented systematic guidelines on mourning-related matters. More important, the tone of official regulations changed in the mid-Northern Song. In the first half of the dynasty, stringent protocols made it almost impossible for civil servants to obtain full, three-year mourning leaves. By the mid-eleventh century, however, such leave was made mandatory. This shift in policy was the result of specific political and administrative considerations, as well as the gradual ascendance of the literati in government.

The second part of this chapter will examine the representation of a variety of mourning practices in Northern Song funerary biographies. While centuries-old literary tropes continued to be employed in the portrayal of a grief-stricken son, the period witnessed the advent of new mourning motifs and a diversity of performances. Several themes stand out. First, young boys were frequently described as exceptional mourners. Second, office-holding men were routinely praised for displaying pain and sorrow while rushing home to tend to parents' funerals or traveling with parents' bodies. Third, at a time when Buddhism and Daoism played a major role in death rituals, some scholar-officials were singled out for actively fighting and correcting unorthodox mourning practices. Unlike the court ritualists and scholar-intellectuals, these men did not elucidate their stances through elaborate treatises. Instead, they deliberately set themselves up as role models for local populations and were applauded by their biographers for transforming the minds and hearts of those around them. The chapter will end with a discussion of the evolution of Northern Song policies on and changing attitudes toward how concubine mothers were mourned.

Mourning in the Classics and in Pre-Song Times

Ritual performance, especially death rituals, occupied a central place in ancient Chinese ethical systems due to its utility in defining patterns of human relationships and supporting ancestral worship practices. The three-year rites, the highest in the graded mourning system, required sons to grieve for the passing of parents for twenty-five to twenty-seven months, during which the dead were transformed into ancestors while the sons and the rest of the family gradually transitioned back to normal life.[3] All major Confucian thinkers commented on extended mourning as a sacred filial obligation. Confucius highlighted the three-year rites as "a universal custom," specifically stating, "When it comes to mourning, it is better to be overwhelmed with grief than overly composed."[4] Mencius similarly declared the three-year rites to be the obligation of all sons, "from the Son of Heaven down to the commoner."[5] Xunzi (ca. 313–238 BCE), who placed much emphasis on the performative aspect of death rituals, characterized coarse garments, the deprivation of material comforts, and various forms of the public display of sorrow as the means "by which one responds to threatening events and by which one pays homage to ill fortune."[6]

Confucian classics and rituals manuals, most prominently the *Yili* (*Ceremonies and Rites*) and *Liji* (*Book of Rites*), offered exhaustive prescriptions for proper mourning. Beginning with the end of soul-calling, the chief mourner, overwhelmed by grief, would experience intense sorrow and become emaciated from eating coarse, vegetarian food, and wailing. Throughout the grieving period, he would wear a white hemp garment (*zhancui*) with rough sleeves. This explains why the end of mourning became known as "taking off the mourning clothes [*chufu*]." The son was also expected to remain in social isolation, characterized by living in a thatched hut next to the tomb (*lumu*). The phases of the three-year mourning period are designated by *zuku* (to stop wailing nonstop), which marks the hundredth-day anniversary of a parent's passing; *xiaoxiang* (the small sacrifice); and *daxiang* (the great sacrifice); the latter two represent the thirteenth- and twenty-fifth-month anniversaries respectively.[7]

Two points merit further explanation. First, despite the prescribed length and austerities, ritual texts generally discouraged sons from mourning in excess of the rites. In fact, dying from emaciation was considered a failure in filial fulfillment. Second, the father-son relationship took priority over the mother-son relationship. A noble son, for example, would wear the white hemp garment with rough sleeves for his father but the same white hemp with smooth sleeves (*qicui*) for his mother. If the father was alive, the son would shorten the mourning period for his mother to one year.[8] The mother's ritual status improved over time. It was not until the late seventh century, however, that Empress Wu proposed that a full three-year mourning period be observed for a mother even if the father was still alive.[9]

The above ritual protocols remained the standard rhetoric in both official pronouncements and literary works regarding proper mourning throughout imperial times. How widely the three-year rites were practiced and to what extent sons followed the classical prescriptions remain subjects of ongoing scholarly debate. Extant records from the Eastern Zhou (770–256 BCE) to the Han suggest that members of the royal and noble families usually stopped wearing mourning at the completion of a parent's burial, which typically took three months to a year.[10] Few men, for example, were known to have worn mourning for three years in the Western Han. In fact, both Western Han thinkers and official rhetoric regarded impartial public service, rather than extended mourning, as the most important filial expression. In the Eastern Han, the changing balance of power between the Han court and the local elites resulted in shifting views on the relationship between official and domestic responsibilities. Extended mourning subsequently gained visibility as a crucial filial obligation.[11]

The centrality of mourning as a fundamental filial duty continued in early medieval times. As Keith Knapp has observed, "When early medieval people wanted to describe how filial a person was, they would talk about the behavior he or she exhibited while mourning."[12] As a result, even though the classical ritual texts warned sons of excessive mourning for fear of fatal damage to the body, those honoring the memory of a parent by depriving themselves of food, staying in perpetual mourning, living in a thatched hut next to a parent's grave, and becoming emaciated or even dying from grief were singled out as the ultimate filial exemplars in contemporary filial tales.[13]

The elevation of extended mourning gradually found its way into state policies in the Period of Disunity. For the first time in Chinese history, the Northern Wei government (386–534) incorporated three-year mourning into its code of law. Pursuing government service during mourning carried a penalty of a five-year imprisonment.[14] The institutionalization of mourning rites for elites as well as the general populace continued in Tang (618–907) legal and ritual codes. The *Great Tang Code* (dated 651) specified a variety of punishments, ranging from exile to heavy beating, for one's failing to observe the mourning rites. The violations included (1) hiding or fabricating the news of a parent's death; (2) wearing auspicious clothes; (3) participating in entertainments; (4) marrying, being in charge of weddings, or serving as a matchmaker; (5) begetting children; (6) pursuing official service.[15] The *Datang kaiyuan li* (*Rituals of the Kaiyuan Period of the Great Tang*, 732) included detailed instructions regarding the mourning behavior of the emperor, members of the royal house, and civil servants.[16]

The inclusion of the three-year mourning rites in official documents did not necessarily lead to their vigorous implementation. Despite stringent wording, the state denied most office-holders full or even partial mourning leaves through *duoqing* (to deprive an official the opportunity to express filial devotion—i.e., to disallow or interrupt a mourning leave) and *qifu* (to recall an official back to office). In fact, *duoqing* and *qifu* were so widely practiced that officials in mourning simply anticipated a quick recall. Some who received a leave were known to have petitioned for a fast reinstatement.[17] Throughout the dynasty, fewer than a handful of violators were punished for mourning-related transgressions.[18] It is therefore reasonable to conclude that extended mourning was not a genuine concern for either the state or the majority of Tang officials.

Northern Song Policies on Mourning Leave for Civil Servants

The *Song Penal Code* contained almost the exact same regulations regarding office holders' and commoners' mourning obligations as the *Great Tang Code*.[19] Those detailed stipulations were supplemented by the issuance of edicts and ritual codes and additions from court memorials and ritual debates. Combined, these documents revealed major shifts in official policies on mourning leave for civil servants.[20] Of primary concern was the tension between the official promotion of filial piety and the state's demands on its administrators. As a result, it was not until the second half of the Northern Song that the three-year mourning leave became a universally enforced policy for the first time in Chinese history.

For personnel management purposes, the Song state was deeply involved in the major events in its civil servants' lives. Death was no exception. In 998, an imperial edict required that all civil servants report the passing of parents and the place where they planned to wear mourning to the Ritual Academy (Taichang Liyuan) and the Censorate (Yushitai), which supervised the implementation of leave policies.[21] In the second half of the Northern Song, when the three-year mourning leave became the norm, officials were further expected to submit memorials of gratitude at the end of their leave for reappointment purposes.[22]

Approximately three dozen imperial edicts, promulgated between 985 and 1092, allow us to trace the institutionalization of mourning leave for civil servants in the Northern Song.[23] Except for the very first decades of the dynasty, most civil servants were generally permitted some leave. As brief as they were, two early edicts, dated 985 and 989, hinted that capital officials (*jingguan*), capital and metropolitan officials serving outside of the capital (*wairen jingchao guan*), and ancillary officers serving in prefectures and counties (*muzhi zhou-xian guan*) were eligible for mourning leave. The 985 edict stated, "The three-year mourning rites are commonly observed death rituals. They were the teachings of the sages and have not changed for hundreds of generations. Previously, officials in mourning were often deprived of a leave because the government needed their service."[24] The edict made it clear that the new dynasty had failed to grant its officials mourning leave in the first twenty-five years but stopped short at making any promises. The 989 decree further explicated the rationale behind the earlier prohibition: "By the time an official [who has lost a parent] is replaced [at his local post], his [allotted] mourning leave will be close to its end." This explanation implied that due to slow transportation and communication between the political center and the regional and local offices, it had been unrealistic to grant mourning leaves to civil servants without hindering local administration. The decree did announce that from then on, officials who had a competent associate to temporarily replace them would be allowed to wear mourning. If such a person was not available, the local government would notify the court to ask for a substitute immediately.[25]

If the unavailability of a capable associate and the necessary wait for a replacement already served as constraints on this policy, geographical distance further complicated its implementation. Although vague, an edict issued in 998 suggested that officials who had just been granted a leave might depart their local post for their native region or another destination. There were major exceptions to this allowance. Southerners serving in the north were forbidden to return home for mourning.[26] Officials serving in distant and strategically important areas, including the Sichuan, Guangdong, Guangxi, Jiangzhe, and Hedong circuits, were clearly prohibited from doing so at a time when travel was slow and unsafe and when the timely dispatching of officials to these regions was not in full operation. Another decree, issued in the same year, restated that officials stationed in Sichuan, Shaanxi, Fujian, and southern Guangdong and Guangxi were not allowed to take mourning leaves due to a shortage of replacements.[27]

The above policies explained the widespread use of *duoqing* and *qifu* in the early decades of the dynasty. Zhang Yong's experience best illustrates the ramifications of these official concerns. While serving in Sichuan in the 990s, Zhang suffered the deaths of both parents. Two *duoqing* orders made returning home or temporary dismissal from office out of the question. It was not until years later, when he was finally back in the capital, that Zhang petitioned to observe *xinsang* (to mourn in the heart) for his parents to make up for the negligence of his filial duties.[28] Zhang's filial gesture occurred at a time when government restrictions on mourning leaves for civil servants had been somewhat relaxed. By 1021, officials in all but four prefectures in Sichuan were required to notify and wait to hear from the court following the death of a parent, indicating the emergence of standard mourning-leave policies. In fact, those who requested to be excused from wearing mourning were subject to punishment.[29]

It is important to note that none of the above edicts specified the length of granted leaves. Evidence suggests that it remained brief. A 994 edict criticized officials whose father or older brother had died within one hundred days for visiting superiors at their offices. To the court, such visits were evidence that the mourners had forgotten "the sorrow that they are [supposed to be] experiencing, which tarnishes social customs."[30] The same document nonetheless reveals that it was common for officials in their first hundred days of mourning to be in active service and carry out normal administrative responsibilities. In fact, since the edict targeted only those who had lost a parent within a hundred days, it is reasonable to assume that the period had been the maximum time that most civil servants were granted. That officials normally received one hundred days of mourning leave can also be seen from an undated early Northern Song policy that stipulated that all officials ranked grade seven and above be recalled to service after completing *zuku*.[31] For most, this time would not have been enough to travel to and mourn at the side of the deceased parent. This supposition is confirmed by the 998 edict that required officials to report their place of mourning. Most office-holding men in the early Northern Song, it seems, had worn mourning in their local positions.

In all likelihood, the above policy decisions were responses to popular demand. The early eleventh century saw active efforts on the part of scholar-officials to petition for the implementation of the three-year mourning leave. As early as 1016, Zhang Guo (n.d.) noted that "officials fill the courtyards of the imperial palaces and there are no ongoing military campaigns," so he requested that all civil servants be allowed or required to take the three-year mourning leave in order to uphold the dynasty's claim that it ruled through filial piety.[32] A 1021 request further evoked the value of filial piety: "For not leaving their office upon learning about the death of a parent, [scholar-officials] damage social customs and invalidate government regulations." The memorial also pleaded that the court refrain from recalling civil servants back to work right after they had gone on mourning leave.[33]

Political situations in the early Northern Song, however, dictated the denial of lengthy mourning leaves for most civil servants, especially those stationed in remote or strategically important areas. In the several decades following the founding of the dynasty, the central government was preoccupied with conquering and uniting the empire in multiple regions and with large military campaigns against the Liao (907–1125) and the Xia (1038–1127).[34] A ready supply of and smooth transition among local administrators remained one of the highest priorities. A universal application of extended mourning also required a mature bureaucratic system to handle a heavy load of personnel changes, a steady supply of official candidates, the growing influence of scholar-officials and their insistence on observing proper mourning, and, last but not least, no major domestic unrest or border troubles.[35]

The transition gradually took place within Emperor Renzong's reign (r. 1023–1063).[36] Whereas the above-mentioned 1021 edict confirmed civil servants' eligibility for a mourning leave, a 1036 pronouncement ordered financial assistance for family members of officials who died while wearing mourning. This shows that almost eight decades into the Northern Song, at least some officials were still being denied the full mourning leave.[37] In fact, officials donning mourning clothes remained a visible presence in the capital. One memorial specifically requested that mourners wear regular official robes to work.[38] Another, dated 1047, was even more illustrative. The petitioner observed that many officials in mourning wore caps made of plain silk (susha) to work and requested that they wear headgear made of shiny silk (guangsha). The proposal obviously created a controversy, leading to the intervention of ritual officials, who opined that "mourning clothes should not be worn inside government offices. Those who have been recalled [back to work] while in mourning should wear regular clothes according to their ranks when attending imperial audiences but may wear light colors without gold and jade decorations [in their office]. When at home, they should wear mourning clothes of the proper grade."[39] Officials who wore mourning clothes to work also called into question their suitability to participate in various court activities. For example, a certain Mr. Shi lost his mother while serving as a prefect. When he was replaced and ordered to travel to the capital for evaluation and reappointment, he reported that he did not "dare to attend imperial audiences" while still in mourning clothes.[40]

By all accounts, the 1050s and 1060s represented a watershed in the implementation of official mourning leave. The change was marked by several indicators. First, starting from the 1050s, duoqing and qifu orders applied only to the highest-ranked officials.[41] Second, in 1050, the grand councilor Jia Changchao (997–1065) requested permission to observe the three-year mourning leave for his mother. Jia based his petition on the fact that "I was orphaned when I was young and had only my mother to depend on." Moreover, no military campaigns required his complete dedication to court affairs. In the end, Jia was granted generous gifts for his mother's funeral but not the leave he had sought.[42] Jia's request was nonetheless significant because it was the first on the part of a grand councilor and served as a precedent for others to follow. Third, in 1054, a memorial was presented to Emperor Renzong asking that all officials, regardless of their ranks or positions, be allowed to perform three years of mourning.[43] In the same year, an imperial edict abolished the practice of recalling officials ranked four and above after *zuku*, giving those highest-ranked more substantial leaves.[44] In 1061, Fu Bi (1004–1083) became the first grand councilor to complete the full mourning term for his mother. His official biography recorded that "in the past, grand councilors who had lost a parent were all recalled immediately. The Emperor left the position vacant and recalled Fu five times. Fu insisted that the [*qifu*] practice had been due to the rampant military actions [in the early Northern Song]. It should not be used during peaceful times. In the end, he did not follow the imperial order."[45] As significant as Fu's victory was, it did not establish a permanent pattern. Even in the 1070s and 1080s, it was not uncommon for high-ranking officials to be recalled back to administrative duties from mourning.[46] For the majority of civil servants, however, extended mourning leave became a standard an entire century after the founding of the Northern Song.

It should be noted that the gradual institutionalization of the three-year mourning leave did not please everyone. Despite strong rhetoric on the part of the state and civil servants to stress the importance of following ritual protocols, many were ambivalent for the simple reason that mourning leaves inconvenienced and disrupted their careers. A 1007 edict specifically stipulated that at the time of their evaluation and promotion, officials who had taken mourning leave must have the months and days of their leaves deducted.[47] Another edict, issued twenty years later, highlighted reappointing those who took mourning leaves in a strictly sequential order.[48] These policies would not have had a large impact in the first half of the dynasty because most officials were not granted lengthy leaves. In the second half of the Northern Song, as peace prevailed and redundant officials became a problem, full mourning leaves had a much wider impact on the career paths of the majority of civil servants and therefore were not always considered desirable.[49]

A major indication that the three-year mourning leave was in place is the central government's attentiveness to mourning-related violations. A famous case involved Sang Ze (n.d.), who served in Sichuan for three years in the 1050s without knowing that his father had died at home. Sang was exposed during a consideration for promotion but claimed that he had not received any news from home while in Sichuan. Sang was accused of having failed to keep in touch with his father, a failure that had led to his ignorance of the father's passing. His critic questioned, "Is this the kind of love a son should have shown his father?" The court eventually decided that even if Sang had not deliberately hidden the news about his father's death, he was still an unfilial son. For this reason, he was never reappointed and sent home.[50]

Records of three additional incidents survive. All occurred in the second half of the eleventh century. The first involved Zhu Fu (1048–?). The subject of two memorials in 1098, Zhu was indicted for failing to live with his brothers while mourning his father. For only appearing at sacrificial ceremonies, Zhu was labeled unfilial and subsequently demoted.[51] The second case, undated, concerned Ru Xiaobiao (n.d.), who was dismissed from office for concealing the death of his mother lest his career be interrupted.[52] The third controversy involved probably the most notorious son in the Northern Song, Li Ding (?–1087), who was impeached and demoted for failing to mourn his concubine mother in the 1070s.[53] This case will be further considered below.

The evolution of mourning policies, just like official procedures on granting office holders close-to-home posts and allowing them to bring parents to local positions, reflects the court's shifting attitude toward its civil servants' domestic duties. It was not until the mid-eleventh century that three-year-mourning and the corresponding leave became an official policy. This change was not clearly stipulated in any particular imperial edict but was made clear by the generic use of "the three-year mourning leave" in epitaphs and court documents.

Mourning in Northern Song Funerary Biographies

Funerary inscriptions (*muzhiming*) are the best source for gauging how elite men dealt with the loss of parents and the dominant mourning practices of the time. Below, I refer to 347 epitaphs by seventeen authors to identify some general patterns and trends. In selecting these funerary biographies, I chose authors who lived in different periods of the Northern Song and who had written at least ten epitaphs. The main goal is to locate specific mourning acts rather than terse, somewhat perfunctory, references such as "So-and-so mourned his parent." This generic statement was most often made in the context of "He was serving at such-and-such a position or location when he lost a parent. He mourned the parent and was appointed to another location [to continue his career]." As frequently as they appeared, these accounts are not very helpful for the present study for two reasons: first, they do not necessarily tell us whether the official took a leave of mourning or, if so, where or for how long he mourned; second, they do not include any information about mourning-related filial expression.

As table 1 shows, of the 347 epitaphs under examination, fifty-nine (17 percent) mentioned at least one specific mourning-related filial deed. The uneven distribution of relevant information among different authors makes a simple explanation impossible. Authorial style and the level of familiarity between the writer and the deceased certainly accounted for some of the differences. That said, three observations can be drawn from the above data. First,

Table 1

Name of Author	Number of Epitaphs Authored	Number of Mourning-Related References	Percent of Epitaphs with Mourning-Related References
Wang Yucheng (954–1001)	12	2	16.7%
Yang Yi (972–1020)	10	4	40.0
Fan Zhongyan (989–1052)	24	5	20.8
Yu Jing (1000–1064)	21	6	28.6
Song Qi (998–1061)	21	6	28.5
Fan Zhen (1007–1088)	10	1	10.0
Su Shunqin (1008–1048)	12	3	25.0
Sima Guang (1019–1086)	24	4	16.7
Su Song (1020–1101)	48	5	10.4
Zheng Xie (1022–1072)	15	3	20.0
Liu Ban (1023–1089)	18	2	11.1
Lü Tao (1028–1104)	26	5	19.2
Yang Jie (1022–1091)	10	2	20.0
Liu Zhi (1030–1098)	29	3	10.3
Shen Gua (1031–1095)	17	1	5.8
Yang Shi (1053–1135)	29	3	10.3
Ge Shengzhong (1072–1144)	21	4	19.0
Total	347	59	17.0

unlike in the earlier times, when there were more cases of men performing out-standing mourning for mothers than fathers, there is no obvious imbalance in the Northern Song sources.[54] All together, the fifty-nine funerary biographies referred to sixty-nine instances of mourning, of which twenty-two (31.9 percent) were about mourning a father, twenty-three (33.3 percent) about a mother, and eighteen (26.8 percent) about an unidentified parent (*qin*). Second, six of the fifty-nine men (10.2 percent) were said to have been brought up by their grandparents and performed exceptional mourning for them. This means that a substantial group of office-holding men had lost not one but both parents, including step-mothers and concubine mothers, relatively early and had subsequently directed their filial devotion to grandparents. Third, most office-holding men (83 percent;

288 of the 347 mentioned in the funerary biographies) in the Northern Song did not perform any distinguished mourning. This explains the popularity of such generic statements as "So-and-so was filial by nature" or "So-and-so observed mourning according to the rites" in Northern Song epitaphs. Without being given any concrete details to distinguish the deceased, funerary biographers had no other options but to resort to general all-purpose statements.

Mourning Motifs 1: Continuity from Earlier Periods

When it came to those who had performed outstanding mourning, Northern Song epitaph writers went to great lengths to elevate them. In representing grief-stricken sons, the authors continued to use existing tropes but also created new standard language. This section will introduce two dominant themes that owe their origins to the classical ritual codes and that became established practices by early medieval times. Both focused on sons' intense display of sorrow, from living next to parents' graves (*lumu*) to wailing and abstaining from daily necessities to limitless mourning.

Wailing, Limitless Mourning, and Emaciating the Body. One of the most important motifs from medieval filial tales was the son wailing incessantly and uncontrollably while mourning.[55] This continued to be a staple theme in Northern Song portrayals of the grieving son. The most frequently used expressions included *haojue* (to wail so hard that one stops breathing), *haotong* (to wail and appear extremely heartbroken), *qixie* (to wail so hard that one sheds bloody tears), and *chaihui guli* (one's body wastes away with grief, the bones protruding). All depicted a son's haggard appearance resulting directly from the physical and emotional pain caused by a parent's passing. For example, when mourning their fathers, both Liu Chong (918–980) and Su Qi (987–1035) wept nonstop and expressed such extreme distress that they stopped breathing.[56] A Li man longed for his mother so profoundly that he did not behave like his usual self.[57] Two Zhang brothers mourned in excess of the rites, shedding blood-stained tears for three years.[58] Another Zhang's hair turned completely white overnight following the passing of his mother.[59] Li Feng (1030–1075) wailed day and night when his mother died. After having a dream about her, he recalled his mother's appearance and inscribed a wooden likeness of her. For the remainder of his life, Li waited on the sculpture as if his mother were alive.[60]

Li Feng was one of many who were said to have mourned limitlessly, another mourning motif that had remained popular since the early medieval period.[61] Having lost both parents at a young age, Zhang Huizhi (970–1018) was said to feel the sorrow his entire life.[62] In the case of Zhang Lun (962–1036), even in his old age, Zhang's "filial devotion to his parents remained the same as when he had just lost them. Whenever he talked about them, he would weep. His sadness would move everyone in his presence."[63] After completing mourning for his mother, a Yang man would often cry and shed tears. Whenever he ran into his maternal relatives, he would show strong affection as if his mother were still alive.[64]

Just like their medieval predecessors, Song men were portrayed as emaciating their bodies and dying of grief.[65] They did so even though Confucian ritual codes discouraged, and even forbade, sons to abstain from food and basic material needs to the point of damaging their bodies. After the death of his father, a Wang man kept a vegetarian diet for three years.[66] The famous statesman Wu Kui (1010–1067) did not drink wine or eat meat the entire mourning period.[67] It then came as no surprise that he and others were described as having weakened their bodies to such an extent that they could stand up only with the support of walking sticks. Some were even said to have died from extreme grief. A Shi man perished fifty days following his father's passing due to excessive wailing and longing.[68] A man surnamed Zhang died within a month of his father.[69] Xie Jikang (1027–1083) rushed home upon receiving news of his father's death and did not eat or drink anything for several days while wailing nonstop on the road. He passed away three days after his father's funeral.[70]

The above portrayals of grieving sons are strong evidence that ancient motifs continued to influence mourning performance as well as literary representations of grieving in the Northern Song. In approximately twenty letters addressed to family members and friends, Huang Tingjian described his mother's death in an extremely personal way, using standard language that was reminiscent of classical ritual prescriptions.[71] As soon as his mother passed away, Huang wrote, her sons and grandsons "prostrated ourselves on the ground and wailed at Heaven. There was nowhere to turn to express our pain, worries, and loss. Our hearts and livers have been shattered. Alas! How painful! How painful!"[72] When accompanying his mother's coffin back to their native place in Jiangxi, Huang recorded, "It has been half a year since we traveled on water. . . . Feeling dejected and overwhelmed, I weep whenever I think of her passing. The pain is almost unbearable." While making plans for the funeral and burial, Huang remarked that there were no words to describe the sadness and sense of helplessness that he felt. He was "sick and frail" and was able to eat only gruel.[73] Huang was so weak that from writing this letter, "My wrist was almost wasted."[74]

Lumu and Beyond. With a long tradition in history, *lumu* was a practice in which sons, saddened by the departure of their parents, moved to live in a thatched hut in or near the family graveyard for an extended period. Leaving the comfort of their homes, these mourners would sustain themselves with only the bare necessities such as water, vegetables, and gruel.[75] Due to the physical hardships that were involved in this endeavor, almost all *lumu* practitioners ended up emaciating their bodies and damaging their health. In this sense, they were no different from those who practiced limitless mourning or nonstop weeping. What did distinguish the *lumu* mourners from other filial exemplars was their complete rejection of social interaction, as well as their dedication to the care of the parents' tombs.

Although not a common practice, *lumu* continued to have its followers in the Northern Song. In the introduction to this book, we learned of Wang Anshi eating coarse food and sleeping on a straw mat while mourning his mother. His younger brother went even further by practicing *lumu*.[76] Similarly, Mr. Li lived in the family graveyard for three full years after the death of his mother, during which he did not enter the city wall even once.[77] A man surnamed Hu was praised for "not stepping into the inner quarter for three years when mourning his mother."[78] While living next to his parents' graves, a certain Mr. Sun did not visit any relatives or friends and forgot the flavor of salt and fruit. This did not change for three years. "The entire town applauded his filial devotion."[79]

One particular activity that preoccupied *lumu* practitioners was tomb building or renovation.[80] In a very detailed account, Yu Jing recorded that after Liang Kui's (n.d.) parents died within two years of each other, Liang personally carried enough dirt to construct and rebuild the tombs of six family members. He then erected a shack and lived there, during which he wailed from morning until night. Liang also pricked his fingers, using the blood he drew to copy Buddhist sutras and pray for his grandparents and parents. To sustain himself, Liang grew vegetables and grains, with which he made porridges. For six long years, he did not eat any meat.[81] To Yu Jing, Liang personified the ideal mourning son. In addition to practicing *lumu* and the extreme grief he displayed over an extended period, Liang distinguished himself by paying extraordinary attention to the conditions of the family graveyard, a theme that will be further explored in the next chapter.

From the Han and early medieval times onward, popular lore called attention to the power of filial piety in transforming the natural and human realms in the form of propitious manifestations, such as the appearance of sweet dew and auspicious plants, as well as Heavenly rewards for the filial practitioner.[82] This belief in the efficacy of filial piety remained strong in the Northern Song. Such miraculous manifestations often fell on those performing *lumu*. According to his funerary biography, a Zhang man was so dedicated to *lumu* that a spring with extremely sweet and clear water appeared. He subsequently named it the Fountain of Responses to Filiality (Xiaoganquan) and wrote an essay to mark the occasion.[83] For performing *lumu* and diligently mourning his mother, a man named Zhi grew black hair and new teeth at the age of eighty. More important, his filial deeds inspired unfilial neighbors to change their behavior.[84] When Hu Ze (963–1039) was mourning his mother and living in a shed, not only did auspicious plants and trees grow at his family graveyard, but he also received rewards from the local government.[85] An extremely filial son, Lü Dingguo (1031–1094) was said to have mourned his father without violating any ritual stipulation. When his father was about to be buried, he lived in the family graveyard, where he wailed day and night. Sweet dew appeared next to the tomb. "Those who witnessed it deemed the miracle [Heaven's] response to his filial behavior."[86] Wei Xian (1068–1140) practiced mourning in similar ways. "He exhausted his family's funds to build a Buddhist cloister next to the tomb. Every day, he would live in it and read scrolls of the Tripikata." Auspicious plants and sweet dew subsequently appeared.[87] In addition to rewards from Heaven, Wei also achieved celebrity status for catching the attention of his fellow scholar-officials. "The scholar Zhang Jingxiu [active in 1090] and others composed many songs and poems to record the auspicious responses to [Wei's] filial conduct."[88]

Mourning Motifs 2: New Developments in the Northern Song

In the Han and the Period of Disunity, according to Keith Knapp, "the feats attributed to filial offspring are extremely stereotyped and limited in number." Many filial sons and daughters were credited with performing the exact same exemplary acts. This was especially true when it came to mourning-related performance.[89] This changed in the Song. In addition to the emaciation of the body and the practice of *lumu*, Northern Song funerary biographers also popularized three new mourning themes. The first featured boys as mature mourners. The second depicted office-holding men putting their official careers on hold to observe proper mourning. The third highlighted the grief that sons exhibited on the road.

Boys Mourning as Adults. In early imperial China, precocious children were often portrayed as wise and filial to living parents.[90] The Northern Song witnessed a new development: the representation of children "mourning just like adults." Sons as young as three were extolled for demonstrating excessive sorrow in mourning. At seven, a Zhao boy displayed extraordinary grief following his mother's passing.[91] A Liu boy was remembered for exceeding adults in expressing his distress. "Even after the end of mourning, he would wail whenever he was overcome with sadness and move those who heard him."[92] Similarly, when a thirteen-year-old lost his mother, he grieved so diligently that all near him were affected.[93] As an eleven-year-old, Ge suffered from the passing of his father; he mourned just like an adult and already knew not to eat meat.[94] Girls were occasionally praised for the same quality. A Miss Xu "lost her mother at age seven. She could not stand the sorrow and said while weeping, 'My mother was the reason that I live. Now that I am motherless, how could I continue to live?' She therefore attempted suicide, but her father and brothers stopped her."[95] When a Miss Fang mourned her father at age ten, she was so overwhelmed by grief that she "could not eat. People in the clan considered it unusual."[96]

Children who lost both parents at a tender age and practiced mourning according to the rites were especially singled out for praise. Jia Zhu (962–1008), orphaned at three, "longed for his parents as if he understood [the meaning of death]."[97] Wang Zeng (978–1038), who lost both parents at eight, grieved so intensely that the experience almost ruined his health.[98] Similarly, when a Su boy lost both parents, the grief he displayed inspired people in his community to treat him as a filial exemplar.[99] Tian Jing (991–1057) was relatively old when he lost both parents at sixteen. He "mourned according to the rites," refusing to drink wine or eat meat. Even on the coldest of days, he would not wear fur or padded clothes.[100]

The above examples confirm the frequency of Song people dying at all ages. The phenomenon itself, however, is not sufficient to explain the increasing visibility of the mourning child. After all, life spans in the earlier periods must have been shorter and just as many, if not more, children lost one or both parents at a young age. A more likely reason may be that in the Northern Song, there was a growing interest in children's potential to elevate the family through examination success and official service. Consequently, more attention was paid to their moral and intellectual capacity. As a result, the period witnessed many epitaphs and eulogies for children. These texts, in addition to describing sons, daughters, and grandchildren as filial and obedient, routinely characterized them as intelligent, keen on learning, and lovely and beautiful.[101] Their passing therefore devastated parents and other family members. The famous statesman Han Qi, for example, authored the epitaphs for nine grandnephews and grandnieces.[102] He called one of them, Han Kai (1041–1060), an extremely filial son. Han Qi related, when Kai's father was sick, that Kai "personally presented medicine to and waited on his father day and night. For several months, he did not lie down to sleep. When his father died, he could not control his grief and mourned in excess of the rites. He soon fell ill and did not recover."[103] To Han Qi, Han Kai's early death was a tremendous loss to the family, especially on account of his distinguished virtue as a filial child and his potential for a bright future in public service.

Choosing Mourning Parents over Career Progress. Another newly emerged theme in Northern Song epitaph writing are references to office-holding men prioritizing their mourning duties over their official responsibilities. In the first half of the Northern Song, when restrictive policies were in place, official sons were singled out for submitting multiple requests for even a brief mourning leave.[104] Such filial acts were often portrayed as the equivalent of choosing *yang* over *lu*, as discussed in the previous chapter. Both Su Qi and Wu Kui were known to have petitioned to observe full mourning for their parents.[105] Others went even further. When a Liu man learned about his father's death in 980, he could not help but wail nonstop on his way to the capital in heavy snow. Although government policies did not allow lengthy mourning leaves at the time, Liu sent in three memorials to the grand councilor. His funerary biographer remarked that even though his requests were not granted, those who heard about his deeds approved of his filial devotion.[106] Many others were depicted as having displayed similarly genuine affection. When Gao Ruone's mother passed away, Gao acted exactly as Liu had done, wailing and imploring that he be allowed to wear mourning for three years. His epitaph writer explained that at the time, court policy stipulated that officials be recalled to work after the completion of *zuku*. For this reason, many showed up in court still wearing mourning clothes. As a result of Gao's petition, an imperial edict made changes to mourning regulations. Gao was not only allowed to wear mourning for three years, but was also paid full salary during his leave.[107]

Gao's epitaph did not indicate the specific date of his memorials nor the change in court policies. In all likelihood, the change occurred in the late 1030s or 1040s. As our above discussion on official mourning policies has shown, requests for mourning leave appeared only in the first half of the Northern Song, when a large portion of the bureaucracy was permitted no leave or a very brief one. Exactly because of the limitations, those who insisted on performing full mourning had to show the court, in memorials and through extreme emotional displays, extraordinary resolve. Wailing in office spaces and wearing mourning clothes to work remained two of the most important ways for civil servants to showcase their devotion. When most civil servants mourned parents in the time and place that were stipulated by the state, those who placed their filial obligations above career considerations, even only temporarily, were subsequently lauded as moral exemplars.

The second half of the Northern Song witnessed a large change in the representation of the ideal mourning son when three-year mourning became standard official policy. Official sons would have to find other ways to distinguish themselves now that they had been given abundant time to take care of mourning- and funeral-related matters. The result was the emergence of a new filial trope: office-holding men were commended for their willingness to give up their careers for the sake of residing at their parents' graves for lengthy periods. As mentioned in chapter 1, Bao Zheng chose to practice reverent care and to mourn both parents for full terms over career development. Several of his peers followed his example in the second half of the eleventh century. After completing the three-year mourning, Yang Zonghui (1040–1094) remained grief-stricken and could not bear to leave his father's tomb. He then expressed the wish to stay in his native region. His biographer remarked that it was only at the persuasion of family members and friends that he left for his position.[108] Du Minqiu (1039–1101) demonstrated the same commitment: he was so consumed by the loss of his parents that he did not want to report back to the court after the completion of mourning.[109]

It should be noted, however, that just as in the cases of official sons who sought temporary retirement to practice reverent care, few actually gave up their careers in the end. That only a small number of men were recorded to have even entertained the idea reveals the continuing attraction of government service to the educated and social elites. At the same time, stories like these allow us to appreciate the emotional toll of mourning and the difficult choices that all office-holding men had to make when dealing with the demands of their professional aspirations and domestic responsibilities.

Grieving on the Road. Of the three new mourning practices in the Northern Song, the most frequently cited by funerary biographers were those of sons grieving on the road. Several factors explained the close relationship between mourning and long-distance trips. First, the enforcement of the three-year mourning leave from the mid-eleventh century onward meant that as soon as an official learned about the death of a parent, he would be put on mourning leave, travel to where the deceased was located, and begin funeral planning. Second, with the official retirement age set at seventy, a large percentage of civil servants died while holding official posts. Third, the Northern Song witnessed a general trend of office-holding men retiring in places away from their native regions or places where they were to be buried.[110] This tendency to build a home away from one's hometown resulted in many dying in remote places at advanced ages. Fourth, officials who brought parents to their local posts for reverent care often ended up coping with parents' sudden deaths and the transportation of their bodies over long distances for burial. The experience of Xue Zhongru (n.d.) is especially noteworthy.

When his father, Xue Shu (977–1041), died while serving in Shuzhou (in Sichuan), Zhongru, who was posted at Lingzhou (Renshou, Sichuan), traveled to Shuzhou to collect his father's body for burial in Jiangzhou (Xinjiang, Shanxi). He did this without knowing that his mother, who was living in Daizhou (Daixian, Shanxi) with his younger brother, Xue Zongru (n.d.), had passed away only six days after his father.[111] We can only imagine the emotional loss and physical hardships the two brothers underwent when dealing with the deaths of both parents and the logistics of transporting their bodies home from different directions. The complications created by remote deaths to funeral and burial planning are the focus of the next chapter. For now, suffice it to say that this phenomenon had two consequences: first, it often took a substantial amount of time for sons and other family members to learn about the death of a parent; second, a large portion of a son's mourning leave was spent on the road.

Sons in earlier times had certainly endured the loss of parents in faraway places and having to travel with their coffins. This phenomenon, however, did not become a major subject in writings about mourning until the Northern Song. Song elite men only occasionally touched on this topic in the voluminous personal correspondence that they composed.[112] It was in epitaphs that they recounted how friends and colleagues had learned about their parents' death and their mourning in transit. For example, as soon as he received news about his mother's passing, a certain Mr. Yuan "rode a horse at night and rested during the day [to avoid traffic] to be home in time for her burial."[113] After losing his father, a man surnamed Zheng wailed and howled, rushing home in bare feet.[114] Mr. Deng's mother died in 1087 in the capital, where Deng was serving. Shedding blood-stained tears on the road, he and his brother accompanied her coffin, arriving in Yangzhou via the Bian, Huai, and Si rivers.[115] When Su Mengchen (n.d.) was notified of the death of his father, he traveled for over a thousand *li* in seven days to return to his native place![116]

In addition to highlighting sons traveling long distances and grieving on the road, Northern Song epitaphs detailed the various challenges that the mourners had to overcome. The physical hardships of long trips, combined with the emotional toll of grieving, were said to have been responsible for the deaths of many men. When a Chen man's father died in office, Chen accompanied his father's coffin back to Runzhou. The long-distance journey drained his energy.

Chen fell sick and died on the road.[117] Similarly, when Mao Fu's (996–1033) father was ill,

> Mao personally tasted the medicine before presenting it to his father. [He was so dedicated to caring for his father that] he did not take off his clothes for three months. Since he slept neither during the day nor at night, his eyes were covered with ulcers. Barely a month after the death of his father, his mother also died. Mao wailed with extreme sorrow, refusing to eat or drink. He accompanied his parents' bodies home for burial. When passing by Zhongling, he was exhausted due to excessive mourning and died on the boat.[118]

In addition to identifying Mao Fu as dying from grief, the biographer pointed to the toll that long-distance travel had taken on his health. Mao Fu's epitaph did not specify where Mao was posted at the time of the parents' deaths. Emotionally overwhelmed and physically emaciated, the hardship of long-distance travel was the final blow to Mao's health.

Sons receiving news about the death of a parent and beginning mourning from remote places was such a common scenario that Zhu Xi in the Southern Song included a section on the proper execution of such mourning in his famous *Family Rituals*. Among Zhu's instructions are the following: (1) "Wail when first learning of the death of a parent. . . . After wailing to the full extent of one's grief, ask the cause of death"; (2) Change into mourning garments; (3) Then "proceed expeditiously": "Go a hundred *li* a day, but do not travel at night"; (4) "On the road, wail whenever grief is felt. In wailing, avoid cities or busy places." In fact, more than occasionally, it happened that a son did not return home until after a parent's burial was complete. In that case, Zhu urged sons to "go first to the grave, wail, and bow" before returning home. Proper procedures were also laid out for "coffins being returned for burial from some other place."[119]

In specifying the proper ritual procedures for sons in mourning, Zhu Xi had in mind practices that had already been singled out by Sima Guang for criticism. Zhu wrote, "The Venerable Mr. Sima Guang said, 'These days when people hurry to the funeral or follow the coffin, they cry when they get to the city and stop when they pass it. This is mere show.'" In fact, Sima's low opinion of his contemporaries was not limited to their superficial expression of grief in public. He also disapproved of many other common practices. "Nowadays, scholar-officials wearing mourning would act no differently from [how they would act in] ordinary days when it comes to eating meat and drinking wine. They also banquet and gather with each other and feel no shame in doing so, nor do people consider this strange. Rituals and customs have deteriorated so much that people consider it normal. Alas!"[120]

The Mourning Son as the Moral Exemplar

In their representation of a mourning son publicly displaying his grief, Northern Song epitaph writers did not stop at lauding the filial paragon; they also were keen on demonstrating the way his moral power inspired those who happened to have witnessed his expressions of devotion. When grieving the loss of his father, Li Hang (947–1004) traveled for almost two thousand *li* from the capital to Qunshu (Shucheng, Anhui). Day and night, he shed bloody tears. "The sadness he manifested moved those on the road."[121] Accompanying his mother's body from Zhengzhou (in Henan), Jia Changchao was said to have walked two hundred *li* and subsequently became emaciated and dark in color. "Those who saw him wept."[122] From the perspectives of their funerary biographers, Li's and Jia's genuine expressions of grief were what drew the attention of their spectators, even though Sima Guang and Zhu Xi might have suspected that Li and Jia were putting on a show for public consumption.

A general development in Northern Song epitaph writing was the growing attention to mourning sons strictly adhering to ritual protocols, as well as the role the mourners played in reforming the minds and behavior of family members, friends, and neighbors. When grieving the loss of his mother, Mu Xiu (979–1032) was praised for walking barefoot and personally carrying her coffin for burial. "Every day, he would read the *Classic of Filial Piety* and *Records of Burial* (*Sangji*). Throughout the entire mourning period, he never read any Buddhist sutras or offered meals to Buddhist monks [i.e., did not use them in the death rituals]."[123] When mourning his parents, Feng Yuan (975–1037) "changed his clothes according to the ritual prescriptions. He refused to use popular religious ceremonies. At times of sacrificial ceremonies, he would sit with disciples and recite the *Classic of Filial Piety*."[124] Wu Kui was similarly lauded for following authentic sacrificial ceremonies and refusing to perform any Buddhist services.[125] Many others took the same path. Ren Gongzhi (1018–1064) sincerely followed the rites during mourning and won the approval of his fellow scholar-officials.[126] Sima Kang was praised for "following the *Book of Rites* and family instructions. He did not perform any popular services."[127] While mourning his father, Lü Dajun (1029–1080) carried out his mentor's teachings and based everything, including mourning garments, burial, and sacrifice, on the rites.[128]

In addition to lauding these men's commitment to ritual propriety, Northern Song epitaphs celebrated these mourners as role models for family, close friends, clan members, neighbors, and fellow villagers. This connection not only highlighted the public nature of family and death rituals, but also revealed the prevalence of popular practices in local communities.[129] Especially problematic to the state and leading intellectuals of the time was the strong Buddhist influence on funeral and burial activities.[130] A general perusal of Northern Song epitaphs reveals that at the same time that government policies and liturgy writing attempted to correct and eliminate heterodox and vulgar ritual ceremonies, many individuals took personal initiatives through promoting what they considered orthodox performance. If early Northern Song funerary biographers such as Wang Yucheng, Yang Yi, and Fan Zhongyan routinely praised their subjects as filial sons for simply wearing mourning "according to the rites," later writers began to include greater detail about educated men going out of their way to influence the ritual behavior of the local population. Seen from a different perspective, over the duration of the Northern Song, epitaphs became an important vehicle to document the elite efforts at moral education at the "grassroots" level. In the process, epitaph writers played a key role in both propagating ritually sanctioned mourning activities and praising their practitioners.

Below I cite three epitaphs by Xu Jingheng (1072–1128), a native of Rui'an (Wenzhou, Zhejiang), to illustrate this development. In the epitaph for Ding Gangxuan (1066–1120), Xu wrote the following:

> Mr. Ding was extremely filial by nature. He often lamented that the study of rituals was lacking and that popular customs were low and vulgar. [The knowledge and practice of] funerals and sacrificial offerings were especially deficient. When he wore mourning for his parents, he conducted everything according to ancient regulations. His weeping and sobbing sounded so sorrowful that people could not bear to listen to him. He discarded Buddhist rituals and lived in a hut next to his parents' graves. He personally planted all the pine trees at the tomb site. Throughout mourning, he did not eat meat or drink wine. The way he performed the annual sacrifices, his abstinence, and daily offerings, as well as the use of offerings, could all be traced back to ancient styles. He would appear so grief-stricken on these occasions that it was as if his parents were present. Local people subsequently began to understand funeral and sacrificial rituals [based on his performance]. Many admired him and considered him filial.[131]

Based on Xu's depiction, Ding practiced mourning most appropriately. This was seen in the way he wailed, practiced *lumu*, and performed sacrificial ceremonies. In particular, Xu praised Ding for avoiding Buddhist services and following ancient practices. Xu especially noted Ding's concern for the lack of adequate guidance on proper death rituals in his community; it was for this reason that people followed vulgar customs. Ding therefore intended for his own mourning performance to serve as a model for his fellow-natives. Xu pronounced that based on their observation of Ding's proper execution of the mourning rituals, "local people began to know [proper] funeral and sacrificial rituals."

Ding was only one of many who saw a problem and actively pursued a solution. Xu Jingheng remarked again on the large influence of Buddhist and other popular practices in local society in his epitaph for Zhang Yanzhong (1071–1102) and Zhang's determination to fight those vulgar practices. When Zhang's grandmother died at age ninety,

[Yanzhong] mourned her according to the rites. Local customs believed in the teachings of Buddhism and Daoism, which urged followers to recite the scriptures to pray for the dead. Yanzhong thought, "In caring for the living and sending off the dead, the sages taught that one should personally follow [ritual prescriptions] and be prudent in expenses. Why should I not lead the way to practice these teachings?" He therefore gathered those of the same aspiration to read the *Classic of Filial Piety* and said, "I hope our actions can convince local folks to follow our example."[132]

Just like Ding Gangxuan, Zhang Yanzhong made it his mission to revive ancient teachings and reform local practices. Both identified prevalent Buddhist influences and a lack of role models as the roots of confusion in ritual performances. To correct this situation would have required a multi-pronged strategy. Ding and Zheng did not address the problem through liturgical writing or sophisticated treatises. Rather, they rose to the challenge by calling for locals to emulate them.

Xu Jingheng lauded another man, Ding Changqi (n.d.), his wife, and three sons in a similar way:

Since the end of the Zhou, funeral and mourning rites have fallen into disuse. Scholar-officials have all followed popular customs and did not distinguish right from wrong. Changqi and his sons singlehandedly got rid of [popular practices] and exclusively adopted the ancient methods. [At first,] those who heard about their deeds all laughed behind their backs, but his wife practiced the methods without hesitation. People in Wenzhou were confused by Buddhism. His sons often discussed its wrongs. His wife would nod and warn her daughters-in-law not to go against their husbands' way.[133]

In Xu Jingheng's portrayal, the Ding men and women were not only filial, but were also adamant promoters of the sages' teachings and reformers of local society. Their activism and success aside, the task at hand proved more formidable than Xu made it appear. Not all of Xu's fellow epitaph writers were repulsed by the dominance of Buddhism in death rituals. They likewise celebrated filial sons that heeded both Confucian ritual codes and Buddhist teachings. The epitaph for Ge Shusi serves as a good example.

Ge Shengzhong, Shusi's funerary biographer, recorded that Shusi followed the ancient rituals meticulously when mourning his father. In addition to not drinking wine, refraining from sexual relations, and wailing most wretchedly, Shusi did not take off his mourning clothes even on the hottest summer days. After the end of the three-year mourning period, he continued to offer proper sacrifices and would weep at the mention of his father's name. Yet during all these orthodox performances, Shusi was said to have chanted Buddhist sutras every day to aid in his father's good fortune in the afterlife.[134] Ge's mix of both Buddhist and Confucian mourning rituals was a strong indication of the dominant influence of Buddhism in death rituals in local societies. By labeling Ge Shusi as a filial son, Ge Shengzhong readily accepted the coexistence of diverse practices in local societies. Both phenomena justified the Neo-Confucian call for an urgent articulation of acceptable and desirable ritual behavior.

Mourning Concubine Mothers

Given the visibility of concubines in Northern Song elite households, a discussion of mourning practices would not be complete without a consideration of relevant government policies about, as well as the changes in, the portrayal of grieving for concubine mothers. Both the policies and the changes illustrated a major shift in the Song: the gradual acceptance of concubine mothers as appropriate objects of filial sentiment and as ancestors.

Well-to-do men in China had always had concubines. These were different types of women whose role could range from intimate companion to maid to entertainer. Classical texts did not specify the ritual standings of concubine mothers, nor did successive imperial governments maintain consistent policies regarding their legal rights.[135] Understandably, the positions of concubines varied greatly in different households, especially depending on the fortune of their sons, throughout history.[136] In the Tang and Song, courtesans and concubines acquired some prominence in literature and elite social and family life.[137] Following the discussion of official sons practicing *shiyang* toward concubine mothers in the previous chapter, this section focuses on sons petitioning and receiving mourning leave for concubine mothers.

The first extant mourning-related request regarding a concubine mother appeared in 1016. When Nie Zhen (n.d.) lost his concubine mother, his supervisor, Wang Qinruo (962–1025), memorialized that Nie be exempted from wearing mourning since Nie's legal mother was still alive.[138] Nie's case was sent to the Court of Ceremonial Propriety (Liyi Yuan) for discussion. After exploring multiple conflicting practices in pre-Song times, the ritual officers concluded that Nie should be furloughed from office, complete his mother's burial, and observe "mourning in the heart [*xinsang*]" for three years. However, because Nie was participating in the compilation of the largest encyclopedia completed in the Song, *Cefu yuangui* (Prime Tortoise of the Record Bureau or Models from the Archives), the same officials seem to have anticipated that it was unlikely that Nie would be relieved of his editorial duties. They therefore added that should the court decide to disallow a mourning leave of any length, his call should not be phrased as a *zhuichu* (literally, to chase after and call an official back to his office following a grant of mourning leave). In the end, Nie was denied a mourning leave and was ordered to continue his editorial responsibilities.[139]

Nie's case occurred at a time when officials were rarely granted substantial leave following the loss of fathers and legal mothers and were routinely called back to work while in mourning. The court's rejection of any leave for Nie was therefore nothing out of the ordinary. The ritual officials' careful deliberation nonetheless affirmed a son's filial obligations toward his concubine mother, even though in this case Nie was denied what was considered to be ritually proper. Moreover, the case reveals that even though there had not been a clearly worded policy over half a century into the Northern Song, civil servants were expected to inform the court of the passing of concubine mothers.

Accounts of the mourning of concubine mothers continued to appear in the eleventh century. In 1030, Miss Hu, the birth mother of the prominent statesman Han Qi, died in his first official post in Zizhou (in Shandong). Having lost his father at the age of four in 1011 and with his legal mother, Miss Luo, having moved back to be with her natal family and died there, Miss Hu was Han Qi's only possible object of filial affection. Han Qi's epitaph for his older brother, Han Qu (1000–1040), clearly stated that Qu "left office to mourn *furen* (Miss Hu)" and was appointed to a new position when he "took off his mourning clothes."[140] None of Han Qi's biographies mention that Han requested or received any mourning leave, even though his record of conduct (*xingzhuang*) stated that when Miss Hu passed away, Han became emaciated from grief.[141] A Song *biji*, however, recorded that during mourning, Han Qi went to live with one of his older brothers who was serving in Huangzhou (in Hubei) at the time.[142] A poem by Han Qi corroborated the anecdotal story.[143]

Why then had all of Han Qi's biographers omitted this information? It was possible that Miss Hu's concubine status, although widely known, continued to be a somewhat thorny issue. After all, as late as 1062, when Han Qi was at the height of his power and asked Fu Bi to author his father, Han Guohua's (957–1101) *shendaobei* (spirit path stele), Fu left Miss Hu out of the biography.[144] These concrete concerns aside, the above evidence confirms that Han Qu and Han Qi were the first Northern Song office-holding men who had been granted a mourning leave for a concubine mother. What remains unclear is the length of that leave.

A decade and a half separated Nie Zhen's case in 1016 and the allowance given to the Han brothers in 1030. Two additional factors might have contributed to the different outcomes. At the time of Nie Zhen's memorial, his legal mother was still alive, whereas Miss Luo, the Han brothers' legal mother, had passed away more than a decade before their birth mother. The Nies and the Hans also differed in status. As a member of a significant book project, Nie had the support of his immediate supervisor, Wang Qinruo. In fact, Wang personally submitted the memorial that obtained Nie an exemption. At the time of Miss Hu's death, Han Qu and Han Qi were both junior officials serving in less crucial local positions, which might explain the leave granted.

Han Qi further confirmed his filial devotion to his concubine mother fifteen years later, when he had Miss Hu buried next to his father in the new family graveyard that he had built. Han readily accepted that his actions were not in accordance with the rites. Yet, he reasoned, "Rituals are not sent down by Heaven or generated by Earth. They are based on human feelings [*qing*]. That she was buried with my father in this graveyard was meant to comfort the heart of the filial son and to accord with human emotions."[145]

Han's writings revealed the dilemma in which he found himself. On the one hand, both his filial devotion to his mother and the emotional bond they shared stipulated that he give her a proper burial. In fact, he specifically called his decision the result of following his filial sentiments. On the other hand, Han was keenly aware that the burial arrangement he made contradicted ritual prescriptions. He therefore clearly remarked that Miss Hu's burial was a *shizang* (attending burial), characterized by the lower quality of her coffin and the position of her grave, which was moved back so that it was not side by side with those of his father and legal mother. Even though her burial crossed some of the established boundaries, Han made it clear that he and his mother "did not dare to violate [the rites]."[146]

By making public his decision to choose piety over ritual propriety, Han not only succeeded in representing himself as an extraordinarily filial son, but also allowed himself to determine the scale of his filial expression. Han Qi implied that if ritual prescriptions did not take human feelings into consideration, it might simply be time to change the rituals instead of compromising a son's expression of his genuine feelings. Han's action was unlikely meant to create any controversy. Instead, he simply wished to honor and commemorate his birth mother, whose presence was acknowledged in neither of his father's funerary biographies.[147]

Han Qi was not acting alone in his endeavor. By the 1030s, it was not uncommon for office-holding men to get some, albeit very brief, leave to mourn concubine mothers. In 1039, a man named Xue was given three days of leave upon the death of his grandmother, the concubine mother of Xue's father. Xue's memorial was intended to check with the court the grade of mourning clothes he should wear. It is reasonable to conclude, however, that if Xue was given a three-day leave, his father must have received a longer one.[148] At around the same time, a certain Huangfu also received an unspecified mourning leave for his concubine mother.[149]

The clearest reference to a civil servant wearing three-year mourning garments for a concubine mother is found in a document of 1046, when Sun Bian (996–1064) lost his birth mother. "Citing a recent precedent, he expressed the wish to observe three-year mourning. His petition was generously granted. When he completed mourning, he returned to resume his previous position."[150] The reference to a "recent precedent" shows that Sun's request had not been the first, nor was it the first time the court had approved three-year mourning for a concubine mother. What had made Sun's case less complicated was that his legal mother had passed away several years earlier, and he had also taken mourning leave for her.[151]

Sun Bian's case is lacking in greater detail, especially regarding the level of mourning he performed. Did Sun wear sackcloth [qicui] or fine hemp as prescribed? How did sacrificial ceremonies for his birth mother compare to those for his legal mother? Was his concubine mother buried next to his father and legal mother, just as Han Qi's birth mother? Most important, where did Sun Bian grieve for her? These unanswered questions aside, the leave granted Sun shows that at the same time that regular mourning leaves for parents were institutionalized, Northern Song officials were expanding their sense of filiality to encompass concubine mothers.

The growing visibility of concubine mothers in Northern Song men's filial performance can also be seen from two other accounts. In the first case, Xia Bosun (n.d.) was not only praised for performing meticulous care in regard to his birth mother, but he was also said to have perished from grieving her death.[152] The second case concerned Lu Gui (1022–1076), who had his concubine mother buried in the ancestral tomb and was rewarded for his filial devotion by Heaven. During a serious drought, a fountain erupted, providing just enough water for Lu to complete his tomb-building project.[153]

Although sons dying from grief was a literary trope with a long history, Xia was the first who was recorded to have died from mourning a concubine mother. And to Lu's epitaph writer, the erupting fountain was unmistakable evidence that Heaven had acknowledged and commended Lu's filial devotion. Considering that Han Qi had felt the need to justify burying Miss Hu with his parents, this reference to supernatural intervention in Lu's outstanding behavior marked a major development in representing and promoting filial gestures toward concubine mothers. Both Lu Gui, the son who performed the filial burial, and Su Song (1020–1101), the epitaph writer who eagerly promoted the way Lu was rewarded, actively contributed to this development.

The epitaph for Zhou Yanzhan (1063–1124) further reveals the growing importance of concubine mothers in elite filial expressions in the late eleventh century. Zhou's father married twice. Raised by Miss Yu, his father's second wife, Zhou never suspected that he had been born to a concubine mother, Miss Hang, who had left the Zhou household when Yanzhan was a baby. When Zhou was made aware of the fact right after he received the *jinshi* degree in 1097, he swore that he would not accept a position until he had located his birth mother. While traveling around to look for her, he had a dream during which he was pointed to Miss Hang's tomb. The next day, Zhou miraculously found exactly what he had seen in the dream. Upon inquiry, a villager confirmed that the grave was indeed that of a Miss Hang, who had died two years previously. Zhou dug up the grave, obtained a new coffin to hold his mother's remains, and then moved them back to his native region, where he held a burial according to the rites. Moreover, "He mourned for three years, during which he grieved as if he had been brought up by his concubine mother and had been deeply attached to her."[154]

Zhou's case bears a similarity to that of Zhu Shouchang. Upon learning that his birth mother was forced out of the household, Zhu went on a long journey to find her, brought her back into his life, and performed reverent care. Both cases, by highlighting the son's determination to locate his concubine mother, illustrate a change in attitude toward concubines and in sons' filial obligations to birth mothers in the second half of the eleventh century. Han Qi had found it necessary to justify in his epitaph for Miss Hu, the woman who had practically raised him by herself, why she deserved a place in the family graveyard, but times had changed for Zhou Yanzhan and Zhu Shouchang. Both actively sought out their birth mothers, with whom they did not have much physical or emotional connection. Lu Gui and Zhou Yanzhan seemed much more assured when they had concubine mothers buried in family plots. That both acts were recorded in their epitaphs demonstrates a growing tendency on the part of elite men to acknowledge the status of concubines in the household and sons' obligations and willingness to mourn and commemorate their concubine mothers. In praising Lu Gui, Zhu Shouchang, and Zhou Yanzhan, their funerary biographers treated what these men did as the most natural, praiseworthy deed. A concubine mother was a mother—no more, no less. That Zhu and Zhou took pains to locate their mothers decades after they had departed made the two men all the more filial.

The growing importance of mourning for concubine mothers can also be seen in a major political controversy that concerned Li Ding (1028–1087). Since the case has been studied in several contexts, our discussion here will focus on the broader narrative.[155]

In 1070, Li Ding was accused of failing to mourn his concubine mother, Miss Qiu, when she died. This led to Emperor Shenzong's ordering an investigation to determine whether Li had observed mourning and, if not, how he should make up for this breach.[156]

> The Censors said that according to the law, a son born to a concubine mother should wear fine hemp for his concubine mother for three months, be dismissed from office, and practice "mourning in the heart" if he is his father's heir and his legal mother is still alive. If he is not his father's heir, he should wear sackcloth with frayed sleeves for three years before returning to normal clothes. When Ding's concubine mother died, he did not request to be dismissed from office to observe mourning in the heart. Instead, he only petitioned to return home to care for his aged father. Ding should repent by wearing fine hemp, being dismissed from office, and observing mourning in the heart for three years.[157]

Above all, this edict confirms that by the 1070s, the court was willing to mandate a son's mourning duties for his concubine mother, even though the length and grade of mourning depended on his status as heir and the status of his legal mother. Failure to do so was not only punishable by law, but could also make one politically vulnerable in a time of factional strife. At least a dozen memorials, dated between 1070 and 1086, condemned Li's conduct and called for his dismissal based on his failure to mourn his concubine mother.[158] One memorial alleged, "When Miss Qiu died at Ding's home, [Li] Ding was thirty-seven years old. It would have been impossible for him not to have known that [Miss Qiu was his birth mother]. People all think that Li Ding was unfilial."[159] Li Ding was subsequently demoted and died in exile.

That Li gained such notoriety had much to do with his close association with Wang Anshi during a time of rampant factionalism. The politicization of filial piety can also be seen in the way Wang Anshi's opponents promoted the deeds of Zhu Shouchang.[160] In contrast to Li's negligence of his ritual obligations, Zhu was praised for locating his concubine mother fifty years after she was abandoned by Zhu's father and for taking caring of her and her entire family. In comparison, Li Ding's offense was made to seem all the more scandalous.[161] In the wake of Li's impeachment, we learned that a certain Mr. Cai, who had neglected the mourning of his concubine mother, corrected his wrongs.[162]

The positive portrayal of filial sons mourning concubine mothers and the political condemnation of Li Ding's failure to do so coincided with ongoing intellectual disagreements on the issue, making any clear-cut standard impractical. While Sima Guang and the Cheng brothers were concerned with the maintenance of proper hierarchies between the main wife and the concubine, Zhang Zai (1020–1077) advocated that a son should observe a lower grade of mourning for his concubine mother only if his legal mother was still alive.[163] That the mourning of concubine mothers continued to perplex Song elite men is seen from a comment by Zhu Xi in the Southern Song. When prompted, Zhu once responded that a man "was mistaken in thinking that he should mourn his birth mother at the low level specified for 'concubine mothers'; she was his mother, and he should mourn her for three years."[164] Zhu Xi's reconfiguration of mourning rituals, by stressing the concubine's role as mother, further helped strengthen the concubine's status in the family. His supportive stance of concubine mothers aside, the very fact that someone had gone to Zhu for advice and Zhu felt the need to explicate his view indicated the lingering unease and uncertainty among elite men regarding the treatment of concubine mothers. It is probably reasonable to suppose that actual practice may very well have fallen in between these lines of thought, with some sons giving more weight to observing family hierarchies while others were more attentive to their filial sentiments.

*   *   *

This discussion of the practice and representation of mourning in the Northern Song is based on the observation that due to restrictive government policies, most office-holding men did not practice mourning in any exceptional manner. This was especially true in the first half of the Northern Song. In dealing with the conflict between their professional and domestic duties, Northern Song men had to make significant adjustments to the way they practiced mourning. Those who were praised for diligent mourning often performed *lumu* or excessive grieving. In this sense, there were strong continuities in the way ideal mourning was perceived and practiced. However, the Northern Song did witness new practices that gave the mourner a larger, more public presence, attesting to the significant place that grieving occupied in the representation of filial performance. In actively promoting the moral exemplars and aiming to reform local practices, Song epitaph authors increasingly used their work as a public platform for moral education.

CHAPTER 3

When and Where?
Burial and Filial Piety

In 1040, Liu Juzheng (997–1040), a native of Dongguang (in Hebei), passed away while serving in Hengyang (in Hunan), a year after his wife had died there. The couple's only son, Liu Zhi (1030–1098), at eleven, was too young to manage his parents' posthumous affairs. Fortunately, Juzheng's brother-in-law had been living with the family. His own brother soon arrived from Hebei to help. In the following months, Liu Juzheng and his wife were cremated and their ashes brought to a Buddhist monastery at Dongguang for temporary burial. In the meantime, Liu Zhi, instead of accompanying his parents' remains back to Hebei, went to live with his maternal grandparents in Yunzhou (Yuncheng, Shandong).[1]

Liu Juzheng and his wife were not permanently interred for thirty-two years, nor were they buried in Dongguang. In 1072, Liu Zhi divined for his parents' burials and moved their ashes, along with the remains of his grandparents and great-grandparents, from Dongguang to a new graveyard in Yunzhou. Liu undertook this long-distance, massive burial in the wake of a career setback. Earning the *jinshi* degree in 1059, he had served in several local positions before filling an important post in the capital as a supporter of the New Policy program. A disagreement with its leader, Wang Anshi, soon led to Liu's demotion to Hebei.[2] The appointment near his native place proved the perfect occasion for Liu Zhi to tend to his parents' burials. Liu's opponents, however, took the opportunity to label Liu an unfilial son. Word quickly spread that Liu Juzheng's burial was actually a *zhaohun* (literally, a calling back of the soul) ceremony and that his ashes had been long lost.

Liu Zhi did not formally respond to the attack at the time. In the next two decades, his political success provided him with ample opportunities to demonstrate his filial devotion. Liu earned multiple honorary titles for three generations of his ancestors. The family cemetery in Yunzhou was subsequently upgraded to reflect Liu's rising rank. The court further authorized the establishment of four Buddhist merit cloisters, two in Dongguang and two in Yunzhou, for the upkeep of the family's cemeteries.[3] For a brief period, Liu Zhi was even appointed to a post near Yunzhou so that he could regularly visit and offer sacrifices at the graveyard.

Liu Zhi continued to fashion his filial image through the perpetuation of his father's memory. To combat the accusation regarding the loss of his parents' ashes and his unfiliality, Liu Zhi wrote a lengthy account in 1091, upon the completion of a family shrine, in which he detailed his father's death, cremation, and temporary burial. This was followed by the composition of multiple funerary biographies, including Liu Juzheng's record of conduct and epitaph on the occasion of a tomb renovation. Finally, in 1096, Su Song authored Liu Juzheng's spirit path stele inscription, in which he included a meticulous account of Liu Juzheng's life. Equally important, Su praised Liu Zhi's perseverance in managing his parents' burials, attributing the family's ascendancy to, among other things, Liu's sincere expression of filial piety. Liu Zhi died two years later.

Liu Zhi's experience reveals the centrality of burial as a major form of filial expression and the various challenges that it posed. In particular, it brings to light two significant issues. The first is the scale of elite geographical mobility, in both life and death. Liu Juzheng died at his post in Hunan, his ashes were originally transported to Hebei, yet he was eventually laid to rest in Shandong. In the stele inscription for Liu, Su Song explained that the move was due to severe water damage to the family's ancestral graveyard and auspicious divination results for Yunzhou. Questions nonetheless remained. Why was nothing done for decades if flooding had caused problems at the burial ground? What were the specific circumstances that led to Liu Juzheng's and his wife's temporary burials? Given that two Buddhist temples were later built in Dongguang, the family's graveyard had continued to function as a base for the Lius. Why then did Liu Zhi opt for a new graveyard away from his native place?

Equally noticeable in Liu Juzheng's case is the long interval—over three decades—between his death and burial. Losing his father as a boy, Liu Zhi was over forty when he had three generations of his ancestors laid to rest. If we consider the continuing renovations of and additions to the new graveyard and the composition of the multiple funerary inscriptions in the 1080s and 1090s, it is fair to say that managing his parents' burial, constructing the Yunzhou cemetery, and preparing for the commemorative texts defined Liu Zhi's entire adult life.[4]

Using the experience of Liu Zhi and that of his peers, this chapter will focus on elite burial practices in the context of filial performance. It will show that the professional pursuits of Northern Song civil servants and the physical mobility that they experienced, in both life and death, tremendously shaped the temporal and geographical dimensions of burial and the discourse on filial performance. While many sons managed to entomb parents in existing family graveyards in a timely manner, long delays and the construction of new graveyards were common occurrences. Contributing factors varied for different families. The place of death and time needed to transport loved ones' bodies, inadequate space and conditions at existing family graveyards, divination results, and the expenses required of funeral preparations were among the most commonly cited reasons for a long postponement in burial and the creation of new burial complexes.

Broadly speaking, the intertwining of these factors rendered a proper and timely burial a much less straightforward task than was prescribed in the classics and ritual manuals. This in turn led to large changes in the representation of the filial son. Similar to the elevation of the *luyang* ideal, Northern Song office-holding men were celebrated for working against great odds to lay parents to rest, follow parents' specific burial instructions, and be attentive to family graveyards. All could be managed over long distances and extended periods of time. This receptiveness to long delays in burials and the building of new cemeteries accommodated office-holding sons, allowing them to juggle their careers and domestic duties.

Old or New Graveyard? The Geographical Dimensions of Death and Burial

A perusal of Northern Song epitaphs and personal correspondence reveals that one of the greatest challenges for office-holding men and their families was to manage deaths and burials over long distances. The extent of this problem can be seen in broad strokes: ten of the twelve (83 percent), fifteen out of the twenty-one (71 percent), and nine out of the seventeen (53 percent) people whose epitaphs were authored by Wang Yucheng, Yu Jing, and Zheng Xie respectively died far from where they were eventually buried.[5] Women experienced just as much geographical mobility as men. Five of the seven women featured by Su Song and three of the ten featured by Shen Gua died either on the road or at their husbands' or sons' official posts.[6] Subsequently, funeral and burial planning often involved multiple steps, beginning with delivering the sad news to sons and other family members, who were in different places; transporting the deceased's body to the place of temporary or permanent entombment; divining for the time and place of burial; procuring the necessary funds; and preparing for the actual ceremony. For these reasons, contemporary epitaphs exalted sons for fulfilling the above responsibilities with the utmost sincerity and perseverance.

Dying far from home was certainly not a new phenomenon. That many perished while traveling can be seen from the emergence of a term, *guizang* (to return the deceased home for burial) in the Han, when the grave took on a growing significance in ancestral worship. The majority of office holders who died in the capital or elsewhere were interred in their native places.[7] *Guizang* remained the standard practice in post-Han times. The renowned scholar Chen Shou (233–297) was dismissed from office and attacked by his contemporaries for allegedly following his mother's wishes to have her buried where she died instead of in the family's ancestral graveyard.[8] A burial in the ancestral graveyard acquired symbolic significance in the Period of Disunity, when entire clans and communities, in escaping nomadic invasion and chronic warfare in the north, fled southward and practiced "temporary burial," hoping that the bodies of the deceased would be eventually returned to the ancestral home in the north.[9]

Guizang regularly appeared in Tang records concerning the most eminent clans. Its meaning, however, witnessed a major change. Although the Tang aristocrats continued to use their clan names and places of origin, the vast majority had relocated to the capital region by the mid-Tang and severed direct connections with their places of ancestral origin by the ninth century. As a result, the final destination for members of this group ceased to be their native place. Rather, they tended to rest in family burial grounds distributed along the Chang'an and Luoyang corridor.[10]

Compared to the Tang, the Northern Song ruling class originated from more diverse familial and regional backgrounds. Consequently, the continuance of the *guizang* practice necessitated the willingness and capability of this group to maintain ancestral graveyards over multiple generations, even though office holding was responsible for frequent travels and deaths in disparate places across the country. An extraordinarily long-lasting graveyard was that of the Shi family of Laizhou (in Shandong), who managed to use the same cemetery for eight generations, from the end of the Tang to the mid-Northern Song.[11] To give three additional examples, Liu Ye's (965–1026) family maintained its burial ground near Luoyang for ten generations,[12] and Liu Kai's (947–1000) and Han Qi's families held multi-generational burial events in their ancestral graveyards in Daming (in Hebei) and Anyang (in Henan) respectively. It should be noted that all four families lived within a reasonable distance from the capital region, making the continuation of the ancestral graveyard relatively manageable.

Parallel to the *guizang* practice was the tendency for families to establish new burial grounds. In the second half of the Tang the less distinguished branches of the great families had already settled in areas far away from the capital region due to migration, provincial service, and downward mobility.[13] The founding of the Song and the expansion of the examination system quickly drew elite men to the capital cities and the surrounding vicinity for educational and career purposes. For many, this became a journey with no return, characterized by the construction of family graveyards in the capital region. A Wang family from Shanxi began to "bury their ancestors in Henan" when a member entered officialdom.[14] Tian Kuang's (1005–1063) father started a graveyard in Yangzhai (in Henan) due to the father's government service. By his son's generation, the family had built another in Shou'an County (in Henan); both locations were close to the capital.[15] Others moved from Taiyuan and Hezhong (both in Shanxi), Cangzhou and Beizhou (both in Hebei), Leling and Liaocheng (both in Shandong), and Guozhou (Nanchong, Sichuan) to the capital region.[16] All cited office holding as the incentive for the founding of new family graveyards.

Frequent new tomb construction can also be seen in the changing meaning of "ancestral graveyard" in literati writing. In the context of filial performance, tomb inscriptions often praised sons for burying parents at their family's *zuying*, *xianying*, *jiuying*, or *xianlong*. All these terms can be loosely translated as "ancestral graveyard," although, in reality, most burial grounds held only one or two generations of ancestors. Fan Yong's (981–1046) father, a native of Sichuan, died while in office in Hefei (in Anhui) when Fan Yong was ten. Fan Yong later had his father buried in Luoyang (in Henan). By the time Fan Yong himself died and was interred, Luoyang was already identified as the Fans' ancestral graveyard.[17] When Sun Yong (?–1087) died in the capital, he was buried in the "ancestral graveyard" in nearby Xuchang (in Henan), which had been started by his father.[18] Yang Jinglue's (1040–1086) family set up a graveyard in Luoyang when his father buried his grandfather there. When Jinglue died in Yangzhou (in Jiangsu), his sons transported his body to Luoyang and buried him near the family's "ancestral" tomb.[19] Similarly, Fan Chunren claimed that his family had maintained a graveyard in Henan for generations when it was actually set up by his father, Fan Zhongyan, for his grandmother.[20]

What especially distinguished the Northern Song from earlier times was the willingness on the part of the deceased and their families to build new burial grounds not only in or around the capital region, but also far away from it. Many factors played a role in the decision-making process. Some officials became so attached to a place that they had visited or in which they had served that they wished to be buried there. After sojourning in Jingkou, a Mr. Cai fell in love with its natural and social setting and vowed, "I will return here when I am old." His son followed his wish and chose a burial plot in Dantu (in Jiangsu).[21] Teng Zongliang (990–1047) called Chizhou (in Anhui) a place where "those who live here enjoy long lives, and those who are buried here will be preserved." Teng subsequently concluded, "This is where one can live as a recluse and lay his ancestors to rest." He therefore had his father buried there. The new cemetery was firmly established when Teng held a funeral for his mother a year later.[22]

Similarly, because Mr. Li "served in Yanzhou (in Shandong) and loved the place," his sons later entombed him there.[23] Chen Xi (1003–1078) thought that of all the places he had been, Xiangyang (in Hubei) had the best scenery. He therefore wished to be buried there.[24] After serving in Weizhou (Weihui, Henan), Yang Huaide's (1012–1084) father specifically said, "I love the natural conditions and social customs of Weizhou. When I die, return me to this place." Huaide later took his mother to various posts but remembered his father's wish, so he buried both parents there.[25]

Places near major political and cultural centers along the Grand Canal and the lower and middle reaches of the Yangzi River held the most appeal for families from the remotest parts of south China, such as Fujian, Jiangxi, and Sichuan. Li Yin of Fujian, discussed in chapter 1, accompanied his son to Hongzhou and fell in love with its natural and social setting. This led to the Lis' permanent settlement there, marked by the acquisition of an estate and the establishment of a family graveyard. Wang Anshi and his brothers set up a new graveyard in Jiangning instead of returning their father's body to Linchuan, where the Wangs had resided for generations. Huang Shen (n.d.), whose family was originally from Fujian, rationalized the family's move in the most straightforward manner:

> My grandfather did not return to Min [i.e., Fujian] [after entering government service] and was buried in the Lake Tai region [in Jiangsu]. I have come to the north due to court service [and brought my father, who died here]. The mountain roads are long and difficult to travel. Not daring to transport his coffin [over great distances], I have divined [for a new burial site] and received auspicious results for Wangshan in Xucheng of Yunzhou.[26]

Huang Shen made it clear that his family had already started a new graveyard once due to the demands of office holding. Since he had been serving in north China, he tried to find a closer location so that his father's body would not have to endure long-distance travel. In fact, he implied, subjecting his deceased father to such hardships would have been an unfilial act. Huang Shen's reasoning left something unsaid. Not only was it a challenge to transport his father's body from north China back to the Lake Tai region, but burying him there would also have created problems for himself. For office holders who were subject to government personnel policies, taking lengthy trips to visit, offer sacrifices, and maintain family tombs posed a major challenge. Burying parents at a nearby and convenient location would lessen the burden.

The examples mentioned above and many more to come demonstrate an unprecedented and frequent movement of burial grounds for Northern Song elite families.[27] In fact, the necessity, or inevitability, of graveyard movement came to be accepted as a fact of life. To Fan Zhongyan, the reality was the following: "When sons and grandsons enter government service, they are truly people of the north and south." For this reason, the building of new burial grounds was to be expected.[28] Ouyang Xiu similarly considered court service as the key reason that sons did not transport parents' bodies back to their native places. "This is not strange, but the result of changes in human affairs. Sons and grandsons of officials all choose to have their parents buried in the north. This was the case with the virtuous in ancient times." Ouyang Xiu made the above comment while mourning his mother and planning to bury her in Yingzhou instead of in the family's native region of Jiangxi. This explained his sentiment that he could not bear "to return my late mother to our native place either." To Ouyang and his peers, "Due to the long distance [between one's local post and one's native place], sons and grandsons are unable to visit parents' graves regularly. This is extremely sad."[29] By alluding to its ancient roots, Ouyang made new graveyard construction a perfectly reasonable choice for men like him. As the following case study shows, it was based on this understanding that a father specifically instructed his son not to bury him in their native place.

Establishing New Graveyards:
The Sus of Tong'an, Fujian

This section looks at the experience of the Su family of Tong'an (Xiamen, Fujian), who established two new burial grounds in the mid-Northern Song, permanently settling in the Yangzi River Valley. In addition to shedding light on patterns of elite migration in the Northern Song, this case highlights some specific considerations of Song scholar-officials as they coped with parents' burials and their long-term implications.

The most prominent figure of the Su family was Su Song (1020–1101).[30] According to his funerary biography, the Sus settled in Tong'an during the Period of Five Dynasties and Ten Kingdoms (907–960). Su Song's great-great-grandfather and his sons entered officialdom through military service. Although details are lacking, we know that Su Song's grandfather, Su Zhongchang (?–1043), participated in but failed the civil service examinations. It was not until 1019 that Su Song's father, Su Shen (999–1046), became the family's first *jinshi* degree holder.[31]

Both Su Zhongchang and Su Shen spent most of their adult lives serving outside of Fujian. When Su Shen's mother, Miss Liu (?–1027), died at his father's post, he was in the capital but was said to have worn mourning for her in Yangzhou. Su Zhongchang later remarried and died in 1043 while he was posted in Fuzhou (Tianmen, Hubei). Su Shen, again serving in the capital, rushed to Fuzhou and, from there, transported his father's body to Tong'an for burial. There was no mention of whether his mother's coffin was moved home on the same trip. It very likely was, as Su Shen would have passed by Yangzhou on his way to Fujian. We can be certain that the burial for Su Zhongchang was prompt. Su Shen did not sojourn in Fujian. Instead, he spent the rest of his mourning leave in Jiangning, close to Yangzhou, where he had mourned his mother nearly two decades earlier.[32]

While Su Shen was preoccupied with his parents' burials, his younger brother, Su Yi (1006–1077), remained in Fuzhou (in Hubei). Having never held office due to a physical disability, Su Yi had accompanied his father on official journeys. When Su Zhongchang died in Fuzhou, Su Yi, who was married and had several sons, chose not to return to Fujian. He wore mourning in Fuzhou and continued to lead a comfortable life there.[33] Su Yi's permanent settlement in Fuzhou meant that he was not present at his father's burial and never visited his parents' graves to perform any tombside sacrificial ceremonies. He and Su Shen, furthermore, never saw each other again for the rest of their lives. When Su Yi died over three decades later, he left instructions that he was to be buried in Fuzhou, thereupon starting a new graveyard away from the Sus' ancestral home of Fujian.[34]

Extensive official travel, the deaths of his parents in disparate places, and the long journey transporting their remains back to Fujian must have affected Su Shen greatly, enough for him to decide not to subject his own sons to the same hardships. Su Shen subsequently told Su Song: "I made a mistake returning my father to our native place for burial. Your generation should not imitate me. Since we cannot escape government service, you can bury me anywhere [that is convenient for you to visit my tomb]. This is truly my wish."[35]

Knowing and hoping that his sons and grandsons would remain in officialdom, a situation that almost guaranteed their absence from their native place, Su Shen made a pragmatic and considerate decision. After all, his brother Su Yi had chosen to stay away from Fujian. And with Su Shen and Su Yi living in remote places, neither would have been able to take care of their parents' graves and offer sacrifices on a regular basis. By instructing Su Song to choose a convenient location, Su Shen made sure that his descendants would have easier access to his grave.

Su Shen died in 1046. In a long poem, Su Song recollected this tragic episode in his life:

Traveling at night, I rushed to my father's mourning hall;
Shedding tears like it was raining, I guarded his coffin to return [south].
My father had considered the mountain ridges in Min [Fujian] to be too
    remote;
Settling in Jingkou would be close enough.
The graveyard I had acquired was close to a town,
And the tomb land was adjacent to hills.[36]

In the preface to this stanza, Su Song further explained:

As soon as he finished mourning for my grandfather, my father died in
Heyang [Mengxian, Henan]. I escorted his coffin to return south. My
father's thought was that our native place was too distant to return his
body. He ordered that I divine for a [new] burial place. When I passed
by Jingkou, my old friend Qian Zigao [n.d.] was the prefect. He arranged
lodging for me, and there I met a Daoist, Zizhen [n.d.], who was skilled at
geomancy. Zizhen accompanied me to several prefectures near Changzhou
and Runzhou [Zhenjiang, Jiangsu] and selected the current graveyard at
Qingyang [Jiangyin, Jiangsu]. Diviners all thought it was auspicious. I
therefore buried my father there.[37]

Su Song's notes made it clear that as soon as he learned about his father's
passing, he went on a leave of mourning. From Jiangning, where he was serving,
he traveled north to collect his father's body. Knowing full well that Su Shen did
not want to be buried in Fujian, Su Song headed south, even though he had no
specific destination in mind. This indicates that Su Song never intended to establish a new burial plot in north China, even though his father had died in Henan
and his fellow scholar-officials generally considered the capital region to be ideal
for retirement and graveyard building.

Su Song's search went smoothly. With the help of the prefect and a capable
diviner, he surveyed a large area and quickly settled on a plot near Runzhou. In
the epitaphs he authored for multiple non-local families who, just like the Sus,
had started new graveyards in the vicinity, Su Song made a similar point in his
own case: "The soil in Dantu is thick and its water deep. There is not a more
auspicious place for family graveyards."[38] Su made up his mind with the help

of the diviner Zizhen, who specifically predicted that this area would grow in importance and that, given the family's propitious plot, Su Song would rise high in government.[39]

Upon the completion of his father's burial, Su Song assumed a position in the Southern Capital, bringing multiple family members with him. These included his grandmother (Su Shen's stepmother), Miss Weng; his mother; an aunt; and several unmarried siblings.[40] When Miss Weng died in 1083 in the capital, Su Song took a short leave to return her body to Runzhou for burial. This means that Miss Weng, the second wife of Su Zhongchang, was permanently separated from her husband, who was interred in Fujian.[41]

Su Song would return to Runzhou again the following year (1084) when his mother, Miss Chen, died in the capital. He observed mourning in Yangzhou before assuming a position in the capital. Su eventually returned to Runzhou in 1095 at the age of seventy-six after repeated requests for retirement. He died six years later and was buried in the family graveyard that he had established.

The Temporal Dimension of Death and Burial

As large construction projects, funerals and burials took heavy emotional, physical, and financial tolls on sons and other family members. Ritual guidelines and logistical considerations would require months, even years, to prepare and encoffin a corpse, divine for the proper site and date for entombment, construct the tomb, and arrange for a funerary inscription.[42] That many officials and their parents died in transition only added to the time needed for funeral planning. Depending on a variety of factors, including a person's place of death, divination results, the ages and ranks of the deceased's sons at the time of a parent's passing, and a family's financial situation, the time frame for burial varied greatly in the Northern Song.

Of the two thousand epitaphs that I have examined, the two speediest burials were completed twenty and thirty-nine days after the deceased's passing.[43] The slowest took over sixty years.[44] Within this large temporal range, a substantial percentage of the deceased were buried within several months to three years after death.[45] To give a few examples, despite long-distance travel between the capital and Meizhou in Sichuan, Su Shi (1037–1101) and Su Che (1039–1112) had their parents buried seven and eighteen months after their respective deaths. Despite a reconsideration of his mother's burial place, Ouyang Xiu still managed to lay his mother to rest within two years of her death. Sun Bian (996–1064), who specifically told his son that he wished to be buried in Kaifeng instead of his native Sichuan, was entombed nineteen months after his death. Zhang Kang's

(999–1061) five sons had him buried in the ancestral graveyard within four months of his death.[46]

The above timely burials aside, Northern Song epitaphs were replete with references to long postponements. Of the ten epitaphs by Yu Jing that recorded specific death and funeral dates, the time frame ranged from eleven months to thirty-two years. Only four of the ten deceased (40 percent) were buried within two years of their passing. Three (30 percent) were buried within two to three years, and the other three (30 percent), years or decades after their deaths.[47] In the forty-eight epitaphs authored by Chao Buzhi (1053–1110), twelve deceased (25 percent) were laid to rest at least five years after their deaths, with the longest lapse being thirty-three years.[48] Major delays in burials can be seen especially clearly from the experience of the three generations of the Gao family. Gao Shenzhao (935–989), a native of Bingzhou (Yuci, Shanxi), passed away in Weizhou in 989, soon after his wife's death, presumably also in Weizhou. "At the time of his death, his family could not endure more calamities (i.e., his wife had just died, and the family could not afford to have her and Gao buried). The couple's bodies were therefore temporarily buried at Weizhou." Before Gao Huaiyin (n.d.), their only son, could make any burial arrangements, however, he died in 1007 at the age of thirty-nine at an unspecified post, eighteen years after the death of his father. Just like Gao Shenzhao, Gao Huaiyin had only one son, Ruone (997–1055), only eleven at the time of Huaiyin's passing. It was not until 1043, fifty-four years after the death of Shenzhao and thirty-five after that of Huaiyin, that Ruone held a burial of multiple ancestors in Kaifeng.[49]

The Gaos' experience reveals that in the eighteen years that separated Gao Shenzhao's and Gao Huaiyin's deaths, Huaiyin did not or was unable to plan his parents' burial. Barely twenty when he lost both parents, Huaiyin could not have handled the long-distance travel between Weizhou and Bingzhou with his parents' bodies. His developing career and the steep expenses required for the burials may very well have delayed planning efforts. When Huaiyin died and left behind an eleven-year-old son, his funeral, like those of his parents, was put on hold. By any standard, Ruone's task was overwhelming. Having decided to start a new graveyard in Kaifeng, where he had been based and where his mother died, Ruone had to divine for an ideal location, collect the bodies of his father and grandparents from different places, and prepare all the necessary materials. It is very likely that the burials were finally held in 1043 because Ruone's mother had died recently. From one perspective, it may be that the mother's longevity contributed to the deferment of the family's burial event.

There is another twist to this story. When Gao Ruone died in 1055, it appeared that the plot he had chosen was too small to accommodate more graves. His sons therefore obtained a much larger estate for his burial. They also moved Ruone's parents and grandparents to the same burial ground. In contrast to the delays in the burial of the two senior generations, Ruone, just like his mother, was laid to rest only a few months after his death.[50]

When it took families years, even decades, to bury loved ones, where did they leave the bodies? Northern Song epitaphs frequently referred to the "temporary burying or leaving" (*quanbian* or *quancuo*) of bodies at Buddhist temples.[51] In fact, so many bodies were left at temples that a local official, Chen, memorialized that more than eighty thousand unclaimed bodies at a monastery in Chenliu (in Henan) be buried using public funds.[52] Chen's commentary not only points to the common practice of "temporary burial," but it also confirms that the availability of Buddhist institutions somewhat contributed to the long delays in burials. Many families eventually failed to lay their deceased to rest, leaving it to local governments or temples to shoulder the responsibility. For this reason, local officials and local elites were often praised for managing the burial of unclaimed bodies.[53]

Song elite men confessed a great sense of guilt and anxiety regarding the postponement of parents' burials. In an account written for a massive burial event, during which he had over seventy family members entombed, the scholar Shi Jie (1005–1045) wrote the following:

It stipulates in the *Book of Rites* that lords are to be buried in five months, dukes in three months, and officers in one month. For this reason, *The Spring and Autumn Annals* ridicules those who are slow in making burial arrangements. The burial of the Shis can be called slow. My late father spent thirty years but was unable to complete it. At the time of his death, he tried hard to stop his tears. Holding my hands, he ordered, "If you do not realize your father's aspiration, I will not be able to close my eyes."[54]

Shi Jie continued his account, adding that since his father's death, it had taken him another seventeenth months to collect enough funds for the burial, during which he had not once tasted a delicious meal, slept well, or enjoyed a drink. Instead, he "trembled with fear," as if he had "ice and charcoal" in his bosom or was carrying "prickles and thorns" on his back. Shi's writing makes it clear that both he and his father were acutely aware of their violations of ritual codes. His portrayal of his father's dying wish and his inability to rest until the completion of the burial are strong indications of the extent of their failure.

It is not surprising that the long deferments of burials invited strong criticism from the leading intellectuals of the time. Sima Guang remarked:

Those who have lost their parents often do not have them buried for a long time. . . . When ancient kings made rituals, they stipulated that the date of burial could not exceed seven months after a person's death. This dynasty has policies that require that those below the ranks of kings and dukes be buried in three months. In addition, the rites required that before a parent is buried, sons not take off their mourning clothes, eat only gruel, and live in huts because they are saddened that their parents have not been returned to the earth yet. Only after the burial may they gradually change their conduct.[55]

In this passage, Sima Guang pointed out that both the classics and state policies required a prompt burial within months of a person's death. This was crucial because burials were closely associated with the wearing of mourning. Only when a parent was buried could sons take off mourning clothes. In reality, Sima found large discrepancies:

Nowadays people deviate from the rites and violate laws. Not only do they take off their mourning clothes before burying their parents, but they also assume government positions in the four directions. They eat rice and wear brocade while drinking wine and participating in entertainments. How could they have peace of mind? Whether one is powerful or inferior, rich or poor, or lives a long or short life is determined by Heaven. Whether he is virtuous or ignorant is dependent on himself, not on where he buries his ancestors. Even if the diviner is right [that a burial must be delayed], when, as a son, one is supposed to be exhausted by grief, how can he bear to neglect his parents' unburied bodies and focus on gaining fortune and profit?[56]

His nostalgic sentiments about ancient practices aside, Sima Guang identified delays in burial as a serious problem and an extremely unfilial act. Sima's contemporaries echoed his criticism. Lü Tao reproved descendants for being "slow in sending off the deceased," resulting in what Sima had also observed: "coffins being exposed for years and not buried in time."[57] Cheng Yi remarked on an even more serious offense. Some families postponed burials for so many years that it became difficult to "differentiate the coffins of grandparents and great-grandfathers."[58] Delays in burials nonetheless remained a common practice. An imperial edict, dated 1091, ordered the Censorate to impeach or stop the promotion of officials who had not buried parents ten years after their deaths, a strong indication that negligence of a proper burial was a pervasive problem.[59]

Factors That Contributed to Long Delays in Burials

Sima Guang, in the same essay quoted above, listed several contributing factors to long delays in burials:

> When asked [about procrastination in parents' burials], some would answer, "There has not been a favorable time"; some would say, "I have not been able to find an auspicious plot"; yet others would respond, "I have not been able to return home due to official appointments at remote places" or "I am too poor to prepare for the burial." Some end up failing to entomb generations of ancestors in their lifetimes and consequently lose track of the whereabouts of the ancestors' bodies. Is this not lamentable? People desire to have sons and grandsons so that these descendants will inter their bodies. If sons and grandsons behave this way, how is this different from the cases of those who have no sons and grandsons and die on the road? Even then, there may be virtuous people who would have the dead buried.[60]

In addition to scolding sons for delaying or neglecting their parents' burials, Sima mentioned four reasons—two having to do with divination, one with government service, and one with financial difficulties—that his contemporaries used to justify the lengthy postponements in or failures to manage parents' funerals. Similar factors were routinely listed in epitaphs. There was, however, a large difference between Sima's tone and that of the funerary biographers. While Sima condemned the delays as outrageous and inexcusable, funerary biographers recorded such occurrences matter-of-factly, often explaining a major delay without referring to or even impugning the descendants for their unfilial ways. The relationship between divination and long delays in burial will be discussed separately. The rest of this section will focus on the three reasons for delay that were most often cited by funerary biographers.

"Too Poor to Afford a Burial"

The first factor that was identified as contributing to long waits for burials was financial in nature. An analysis of burial costs is made difficult by the lack of comprehensive information about specific households. Extant references to property division, landholding, education, entertainments, and book and antique collections indicate that the economic caliber of elite households varied greatly. Song graves similarly differed in size and structure.[61] This was partly the result of active state regulations, intended to maintain social hierarchies and curb extravagant practices.[62] Leading intellectuals and statesmen also promoted simple burials.[63] Burial-related matters nonetheless remained expensive for both elite and commoner households.[64] Available records do not allow us to pinpoint the exact cost of individual funerals, but there are ways to illustrate their financial implications.[65] Cheng Minsheng has estimated that in the Song, a coffin could cost between one and one hundred strings of cash coins. Burial plots, construction, and the funeral procession could cost an additional hundred strings. Expenses for diviners and religious services, commissions for epitaph writers, and the cost of grave goods varied greatly. Funerals and burials could therefore require hundreds of strings of cash.[66] To put the cost in context, Cheng Minsheng calculated that a "middle-class" family in the Northern Song was worth one to several thousand strings of cash.[67] This means that a family routinely spent a sizable chunk of its net worth on a funeral.

The above calculation leaves out three large expenditures: the cost of travel, a funeral feast, and a massive burial event.[68] The third factor bore special significance. Because people died at all ages, families rarely prepared a funeral for one person. For cost and ritual considerations, funerals for junior family members were routinely held at the same time as those of one or more senior members. For example, Han Qi's family held three large burial events in 1045, 1062, and 1071, interring thirteen, twelve, and nine people of different generations respectively.[69] A Chen man was credited with burying more than twenty family members from three generations.[70] While mourning his mother and preparing for the burial of his parents, a man surnamed Ju traveled to multiple places to collect the coffins of his grandparents, uncle and aunt-in-law, and brother. He had all five of them buried at the same time as his parents.[71] In the 1040s, Shi Jie had over seventy Shi men and women from five generations buried.[72] At Shi's estimate, the funeral, which was held locally and did not necessitate the purchase of more land, would cost about five hundred strings of cash.[73]

The high cost of funerals and burials explained the common trope of a family being "too poor to afford a burial" (pin wu yi zang or pin bu ke zang). "For example, of the thirty-three epitaphs written by Lü Tao, ten explicitly referred to poverty as the reason for postponement.[74] After a man named Fei died in a boat near Yuzhou (Chongqing, Sichuan), his family temporarily left his body at a Buddhist temple in Hezhou (near Chongqing, Sichuan) for fourteen years because "the family had no clan members to rely on, no land to till, and no room to live."[75] A Mr. Wang was said to have saved all his income for years from teaching at the prefectural school to bury his grandparents and parents.[76]

It should be noted that sons and families were not completely on their own. From the beginning of the Northern Song, the court had shown a willingness to subsidize its officials' funeral and burial expenses. Governmental help often took the form of bestowals in silk, silver or cash, and sometimes even burial plots.[77] It is understandable that the largest amounts, worth hundreds of strings of cash, went to the highest-ranking officials.[78] Imperial generosity did consider families in financial stress. As early as 1003, an imperial edict made it a standard practice to award some burial allowances to the families of exiled officials in Guangdong and Guangxi.[79] When a man surnamed Liu died in 1036, the emperor, knowing that the Lius were poor, granted the family 120 strings of cash.[80] An official memorialized on behalf of Mr. Hu's sons and grandsons, who had been too poor to manage Hu's burial for over thirty years. An imperial edict subsequently granted two hundred strings of cash and a plot to help cover Hu's funeral.[81] So did Wen Yanbo on behalf of Cheng Yi when Cheng's father died.[82]

In addition to institutional support, friends and acquaintances also contributed in times of need. An important part of funeral and burial culture since the Han, *fuzeng* (cash gifts) remained a widespread practice in Chinese history.[83] Many Song men were praised for their generosity, especially when a funeral involved multiple deceased. After Shi Jie died, his good friends, Han Qi and Fu Bi, purchased land for Shi's wife and children so that they would not suffer from hunger and cold.[84] Han Qi was also known to have given three hundred ounces of silver and Ouyang Xiu two hundred when Su Shi's father died.[85] The famous "Community Covenant of the Lü Family" (Lüshi Xiangyue) stipulated that for funerals and burials, contributions should range from a few to dozens of strings of cash.[86] In fact, cash gifts were such an important part of the death rituals that Sima Guang included them in his *Letters and Etiquette* (*Simashi Shuyi*).[87]

At the same time that both the state and elite men were commended for their generosity, sons and grandsons were singled out for refusing outside help and managing funerals on their own—another standard trope in Northern Song epitaphs. For example, Mr. Tang's father died at an official post when Tang was only thirteen. "His family was poor. People at the prefecture offered to help. He refused while shedding tears."[88] When the mother of Mr. Yuan died after accompanying him to his official post, he was too poor to hold a funeral. Even though "local gentlemen were all eager [to help him]," Yuan declined their kindness and carried his mother's coffin in a boat so that it could be buried in the family graveyard.[89] A man surnamed Zhang rejected many strings of cash by saying, "I plan to bury my parent according to the rites. Why would I need money from others?"[90] Similarly, when Du Minqiu died, local people, sympathetic to the family's poverty, offered to help. His sons wailed and said, "Our father observed the rites and righteousness. Throughout his whole life, he never took one penny from others. Now that we are suffering this disaster, even though we are poor, we would rather die from cold and starvation. Dare we accept gifts to damage his pure reputation?"[91] By insisting that their father was an honest and upright person who never accepted gifts from others and their willingness to continue the father's legacy, Du Minqiu's sons distinguished themselves and were portrayed as extraordinarily filial.

This image of a son overcoming financial difficulties and taking his time to manage a parent's burial with propriety and devotion remained popular throughout the Northern Song. By concentrating on the son's devotion to his parents' burials without outside help and his going to great lengths to save for funeral expenses, Northern Song funerary biographers were able to "explain away" the long delay in burials while elevating the son's filiality.

Waiting to Bury Parents at the Same Time

The second factor that led to long delays in burial was that sons, and in some cases grandsons, were keen on having parents and other senior family members entombed at the same time. For example, Li Chui (965–1033) died while in office at Wudang (in Hubei) in 1033, and his wife died in the eighth month of 1045 at her son's office in Ningzhou (in Gansu). Planning for the couple's burial began immediately in the ninth month of 1045, when two of Li's sons accompanied their mother's coffin and one their father's from two directions and had the couple buried in Dengzhou (in Henan).[92] When Miss Zhu died in 1053 in Wujiang (in Jiangsu), where her husband, Zeng Gongwang (1010–1066), was in office, her body was moved to Hangzhou (in Zhejiang) for temporary burial. However, it was not until thirteen years later, when Zeng died in Guangzhou (Huangchuan, Henan), that their sons divined and prepared for a funeral. The couple's bodies were subsequently brought to Zhengzhou (in Henan) for a co-burial.[93] In another instance, a man named Li died in 1093, but it was not until his wife's death in 1110 that preparations for their burial began, with the actual entombment completed in 1114.[94] Similarly, as soon as Mr. Zhang, who had survived four wives, died, the family held a massive funeral for all of them. While the promptness of this burial was singled out for praise, it still meant deliberate, long delays in the burial of his wives.[95]

The above examples share two similarities. First, sons postponed the funeral of one parent in order to wait to bury both parents at the same time. Second, two parents often died at different places and were buried at a third location, necessitating time-consuming preparations often made through personal correspondence. Other, more specific considerations also played a part. In some cases, when the first parent died, the family members might not have determined whether they were going to continue to use the ancestral graveyard or to start a new one.

In others, sons serving in disparate places or parents dying far away from home made a prompt funeral impossible. Waiting for the second parent's death and holding a joint funeral subsequently became a more practical option. Financial considerations—that one funeral for both parents was normally cheaper than two separate ones—must also have been a factor in the decision-making process. In addition, waiting to bury both parents at the same time was the best guarantee that they would rest in the same burial ground, sparing the sons' and the senior couple's anxiety as to whether they would end up being entombed hundreds of miles away from each other.

A related burial-postponing scenario occurred when sons waited to earn honorary titles for their parents in order to demonstrate their *luyang* achievements, as well as to entomb parents according to the standards set for parents of higher-ranked officials. One family was said to have waited nineteen years for this honor.[96] Another put off a parent's burial for seven years for similar reasons.[97] Ironically, the wait often corresponded with more deaths in the family and growing pressure for a larger-scale burial. And often enough, sons who failed in the end to obtain the highly coveted titles for parents found themselves in an awkward position when it came to justifying the delay. Chen Shunyu (1026–1076), in a long and moving letter requesting an epitaph from Ouyang Xiu, stated that he had waited thirteen years because he had wanted to earn his father an honorary title at the time of his burial.[98] Presumably not having heard from Ouyang, Chen wrote again two years later, asking if Ouyang would be willing to write his father's epitaph. This way, he could "redeem his crime for having not held a burial for his father for fifteen years."[99]

Parents Dying with Young Sons

The third reason for long delays in burials concerned parents who died with young sons or no sons, as already noted in several cases discussed above. In yet another example, Liu Jian (1042–1075) died in 1075 at age thirty-four; he had three young sons. It was not until thirty years later that one of the sons proposed, "Our father unfortunately died young, and our mother also passed away. Our great-grandparents, grandparents, and parents have not been buried. Let us exhaust everything we have to complete their burial so that when we die, we will have no regrets." The brothers subsequently divined for an auspicious plot and built seven pits within two years.[100]

Liu Jian's case indicates that when he died, his widow and young sons were incapable of managing his burial. With his wife continuing to live, presumably to a ripe age, the sons were in no rush to prepare his funeral. Chao Buzhi, Liu

Jian's funerary biographer, did not dwell on the delay in Liu's burial. Instead, he focused on the sons, who demonstrated extraordinary filial piety for having the determination and willingness to exhaust the family's resources for the burial of seven ancestors. The Lius' experience reminds us of that of the Gaos, discussed above. Both cases show that the more ancestors remained unburied and the longer the lapse between death and interment, the more daunting the task became. And dying prematurely with young sons certainly added great uncertainty to the already expensive and complicated matter of funeral planning.

In epitaphs, authors often highlighted the disastrous effect on boys and young men who had lost their parents in order to stress the junior men's filial devotion. In his epitaph for Ren Ju's (n.d.) father, Yin Zhu (1001–1047) cited extensively from Ren's letter to highlight Ren's devotion:

[Ren] Ju said, "I unfortunately lost my father when I was little and was brought up by my mother. When I was old enough, I learned that my father had not been buried, but I was too weak and poor to manage the matter at the time and worried that I would not be able to have him buried [should some disaster befall me]. Heaven has assisted me to serve in counties and prefectures. I now earn a monthly salary, which affords me a way to realize my original aspiration. I plan to have my father buried on [a certain] day of [a certain] year. I would like to request an epitaph from you to record my father's life and deeds."[101]

Yin's epitaph reveals that it had been over forty years since the senior Ren's death. Instead of blaming Ren Ju for concentrating on his official pursuits and neglecting his father's burial after he reached adulthood, Yin applauded Ren's perseverance and filial devotion: "I sympathize that Ju has gone through poverty and hardships but has remained determined and has finally established himself." In particular, Yin Zhu remarked, he had agreed to write a *muzhiming* because Ren "could speak about his father's deeds and conduct [even though he was only a young boy at the time of his father's death]," an indication that Ren had not forgotten his father, yet additional evidence of his filial piety.[102]

In the same epitaph, Yin Zhu specifically addressed the issue of long delays in burial:

Recently, many, being sticklers for divination theories, have failed to manage the burial of two generations of ancestors. Is this not extreme? There are others who simply are not competent. In the case of Ren Ju, who did not take on his father's burial until four decades later, it is not that he had not wanted to. It is because he could not. This is different from those I have just ridiculed.[103]

Yin Zhu acknowledged that long delays in burial were common, but they were widely practiced for different reasons. Unlike those who were negligent or easily restricted by superficial reasons such as divination, Ren Ju did not take care of his father's funeral earlier because he had not been able to; he was young when his father died and had suffered much hardship before he turned to this large responsibility, yet Ren had never forgotten his father. To Yin, that Ren eventually fulfilled his duty after acquiring official rank was clear evidence of his filial piety.

Yin's justification of Ren's delay in planning his father's funeral was not at all uncommon. Even Sima Guang, who, just as Yin Zhu, lamented that sons were neglecting their parents' burials, also wrote epitaphs celebrating sons who were too young to handle funeral-related matters. In a detailed case that can be reconstructed through three epitaphs, Sima wrote about the filial piety of a certain Wu Jifu (n.d.).[104]

Wu Jifu's father, Wu Yuanheng (991–1031), died in 1031. His coffin was temporarily left at Luoyang. When Jifu's older brother, Wu Hao (?–1033), died two years later, his coffin was similarly left at a temple, but in Ruzhou (in Henan). Another three years later, Jifu suffered from the death of his mother, Miss Nie, who was temporarily buried at an unspecified place. It was not until 1060, when Jifu was about to take up a post in Sichuan, that he had his parents and older brother buried in Liangxian (in Henan). For laying his parents to rest thirty years after the death of his father and twenty-five after that of his mother, Sima celebrated Jifu as a filial son. Just as Yin Zhu had done, Sima quoted Jifu as saying, "I was often afraid that I would fail to bury my parents and perform ancestral sacrifices." In fact, "the pain caused by the thought of my parents having not been buried yet" grew to be an unbearable emotional and psychological burden. Jifu mentioned that he simply could not go to remote Sichuan with this hanging over his head, implying a fear of perishing on the long journey. This would have greatly exacerbated the difficulties of the burial matter for his descendants, likely causing a massive, multi-generational event years later.[105]

In celebrating Jifu's filial endeavor, Sima was willing to ignore the fact that Jifu did not bury his parents earlier because he had been busy pursuing an official career, something of which he specifically did not approve. In the end, to Sima as well as Yin Zhu, what mattered the most was that the son in question eventually managed to have his parents buried, but Sima's praise for Wu Jifu was further justified by the extra effort that Jifu put into this cause. While planning for his parents' burial, Jifu also looked for his grandmother, Miss Liu's, coffin, which had been temporarily left in the Guangji Temple in Kaifeng. The search went on for years because, it turned out, there were two temples of the same name in the capital, each with an enormous number of unattended coffins. And decades after Miss Liu's death, few could give Jifu any clue as to the whereabouts of her remains. In the end, Jifu was assisted by an old monk who happened to remember that Jifu's father had left Miss Liu's coffin there because he (the monk) happened to share the same family name with the Wus. By the time Jifu was able to bury his grandmother, forty-two years had passed since her death. Miss Liu, however, was entombed near Luoyang while Jifu's parents and older brother were buried near Ruzhou.[106]

Sima Guang voiced no disapproval of the delay in the burial of Wu Jifu's parents and grandmother and the separation between their grave sites. Instead of criticizing Wu Yuanheng for leaving his mother's coffin unattended and not holding a timely burial for her, Sima celebrated Wu Jifu's filial piety. If it had not been for Jifu, Sima wrote, Miss Liu's coffin would never have been recovered. And to whom should this success be attributed? Sima reasoned that it must have been Yuanheng's spirit that had guided Jifu, pointing him to the right monastery and the old monk. From this, Sima concluded, "It is true that genuine filial piety can move ghosts and spirits."[107]

Two Extraordinary Burial-Related Filial Deeds

As the above discussion has shown, Northern Song elite men took it for granted that in addition to mourning parents with sincerity, a son was expected to lay the deceased to rest with propriety. The reality of people dying at all ages, as well as far away from where they were to be buried, and sons being posted in remote places at the time of a parent's passing tremendously complicated the burial process, making long delays and the establishment of new burial sites commonplace phenomena. In the funerary biographies they composed, Northern Song writers included meticulous details about burial-related activities, actively praising their fellow scholar-officials for dedicating themselves to parents' funerals and burial matters against great odds. They especially identified two new endeavors in their construction of the filial son. The first involved sons following parents' instructions on posthumous arrangements. The second featured sons' continual care of the family graveyard in the aftermath of a burial.

Northern Song epitaphs contain rich evidence regarding the role of elite men, and occasionally women, in planning their own posthumous matters.[108]

References of this nature often appeared in the context of commending sons for satisfying parents' wishes, even though fulfilling such requests would complicate their handling of the burial. Many deceased, for example, were said to have been adamant about being buried in the ancestral graveyard, even though this would entail long-distance travel for their children.[109] A man named Yuan instructed that when he died, he was to be buried in the same graveyard with his father and brothers so that if "spirits have consciousness, I can wait on my parents underground."[110] Another man, Wu, left clear orders for his sons to "return his bones to the ancestral graveyard. His sons followed his dying words."[111] A woman traveling with her son to his official post told her son, "I would rather return home so that I can sweep the ancestral graveyard and die peacefully among neighbors and clan members." Although circumstances did not allow her return and she eventually died at her son's office in the capital, the son made sure to have her buried in their native place.[112]

Parents were portrayed as similarly vocal in their wish to be buried away from the ancestral tombs. Their descendants were likewise labeled filial for meeting this demand. A certain Mr. Sun's descendants were commended for following his instructions to start a new graveyard in Kaifeng.[113] Before her death in the capital, Mr. Wen's mother specifically ordered that she not be returned to their native place. Mr. Wen subsequently constructed a new cemetery near the capital to honor his mother's wish.[114] Originally from Fujian, Zhang Dexiang's (978–1048) mother traveled with him to many localities. Before dying in the capital, she specifically ordered that her body not be sent back to Fujian. A new tomb site was created in Xuzhou (Xuchang, Henan), where Zhang buried his mother and two wives.[115] Shi Changyan (995–1057), a native of Sichuan, buried his wife in the capital region and asked his sons to do the same when he died.[116] Similarly, Sun Bian, also a Sichuanese, left final words that he wanted to be buried in Kaifeng, where he was, nineteen months after his death.[117]

For honoring their parents' wishes, sons were seen as nothing but filial. A decision to do so, however, had major implications, especially in terms of the physical separation in death of parents and sons and husbands and wives. By instructing her son to bury her away from the ancestral tomb, Zhang Dexiang's mother clearly understood that her son would be permanently separated from his father and other ancestors and she from her husband. Unlike Yuan, who insisted on remaining physically close to his family in the afterlife, Zhang's mother manifested a different understanding of the issue: "The energy of one's *hun*-spirit can move everywhere. Why would only a co-burial be called 'returning?'"[118] Zhang's mother asserted that it was important to maintain connections with one's family, both in this world and in the afterlife. What was crucial, however, was not the physical but the spiritual and emotional links among its members. To her, even if she, and understandably her son, would not be buried with the rest of the Zhangs, in spirit, they would remain close.

This new model of office-holding sons who followed parents' wishes to build a new graveyard paralleled with the emergence of the *luyang* ideal. New graveyards away from the native place, just as the *luyang* rhetoric in regard to the sons' reverent care duties, relieved official sons from the obligation of returning deceased parents to a distant native place and of trekking long distances for the fulfillment of ancestral worship-related rituals and ceremonies, performances that were made impractical by their careers. A question then follows: to what extent should we believe that parents were actually the ones who approved, and even insisted on, such new tomb complexes? As our discussion will show, words might have been put into parents' mouths in some cases. Some families, such as the Sus of Tong'an discussed above, clearly started new tomb sites out of practical considerations. In other instances, parents and sons deliberated and reached a mutual understanding.

In addition to commending sons for following parents' instructions regarding their final resting place, Northern Song funerary inscriptions celebrated filial offspring who moved or repaired damaged graveyards while tending to their parents' burial. Despite technological improvements that made graves stronger and more waterproof, references to deteriorating tombs, especially due to water damage, were common in the Northern Song.[119] As a result, what made a son especially praiseworthy was his attentiveness to graveyard maintenance. This included fixing minor problems and conducting periodic renovations. The most significant effort, however, was *qianfen*, which involved moving some or all of the ancestors' tombs to a different location, either locally or over long distances.

Frowned upon in the classics, *qianfen* first appeared in official policies in the eighth century. Three chapters in the *Datang kaiyuan li* specifically dealt with *gaizang* (reburial), which could be held locally or over long distances.[120] It was not until the Song, however, that such expensive, time-consuming endeavors were widely represented as filial acts in contemporary records. As noted, many sons were commended for moving and rebuilding damaged graves.[121] In a particularly detailed case, we learn about the undertakings of the Chao family, natives of Henan, from Chao Ciying's (1046–1113) epitaph.

Ciying's grandfather, Chao Tejin (n.d.), was buried in Kaifeng. For many years, Ciying's father, Chao Zhongcan (n.d.), had planned on divining for a new plot and moving Tejin's water-damaged coffin for a reburial. Unfortunately, Zhongcan died before carrying out his plan and was buried in Rencheng (Jining, Shandong). Remembering his father's wish, Ciying prayed at the family shrine.

Upon receiving the approval of his ancestors, he walked four hundred *li* and transported his grandparents' coffins to be buried beside his father. Li Zhaoqi (?–1126), Chao Ciying's funerary biographer, recorded that some unidentified people disapproved of Ciying's project:

> Some said, "In ancient times, people did not repair tombs. Why are you moving your family's?" Ciying said, "When filial sons bury their parents, they cannot bear for dirt to touch their parents' skin. Unfortunately, my grandparents' coffins are now rotten and submerged in water; how could I stand this? Even if the sages came back to life, they would approve of my petition. Leaving a place that is low and damp and [moving ancestors to] an elevated place so that sons and grandsons can depend on each other and clean the graveyards and offer sacrifices, this is my ancestors' aspiration. What is wrong with what I have done?"[122]

The opposition that Chao Ciying faced reveals both the commonplace occurrence of reburials and the movement of graveyards and the ambivalence toward such undertakings. The rationale of the opposition was that the ancients did not repair tombs, not to mention dig up ancestors' remains and move them over long distances. Ciying's defense rested on three points. First, there was serious damage to his grandparents' graves. The new construction was on high land, a site that would alleviate worries of further environmental degradation; second, by moving their remains, he was uniting parents and sons; third, this move would make sacrifices easier. Ciying felt so justified that he declared that even if the sages came back to life, they would approve of his initiative.

Chao Ciying's words allow us to appreciate the changing perceptions about the meaning of proper burial and care of family graves. Two things especially merit discussion here. First, Ciying was portrayed as following his father's desire to repair the damaged graves of his grandparents. The second, more telling aspect is the prominence Ciying's decision occupied in his epitaph. Despite the disapproval from others, Li Zhaoqi, the epitaph writer, was apparently in support of Ciying, lauding Ciying's dedication to honor his father's wishes.

A very similar case concerned the Zhao family. Zhao You (1001–1045) was buried in Hebei. His son, Zhao Zi (?–1087), had divined to move the family graveyard to Xin'an (in Anhui) due to water damage, but he died before anything was done. Just as in the Chaos' case, Zhao Zi's final words to his sons were to urge them to finish the project so that "I would not be blamed [for being unfilial]." His sons followed his wishes, bringing the remains of two generations of their ancestors to Xin'an and having them buried in 1109.[123]

That the Chaos' and the Zhaos' endeavors took two generations decades to complete demonstrates the significant role that burial played in elite men's filial performance. Both cases involved sons moving graveyards out of concern for water damage but dying before they could complete the project. The grandsons, in continuing their fathers' endeavors, manifested their devotion. Equally important, both cases highlight the scale of geographical movement of elite families.

For the Chaos and Zhaos, the reburials were at the same time a relocation of the family graveyards. Questions then arise: given the scale of the project, why did the Zhaos not limit it to a local one? The official reason for their choice of the Xin'an site was an auspicious divination result, which, as our discussion below will show, was taken seriously. A closer examination, however, offers other possibilities. The epitaph for Zhao Zi's wife, Miss Li, states that after Zi's death, his two younger brothers sought a property division and bullied his widow and sons.[124] Subsequently, Zhao Zi's sons might have decided to get away from their uncles. In fact, it was possible that Zhao Zi and his brothers had not been getting along. The claims of both water damage and divination for a new burial ground could have been pretenses to get away from his brothers. Moreover, the large (re)burial event was undertaken following the death of Zhao Zi's wife. It was therefore possible that even though Zhao Zi's sons were having problems with their uncles, they had chosen to wait for the passing of their mother before embarking on this large construction project.

In praising the junior Zhaos' filiality, the epitaph writer implied that Zhao Zi's brothers, for ignoring the damage to their parents' tombs and taking advantage of their young nephews, were unfilial. The Zhaos' case makes us wonder about how disputes among brothers, especially when they involved property issues, affected filial performance and its representation. Unfortunately, while Song elite men were critical of property disagreements among their local subjects, they rarely talked about similar matters in their own households.[125] They did, however, imply that such discord existed. In a letter to his brothers, Zhu Changwen (1039–1098) mentioned that when their father died, the family suffered from poverty. "Our two uncles sympathized with us and helped out by giving some of the old estates of our grandparents for us to use." Here Zhu praised his uncles for aiding their nephews in need. He did suggest that as his father pursued an official career, the two uncles made the family estate their own.[126] This, in addition to the literary trope of glorifying elite men for not minding money or property-related matters, giving their brothers or nephews the best or larger shares of the family estate, and helping out kinsmen in financial difficulties, make us suspect that actual circumstances for individual families were much more complicated when it came to the allocation of family properties and the fulfillment of filial duties.[127]

Three Burial-Related Unfilial Acts

NEGLECTING THE FAMILY GRAVEYARD

Northern Song scholar-officials, among them Fan Zhongyan and Ouyang Xiu, acknowledged that starting new burial grounds away from the ancestral grave-yard had become an inescapable reality because it was impossible for office-holding sons and grandsons to tend to ancestral graveyards and hold graveside sacrificial offerings on a regular basis.[128] More than occasionally, descendants neglected the ancestral tombs for so long that they were no longer able to identify the graves of grandparents and more remote ancestors.[129] Individual experiences certainly varied. One noticeable pattern, however, emerged: just as the *luyang* rhetoric transferred the physical care of parents to women and non-office-hold-ing sons, official sons increasingly relied on others for the upkeep of graves and seasonal sacrificial offerings.

Song men wrote extensively about their negligence of ancestral graveyards because of their official careers. In 1050, Ouyang Xiu wrote to his clansmen, "Because my mother is old and sick, I have not been able to return home to tend to the family graveyard. Please help care for it."[130] After his mother's burial in Jizhou in 1053, Ouyang submitted seven petitions for a close-to-home position.[131] The main rationale was that "my parents' graves are located south of the [Yangzi] River, but there are no able family members to take care of them."[132] In another memorial, composed seven years after his mother's burial, Ouyang specifically requested to be posted near Jizhou in order to complete a renovation of his par-ents' graves. "Such matters as planting pine and cypress trees, purchasing tomb land and hiring tenants, building ancestral shrines, and inscribing steles are not to be rushed. I should be able to complete these in one to two years."[133] In the end, Ouyang was unable to visit his parents' tombs for the rest of his life. In 1070, on the occasion of earning additional honorary titles for his parents, he had a stele inscription erected at his parents' graveyard with the help of clan members.[134]

Ouyang's experience was anything but unique. Zeng Gong appears to have performed tombside rituals only twice, made possible by official appointments that brought him close to his native place.[135] Li Shu (1002–1059), on the basis of long absences from home, once requested a leave for the purpose of tomb clean-ing.[136] Following the completion of his father's burial in 1067, Su Shi did not once return to Meizhou, even though he wrote profusely about missing home and made multiple requests for close-to-home posts. In several letters, he gave instructions to and thanked clansmen, Buddhist monks, and even the local magistrate for helping take care of his family graveyard.[137] Among the gifts and monies he sent home were funds for tomb maintenance.[138] Because he served in officialdom, Su Song wrote, it was really the tomb land tenants who cared for the graveyard. For this reason, he asked that they be treated as family by his descendants.[139] In fact, so rarely did office-holding men visit their parents' graves that Zhang Shixun (964–1049) was singled out for praise because he had managed to return to his native place to perform tomb cleaning every other year.[140] In the 1070s, an official named Chen was given the privilege of visiting his family graveyard, located in Zhenjiang, twice every year while he was serving in Yangzhou.[141] Such a privilege was widely celebrated as an extraordinary gesture of imperial generosity, but the anecdote nonetheless reveals the extent to which Chen might have neglected the family graveyard, even though it was only about twenty-five miles from his office.

Office-holding men suffered emotionally for their absence from homes and family graveyards. A case in point was Chao Buzhi. Chao recounted that it took him nine years to have his father buried. Only three days after the entombment, he left home to continue his career pursuits; it would be another eleven years before he was able to return to offer sacrifices.[142] If Chao stopped short at calling himself unfilial, Liu Anshang (1069–1128) was more up front. In several elegiac essays, Liu recorded half a dozen deaths of senior family members and his absence from their funerals and burials. Specifically, Liu confessed that due to government service, he did not visit the family graveyard, where his grandfather and father were buried, for seven years. When he finally managed to do so, it was only because his mother had died and funeral planning was in order. For being obsessed with earning rank and honor, Liu labeled himself an unfilial son.[143] Ouyang Xiu, Su Shi, and Su Song would have understood and shared the same pain and mortification.

Some descendants failed to visit or maintain their ancestral graveyards for so long that they lost track of their locations. Those who did look for and find the sites were subsequently celebrated as extremely filial. In the mid-eleventh century, a certain Zhou Yuan (1026–1076) promised his father, Zhou Weihan (n.d.), when the latter was dying, that he would locate the family's ancestral tomb site. According to Zhou Yuan's epitaph, the Zhous were natives of Qiantang. Zhou Yuan's grandfather, Zhou Renli (n.d.), was very young when his own father died at the end of the Period of Five Dynasties and Ten Kingdoms, following a career in officialdom. Due to migration, the family had lost track of the graveyard's location by the early Song. It was Renli's dying wish that Weihan find the original site. The only clue that Renli gave Weihan was that the graveyard was located at a place named Huangshan (not to be confused with the famous Mount Huang).

Weihan, having failed to locate the site, asked his son Zhou Yuan to continue the nearly impossible task. Zhou Yuan subsequently spent years traveling around the Qiantang area (in Zhejiang). He eventually realized his father's wish with the help of a ninety-year old man.[144]

The gist of this story was to praise the filial devotion of three generations of Zhou men. The family's ordeal also reveals that losing track of one's ancestral graveyard was far from unheard of. At a time when people died at all ages and families changed the location of their graveyards every few generations, it remained a great challenge to stay connected to one's ancestral tomb site.

CREMATION

In addition to neglecting family graveyards, another popular practice, cremation, caused much controversy in the Northern Song. The history of cremation in China had much to do with the rise of Buddhism and escalating land prices; changes in mortuary customs; a decline in the use of grave goods; and other folk beliefs about bodies, ghosts, and graves.[145] In this sense, cremation was adopted as both an expediency and an act of Buddhist piety. By the Song, the custom had long been practiced and was impossible to ban despite opposition from the state and scholar-intellectuals. The earliest imperial edict against cremation was issued in 962; it claimed, "In recent times, people follow foreign practice and often resort to cremation. This is a great violation of the classics and rituals. From now on, it should be banned."[146] Similar regulations followed.[147] The state's stance can also be seen when local officials were praised for correcting vulgar customs, including cremation, at their local posts.[148]

"Neo-Confucian objections to cremation were based on sectarian opposition to Buddhism, on belief in the transformative powers of adherence to ancient ritual protocols, and on deeply felt ideas about respect for ancestors."[149] In a long memorial entitled "On Prohibiting Cremation," Jia Tong (n.d.) confirmed the commonplace practice of cremation in office-holding families and considered it a greater offense than unfilial sons discarding parents' bodies to be consumed by animals.[150] Song Qi offered an even more graphic description of cremation and its dire consequences. People's "clothes are left to smoke and ashes, and their bones and flesh roast in firewood and charcoal. Spirits and divinities fear greatly. . . . If this is not banned, I am afraid that filial sentiments will decline. I request that the court implement clear policies and have them widely circulated" in order to fulfill a filial son's wish to repay his parents' loving kindness.[151]

To cope with the difficulty of finding a proper way to handle parents' bodies when they "die[d] in remote places and one was too poor to carry them home," Jia Tong advocated that, as an alternative, sons performed mourning and temporary burials before returning parents' remains to the family graveyard. Jia asked in the most straightforward manner, "Is this not doable?"[152] As our discussion below will show, some families indeed did what Jia Tong recommended, and often enough what was intended as a merely temporary burial became permanent.

Leading intellectuals of the time saw a larger problem for sons who practiced cremation. Cheng Yi famously said, "Those who cremate [parents and family members] do so because they cannot help it. [The problem is that] the ashes of the deceased cannot be moved and buried [in the ancestral graveyard].[153] Here, Cheng Yi acknowledged that cremation as a last resort was somewhat understandable, but he did not see a compromise between cremation and a proper burial for parents; it was simply out of the question to bring the cremated into the ancestral graveyard.

Neo-Confucian opposition to cremation as "cruel, a desecration of the corpse, barbaric, Buddhist, and unfilial" did not lead to its decline.[154] Sima Guang lamented, "Recently when those who serve in remote places die, their sons and grandsons often have them cremated, returning their ashes for burial. This is so commonly practiced that no one bothers to ridicule it anymore."[155] Here Sima, just like others, not only recognized the obstacles of returning the dead home, but he also specifically identified official service and long-distance travel as the main causes for the decision to cremate. The sense of helplessness in Sima's tone is most significant: so many chose cremation as an alternative that people stopped objecting to the practice. In the case of Liu Zhi's father—and if we believe Liu Zhi that his father's ashes had indeed been preserved—the fact that Liu Juzheng was cremated did not stop Su Song from praising Liu for having given his father a proper burial and calling Liu a filial son.

As popular as cremation appears to have been in funeral and burial practice, families and epitaph writers rarely mentioned individual cases. We might not have learned about Liu Juzheng's cremation had it not been for the factional politics of the time and Liu Zhi's defense of his father's cremation. Consequently, when the issue of cremation appeared in Song epitaphs, it was often in the context of praising a deceased's son for resisting having his parents cremated. Sima Guang, for example, wrote the above passage when juxtaposing the filial conduct of a certain Mr. Su. In response to suggestions that his father be cremated, Su said, "A son who bears to do this, is his heart that of a human?" According to Sima, Su eventually traveled thousands of li to bring his father's body home for burial.[156]

DIVINATION

In addition to cremation and the neglect of family graveyards, a third controversial practice, divination, was closely associated with changing representations of filial performance in the Northern Song.[157] Despite stern criticism from leading scholars, divining for a proper time and burial site not only remained a common practice, but was also a leading cause for long postponements in burial. Moreover, there existed a large discrepancy between the rhetoric of the educated elite, which tended to be critical of geomancy, and their actual behavior in burial arrangements. It is interesting that both sides based their argument on the principles of filial piety.

Ancient Chinese believed that the living benefited when their ancestors rested in peace. By the Tang, divination had become a conventional practice in death rituals.[158] Recent studies have shown the prevalence of geomancy culture in all levels of Song society, evidenced in the large number of practitioners, the "professionalization" of those specialized in identifying auspicious burial sites, the publication of key texts, and the close association between elite men and geomancers.[159] Many geomancers even followed the physical movements of the elite and adapted their prophecies to the tastes and social experiences of both men and women in elite households.[160]

The popularity of divination invited contemporary criticism from scholar-intellectuals, who brought in historical, canonical, and ethical arguments.[161] Of all the Northern Song figures who wrote systematically about divination, Liu Kai was the first to address its relationship with filial piety. Liu began by pointing out a common practice of the time: "Sons say to themselves: 'My parents have to be buried in an auspicious place so that their sons and grandsons will be rich and powerful.' Those who are already rich and powerful say, 'My family has never lacked anything for generations. This is because we have located the right pit in which to bury my parents.'" Liu reasoned, when it came to burial, if one thought only about benefiting oneself and one's posterity, "How could this be called filial?" "How could I bear to use my parents to make up for my inadequacy?" In addition to labeling the contemporary practice as unfilial, Liu Kai called into question the efficacy of divination. If divination was so useful, Liu Kai asked, "Why do we not see sons of diviners becoming powerful and successful?"[162]

Major intellectual figures in the mid-Northern Song, such as Sima Guang, Zhang Zai, and Cheng Yi, took a similar stance, indicating a general concern that most sons and family members were not acting in the interest of the ancestors and were using divination as an excuse for other ulterior motives.[163] In his famous "Treatise on Burial," dated 1084, Sima wrote the following:

Nowadays, people who manage burials do not follow ancient practices. They go to extremes when it comes to rigidly adhering to *yin-yang* principles and avoiding other taboos. In the ancient times, although people divined for the [auspicious] sites and times for tombs, they turned to divination only after having considered the convenience of human affairs. The purpose was to make sure that there would be no hardships in later times. The focus was not on specific times and sites. The burial books of the present day concentrate on divining the shapes and appearances of mountains and rivers, examining the heavenly and earthly branches of the month, day, and time. They claim all these relate to the status, fortune, lifespan, and intelligence of sons and grandsons. A burial cannot be held if it is not at the exact place and time prescribed by the diviner. All in the world are confused and believe them, and as a result, those who have lost their parents delay in holding funerals for a long time.[164]

Both Liu Kai and Sima Guang agreed that the close relationship between familial graveyards and the fortunes of a family's posterity was nonsense. Sima Guang especially found the rigidity with which people followed a diviner's instructions to be outrageous. He further illustrated his point based on his personal experience. For one thing, both his grandparents' and parents' generations had simple burials, implying that no diviners had been used. Even though the Simas had never subjected themselves to the manipulations of a diviner, the family had been prosperous. Sima Guang continued, "I now write this essay on burial so that descendants will hold burials in a timely manner [instead of putting off burials in compliance with diviners' instructions]. To understand that burial goods do not have to be luxurious, one needs only to look at my grandparents' burial; to understand that burial manuals are not reliable, one needs only to look at my family's experience."[165] To Sima, that his family continued to prosper, with many among them living long lives and having successful careers, was strong evidence that his ancestors' spirits were in peace, which in turn explained the family's good fortune. In this sense, one really should not feel constrained by strict divination principles. In fact, Sima "once petitioned that all burial books be banned, but the grand councilor of the time did not agree with me."[166]

Sima was not trying to convince his readers that they should all do away with divination and divination books. Rather, the "Treatise on Burial" insists that a filial son's primary concern should not be adhering to yin-yang principles and that he should not be manipulated by divination manuals and professionals. Rather, his priority should be to give his parents a proper and timely burial, not to see burials as opportunities for him to gain wealth, fame, and long life. Cheng Yi's writing echoed Sima Guang's concerns. In "Discourse on Burial," Cheng wrote the following:

To divine for a burial place is to divine whether the place is good or bad, not what diviners call [whether the place is going to bring the family] fortune or misfortune. If a location is good, the deceased's spirits will be peaceful, and his descendants will prosper. This is the same principle as if one cultivates the roots of a tree, its branches and leaves will flourish. An inferior plot will cause the opposite, but what is a good plot? Evidence [of a good place] can be seen in the appearance of the soil and the luxuriance of the plants and trees growing on it. Fathers and grandfathers and sons and grandsons share the same energy [*qi*]. If the former are in peace, the latter will be as well. This is based on the same principle. Those sticklers misunderstand [the principles of geomancy], thinking it is determined by the location of the place selected or the auspiciousness or inauspiciousness of the chosen time. Is this not too much? Worse still, there are those who do not consider worshipping their ancestors to be their priority. They instead worry about ways to benefit their descendants. This, especially, is not the intention of the filial son in putting parents to rest.[167]

Liu Kai, Sima Guang, and Cheng Yi all agreed that sons and grandsons misunderstood the principles of divination. In employing them for their selfish desires, they failed to act filial. Of the three, Sima was probably the most critical of divination practice. As far as he was concerned, it was all right to go without divination altogether. Liu Kai and Cheng Yi, however, acknowledged the utility of divination: the top priority of a filial son should be to put parents' spirits to rest. Cheng Yi went one step further in his support of divining for the proper location. After all, "To bury means to hide. Once a burial is completed, it cannot be changed. It is therefore important that a burial plot can assure the deceased's lasting peace. For this reason, filial sons and loving grandsons must be extremely careful. If one wants a peaceful plot, it is most important to know the underground water conditions. As long as the water conditions are good, there will be no other worries."[168]

In another essay, Cheng Yi further highlighted that two things were primarily responsible for damage to coffins: water and pests. It was his opinion that cypress wood (with lacquer) was the sturdiest and most consistent in preventing damage from both. In addition to the digging of deep pits and the avoidance of large boulders to prevent water damage, Cheng suggested that sons eliminate what he called the "five worries" at the time of graveyard construction. Ancestral graveyards should be built far from major roads, city walls, and ditches. Sons also needed to make sure that the land on which the family graveyard was located would not be seized by powerful families and would not be turned into agricultural land.[169]

Northern Song writers continued to elaborate on the meaning of a proper burial, the intentions of divination, and the importance of choosing the right plot. In a long letter from Xu Jingheng to Ding Gangxun (n.d.), Xu reiterated that (1) the primary goal of a burial was to assure peace for the deceased; (2) one should avoid rocky and wet places; (3) it was equally important to treat parents properly after death as it was when they were alive; (4) the purpose of divination was to get rid of any feeling of uncertainty on the part of the family; and (5) one should not consider expense to be a primary reason to find a close-by site.[170] In particular, Xu agreed with Cheng Yi on a variety of potential worries in choosing the location of a grave:

An ideal place would be where the soil is rich and deep, where there is no sand, rocks, or springs, and where it is not close to ditches and marshes. This way, there will be no worries [about water damage to coffins] due to the moisture in low places. If it is close to roads and markets, one cannot avoid problems arising from unexpected situations. For this reason, when sons bury their parents, they should be careful and treat it as a matter of serious consequence. They should not make decisions based on their own subjective judgment. Sages have instructed that one must divine before holding a burial. The deceased will be at rest after being buried if the [chosen] plot is good. The deceased will be restless if the plot is inferior. If the deceased is at rest, how could the living be restless? If the deceased is not at rest, how could the living be? This is not an [abstract] theory on good and bad fortune but the principle [of burial-related matters].[171]

In continuing to talk about high- and low-quality soil and its relationship with the state of the deceased's spirit, Xu Jingheng advocated for the necessity of divination. He, just like Liu Kai and Cheng Yi, insisted that the primary reason for divination was the restfulness of the ancestral spirits, not for the benefit of the living. Xu did acknowledge, and even highlight, the close relationship between the state of the ancestors' spirits and those of their descendants. This made divination for a proper burial plot all the more important.

Discourses on divination by leading intellectuals, and especially their reservations and opposition to it, did not seem to have a direct impact on the way divination was practiced or on the understanding of its utility.[172] Even Sima Guang admitted that when his clansmen could not have peace of mind without the confirmation of a diviner, his cousin succumbed to pressure by bribing a diviner to rubber-stamp the lot that he had chosen, an incident that further confirmed strong popular beliefs in the efficacy of divination.[173] In Liu Kai's case, despite his rigorous opposition to blindly follow geomancers' words, Liu did heed the advice of the local diviner and waited for eight years to conduct a massive family burial event.[174]

In contrast to the critical tone of the scholarly discourses, Northern Song funerary biographers routinely referred to divination in a matter-of-fact manner and displayed few reservations in praising sons for making use of geomancers to assure the proper time and location for parents' burials. More specifically, divination was often used as a justification for the building of new burial grounds. For example, Wang Li (955–1026) was buried away from his ancestral tomb due to an auspicious divination by his son.[175] Liu Caishao (1080s–1150s) was called filial for moving his parents' coffins to a new site, with which his father was familiar and of which he approved, because the old one was not auspicious.[176] Xin Youzhong (999–1066) buried his father in Yangzhai (in Henan) instead of Xuzhou, where his grandfather had been entombed, due to an inauspicious divination result.[177] In a particularly well-recorded case, we learn that Guo Yuanming (1022–1076) died at his official position in 1076. His sons, after moving his coffin back to his native place of Yunzhou, left it at a local monastery. It was not until Guo's mother, Miss Li, who outlived her husband by over thirty years, died in 1084 that a funeral was arranged. The family had originally planned to have a joint burial for Miss Li with her husband, but the diviner insisted on a new location because "the old burial ground was low and its soil inferior." Guo's sons eventually settled on a place that was ten *li* north of the old graveyard, to which they moved the remains of their grandparents and father. "Those who have expertise on soil and burial all called it suitable, so they buried the mother there."[178]

Families routinely started new graveyards locally when the old sites ran out of space or when new branches established their own cemeteries. The Guos' case was unusual because Guo Yuanming's sons, having not planned a new burial ground, readily followed the diviner's advice in establishing one nearby. Additional expenses aside, this case allows us to see yet another major challenge that sons faced in giving their parents a proper burial. If the old cemetery was located at low ground and its soil of poor quality, had it always been so? Why did it take the family and two geomancers more than thirty years to discover this? What if the same were to be discovered of the newer location at some point in the future? Guo's epitaph does not provide any clues to these questions. It does, however, help explain why so many families founded new graveyards based on geomancers' advice.

While the Guos simply founded a new local burial ground, a Li family went to greater lengths. Having maintained an ancestral graveyard in Hailing (Taizhou, Jiangsu), Li Xixun (1029–1090) came to a realization: "The township was remote and small. As time went on, more people lived there [so it was becoming very crowded]. The land next to the sea was salty, low, and infertile. Furthermore, it lacked hills and auspicious land for burial." After traveling widely and seeing the local conditions of many different places, Li found Hailing even more unsatisfactory for burial purposes and eventually decided to start a new burial ground in Jingkou (near Nanjing, Jiangsu). Although Xixun made clear his wish to retire and be buried there, he died before he could make any concrete plans. His son, having known Xixun's aspiration, fulfilled his final wish.[179]

According to Su Song, the author of Li Xixun's epitaph, Li's son specifically asked that Su include this episode in Xixun's epitaph. Su Song's detailed account did not mention a divination, although it was very likely that Li and his son had turned to a geomancer. Instead, it was Li Xixun's own understanding of basic geomantic principles, many of which had been referred to by Cheng Yi and others, that convinced him of the inferiority of Hailing as a location for his family's graveyard. Equally important, in relinquishing the family burial ground, Li did not refer to his ancestors' well-being, nor did he intend to move the remains of the ancestors to the new location. This in no way seemed inappropriate to Su Song, the epitaph writer. After all, as the above discussion has shown, Su himself was personally responsible for following the recommendations of a geomancer and starting a new graveyard away from the family's native place.

This chapter has focused on the complexities and challenges of burial planning. Song educated men took it for granted that giving parents a proper burial was a major filial duty. In real-life scenarios, a wide variety of factors, including a family's financial situation, the number of sons a couple had, the times and places of a couple's deaths, a family's native place, and the location of the ancestral graveyard greatly diversified the experiences of different families. Similarities did exist. Long delays were common, as was the frequent movement of ancestral graveyards, practically rendering many office-holding men unfilial sons. Contemporary observers offered stringent criticisms of these practices, even though they agreed that such phenomena were inevitable outcomes of civil service. Paradoxically, those who did manage to lay parents to rest in a timely manner were rarely singled out for praise in epitaph writing. It was the sons who had overcome extreme circumstances and demonstrated extraordinary perseverance that were recognized as filial paragons. A similar trend can be observed in the commemoration of parents, the focus of the next chapter.

CHAPTER 4

Remembering and Commemorating

Epitaph Writing as a Form of Filial Expression

In 1061, Mr. An's mother, Miss Zhao, died at his local office. In the midst of planning for her burial, An prepared his mother's record of conduct (*xingzhuang*) and had it sent to Qiang Zhi (1022–1076) with the following request: "I was not able to elevate my parents by obtaining honorary titles for them while they were alive. Now that my mother has passed away and is about to be buried, if her wifely virtue and motherly comportment are not recorded and are subsequently forgotten, it would double my endless regret. Would you be able to bear not to write an epitaph [*muzhiming*] for her?"[1]

The above request was one of thousands made by Northern Song office-holding men in preparing for parents' burials. An's original letter did not survive. The fragments preserved in Qiang Zhi's epitaph for Miss Zhao nonetheless reveal the importance of epitaph writing as a form of commemorative culture and filial expression. To An, securing his mother an epitaph was what a filial son should and must do, especially after he had failed to earn her any honorary ranks. An therefore prepared a sketch of his mother's life and deeds and turned to a friend for help. On his part, Qiang Zhi understood An's expectations and dutifully portrayed Miss Zhao as a highly virtuous woman. In addition, Qiang's writing applauded a filial son's eagerness to perpetuate his mother's memory. A significant component of Miss Zhao's epitaph is Qiang's account of An's request and the relationship of the two men. Given his admiration of An's character, Qiang wrote, "How could I possibly decline the petition of a principled scholar-official who wanted to honor his mother with the utmost sincerity?"[2]

Drawing on hundreds of epitaphs, personal letters, and formal essays, this chapter will explore the establishment of epitaph writing as a major filial deed in the Northern Song. This development can be observed from three respects. First, funerary biographies of the time contained extensive discussion of an epitaph's functions and a son's duty to obtain one for parents. Second, the same texts routinely detail the circumstances under which the epitaph requester, often an office-holding son, approached the author and the extraordinary filial sentiments that he displayed. Consequently, the official son emerged as *the* filial exemplar in his parents' commemoration. Third, funerary biographers typically explained their relationship with the deceased and the epitaph requester in their work. By doing so, they fashioned themselves as strong advocates of the son's filial performance and of the epitaph as an ideal and legitimate vehicle for its expression.

In addition to highlighting the significant place of epitaphs in elite conceptions of filial performance, another goal of this chapter is to illustrate the many factors that complicated the epitaph-writing process. Procrastination and perfunctory work on the part of an author and excessive and unreasonable demands from the deceased's family were responsible for long delays and unpleasant interactions between the two parties. Many sons ended up failing to procure an epitaph for their parents due to insufficient social or literary connections. Other uncertainties in life, such as political exile and untimely deaths, added more difficulties to the already formidable task. All these occurrences had serious implications to the timely completion of burial and death rituals and the portrayal and self-identification of the filial son.

Epitaph Writing: A Brief Introduction

Conventionally translated as "epitaph," "funerary inscription," or "funerary biography," *muzhiming* has a long history in imperial China. In its mature, standard form, it refers to a square-shaped piece of stone engraved with a biography of the tomb's occupant. The staple elements include the name of the deceased, death and burial dates, ancestral and biographical information, outstanding virtues and talents, and a rhymed elegy. The completed stone inscription is protected with a cover made of the same material. At burial, this pair of engraved slabs is placed next to the deceased.[3]

An epitaph required multiple steps to produce. The process began with the preparation of the deceased's record of conduct by a family member or close friend. This was followed by the selection of a potential epitaph author, normally a friend or relative of literary repute. When the biography was completed, the deceased's family had the option of either using the brushwork of the author or commissioning a calligrapher. The finished product was then committed to stone by local artisans. Every step of this process was at the expense of the deceased's family. Suffice it to say, the costs and time needed for epitaph preparation were responsible for budgetary concerns and long delays in postmortem arrangements.[4]

Broadly speaking, epitaphs flourished in Chinese history because they grew to satisfy a variety of religious, social, and cultural needs of individuals and families. As burial objects, they first and foremost marked the location of a tomb and helped record the deceased's identity. They also served to protect the deceased from harmful forces and claimed ownership of the burial plot for the deceased's physical remains and spiritual essence. Moreover, the account of the deceased's virtues and accomplishments was intended to comfort and please the dead, as well as inform the underworld authorities of the occupant's status. For the living, epitaphs functioned as a powerful tool of remembrance and family preservation. The process of epitaph preparation allowed blood relatives to muse over, commemorate, and cherish their ancestor's words and deeds. In addition, genealogical accounts and narratives of ancestral virtues in the epitaph helped strengthen kinship solidarity and create a shared identity.

The earliest extant epitaphs were dated to the Han, even though the more dominant forms of remembrance at the time were the aboveground tombside stelae engravings (mubei).[5] The ban on lavish funerals and commemorative activities by the Wei (220–265) and Jin (265–316) courts resulted in the flourishing of various underground inscriptions. By the second half of the fifth century, not only did epitaphs supply detailed genealogical and biographical information—including names, ancestry, marriage alliances, wives and children, agnatic and affinal kin, and office-holding records for men—but they also highlighted a deceased's moral character and accomplishments.[6]

Muzhiming thrived and reached their highest point in the Tang and Song dynasties.[7] Two periods, the late eighth to early ninth centuries and the early to mid-eleventh century, were particularly important in their history. Compared to the several hundred extant pieces from earlier times, thousands of epitaphs have survived from the Tang and Song; starting from the second half of the Tang, both their length and physical size grew substantially. While the capital areas had the largest concentration of burial plots for members of Tang great families, in the Song, epitaphs were prepared for people from much more diverse regional backgrounds by authors who hailed from equally disparate places. More men and women of moderate elite backgrounds had epitaphs in the Song.[8] Almost all prominent late Tang and Song essayists tried their hand at epitaph writing.[9]

Perhaps the largest change in epitaph writing in the late Tang and Song concerned their function: while epitaphs continued to occupy a key place in mortuary rites and as a major form of commemorative culture, participating in their production and consumption increasingly took on a larger, more tangible significance for the living. For sons and families as well as epitaph authors, funerary biographies became a somewhat public platform to mark family status, as well as promote social and cultural ideals. Tang and Song epitaphs grew lengthier and more biographical, but there was a steady decline in the attention paid to remote ancestors, indicating the decreasing importance of pedigree in the determination of social status. In its place were the descendants and their achievements. Elite men were typically praised for their examination and scholarly successes, administrative skills, and extensive social and cultural activities. Women were consistently portrayed as having played key roles in the education of their children, the care of in-laws, and the operation of household affairs. By the mid-eleventh century, a typical epitaph would include complete information about the marriages of a deceased's sons and daughters; his or her grandchildren; and sons' and grandsons' schooling, examination endeavors, and official service records.[10] Degree- and office-holding sons therefore occupied a prominent place in parents' funerary biographies.

Tens of thousands of epitaphs have survived from imperial China. The *The Complete Prose of the Song Dynasty* (*Quan Song wen*) alone contains about forty-five hundred funerary biographies, with over two thousand of them dated from the Northern Song. This study is based on the latter.

Epitaphs as a Major Form of Filial Expression

A key change in the content and function of epitaphs in the Northern Song was their emphasis on filial performance. For both the deceased and their descendants this included meticulous descriptions of their extraordinary reverent care, mourning, and burial efforts (the focuses of the previous chapters). Another noticeable development was a profuse discussion of the relationship between epitaphs and filial piety. In an epitaph completed in 1037, Fan Zhongyan wrote the following:

> To bury is to hide so that people cannot see [the remains of the deceased]. A gentleman's longing [for his parents] is enduring, so he divines [for a burial place] in a mountain or near a spring, then has [an epitaph] engraved and interred with his parents' bodies. This is done so that even after much chaos has come to pass, when people from a hundred generations later see the inscription and the deceased's deeds, they will not dare to destroy the grave. This is the intention of the filial son. It is explained in the Great Fault hexagram of the *Classic of Change*.[11]

To Fan Zhongyan, without an entombed inscription to mark the deceased's identity and accomplishments, people from decades or centuries later would not recognize his or her deeds and have no reason to leave the body intact. How could such a thought not generate fear and anxiety in the minds of the descendants? A filial son's duty was therefore not only to give his parents a proper burial, but also to make sure that their remains would be permanently identifiable so as to be spared destruction.

Fan Zhongyan was not alone in promoting epitaph writing as a filial duty. Liu Ban (1023–1089) was even more straightforward: "The most important responsibility of a filial son is to bury his parents [properly]. To make the parents' reputation last, there is nothing more crucial than preparing an epitaph for them."[12] Here, Liu specifically placed death rituals above reverent care as a key filial duty. In juxtaposing burial and epitaph writing, he also recognized the latter as important an obligation as the interment itself.

Sons elaborated on the same sentiments in their epitaph-requesting letters: "Without interring an epitaph [in my parents' graves], my longing could never be satisfied."[13] In a letter to Fan Zhongyan regarding the epitaph for his father, Hu Ze (963–1039), Hu Kai (n.d.) accepted that preparing an epitaph was his filial duty by making a direct connection between commemoration through epitaph writing and classical ritual stipulations. Echoing Fan's emphasis on the durability of the written word and the stone inscription, Hu wrote, "According to the *Book of Rites*, to promote the good deeds of one's ancestors for them to be remembered by later generations is the intention of filial sons and grandsons. If the words of remembrance are not strong, the ancestors' deeds will not last long."[14] Fan's and Hu's belief was shared by others. To Lü, the permanence of an epitaph not only ensured that his mother would continue to enjoy the honor she deserved, but also brought peace to him, the helpless orphan. For this reason, the epitaph author, Liu Yan, extolled the "stone slab" for realizing the filial son's wish.[15]

That epitaph writing was as much about demonstrating a son's filial devotion as it was about commemorating the deceased was further elaborated by Su Shunqin. In the epitaph for his father, dated 1039, Su wrote: "Ancients recounted the deeds of their ancestors. People then considered them filial. I did not dare to fabricate anything [about my father's life]. My words can therefore be circulated as reliable information for later times." Here, Su made it clear that his epitaph for his father had two goals. First, he wanted to assure his reader of the reliability of his account. Second, by narrating his father's life, he did what a filial son from ancient times would do. Su continued: "Even if my writing is not powerful enough to illustrate my late father's glory, at least I have fulfilled the aspiration of a son."[16] To Su Shunqin, it was one thing that his father's words and deeds were not preserved due to his lack of literary talent. It would be a major offense if he did not try to make his father's deeds public and memorable.

Some of Su's fellow scholar-officials were even more adamant in seeing an epitaph as a son's last chance to pledge his devotion to parents. When requesting an epitaph for his mother, Mr. Chen claimed that he had been unfilial "because I did not support my mother [with official emoluments]. I am ashamed of not having been able to find a way to fulfill my filial intentions. Fortunately, I still have this [last] opportunity to obtain an epitaph for my mother to be buried underground so that people from later generations will know about her. This is a wish [that I hope you, the writer, help me realize]."[17]

Epitaph writers like Qiang Zhi, quoted at the beginning of the chapter, readily acknowledged their admiration of sons' filial sentiments. In Hu Ze's epitaph, Fan Zhongyan quoted Hu Kai's letter extensively, specifically noting that he had agreed to compose Hu Ze's epitaph because he was moved by Kai's devotion: "Confucius would perform a proper ritual every time he saw a person in mourning. He did this because he respected those who were filial to their parents. How dare I not agree [to a filial son's request to immortalize his parent]?"[18] In referring to the level of respect that Confucius showed to filial sons, Fan implied that he had no other choice but to honor Hu Kai's wish, just as Qiang Zhi had done with An's. In this way, Fan's epitaph for Hu Ze became a commendation of Hu Kai's filial piety, permanently inscribed on his father's epitaph, and evidence of Fan Zhongyan's advancement of funerary biography as a form of filial performance. This aspect of epitaph writing will be further explored below in the chapter.

Sons Securing Epitaphs for Parents

Not only did Northern Song funerary biographies frequently refer to the close relationship between epitaph writing and filial performance, but the same texts also routinely featured the grief-stricken son manifesting utmost filial sentiments to procure an epitaph for parents and the epitaph author's eagerness to help preserve the deceased's memory as well as elevate the son's filial reputation. As a result, the epitaph-obtaining son gained a prominent place in his parents' epitaphs.

Before delving into the procedure for epitaph acquisition and the challenges that the process posed, let us first look at Northern Song epitaphs in terms of their authorship. This approach is necessary because many Northern Song men who went to great lengths to secure epitaphs for parents were prolific funerary biographers, so they could very well have authored their own parents' epitaphs. Most, however, did not. All together, the *The Complete Prose of the Song Dynasty* contains about 2,100 epitaphs by over 370 authors in the Northern Song.[19] Only fourteen men, or 3.8 percent of the writers, composed an epitaph for a parent.[20]

How do we make sense of this seeming unwillingness on the part of well-educated men to honor their parents using the most popular form of commemorative literature? As our discussion will show, several considerations were at play. Some men were too young when their parents died and unable to fulfill this filial duty. With the passing of a parent, a son was expected to focus on mourning so might be too emotionally overwhelmed or physically emaciated to write. As commemorative literature, one primary function of epitaphs was to glorify the deceased's outstanding virtues, a task that was better left to others to avoid charges of the son's self-promotion. Moreover, the more famous the epitaph writer was, the more likely it was that an epitaph would survive and circulate. Last but not least, given that epitaphs routinely included detailed information about the deceased's descendants and their accomplishments, an unspoken desire to hear himself praised must have stopped many a son from composing a parent's epitaph.[21]

Overall, the majority of Northern Song epitaph writers came from three overlapping pools of the deceased's or the son's social network: close personal friends, former or current colleagues, and relatives.[22] In all of the twelve epitaphs authored by Wang Yucheng, Wang referred to having socialized with either the deceased or their sons. He therefore admitted that he felt obligated to help perpetuate the deceased's legacies.[23] Similarly, eight out of the eleven epitaphs by Yang Yi and eight out of the thirteen epitaphs by Hu Su stated that the authors personally knew the deceased or the deceased's sons.[24] This was true of almost all the epitaphs written by Su Song, who explained the close relationship he and his family had with the deceased, ranging from his father's friends and colleagues to his own and from relatives to agnatic relations.[25] When Su was asked to write the epitaph of Mr. Yang, he especially highlighted that the Sus and the Yangs had been associated with each other for four generations. He was therefore happy to "record what I had personally heard and seen . . . to fulfill the wish of the filial children."[26] In his epitaph for Song Minqiu (1019–1079), Su Song similarly claimed that he and the deceased "had associated with each other for three decades. Our interests were similar, and our official careers were comparable. I am thoroughly familiar with his beautiful writing and virtuous deeds." For this reason, Su acknowledged that he was the "natural" candidate to write Song's epitaph.[27]

Su Song's emphasis on the social closeness between him and Song Minqiu went hand in hand with his elevation of Song Minqiu's epitaph-seeking sons. In vivid language, Su recounted that shedding bloody tears, Song's sons arrived at his residence with Minqiu's record of conduct and pleaded with him. Since Su had known Song Minqiu longer than anyone else and had been a close friend, "We would like your biography [of our father] to be engraved on stone. This was also our father's wish."[28] In disclosing the way Song Minqui's sons had approached him, Su indicated that he had agreed to author Song's epitaph in order to memorialize his friend as well as to honor Song's sons for their genuine display of grief. As the rest of this chapter will show, such descriptions of and attention to the filial son became a standard component of Northern Song funerary inscriptions.

Letters as a Tool to Realize One's Filial Aspirations

A large proportion of Northern Song epitaphs were requested through personal correspondence and delivered over long distances. In their epitaph-seeking letters, sons routinely demonstrated exceptional filial sentiments in the hopes of persuading potential authors. In the epitaph for Mr. Peng, Yang Yi stated that he and Peng were from the same region and connected through marriage. "Peng's son wrote me while shedding blood-stained tears, pleading that I write his father's funerary inscription." It was due to his friendship with Peng and Peng's son's filial intentions, Yang Yi remarked, that he had agreed to the request.[29] Fan Zhongyan described a similar experience in his epitaph for Zhong Shiheng (985–1045). Fan noted that not only had he known Zhong well, but he was also moved by Zhong's son, who begged for an epitaph while shedding bloody tears, lest his father's extraordinary deeds be forgotten. Fan wrote that for these reasons, he had to oblige.[30] Parallel examples are plentiful. When entrusting his parents' epitaphs to Chao Buzhi, a man named Hu wrote, "I have been unfilial and am going to die before being able to bury my parents. I worry that my sons are not capable and may discard my parents' bones in the wild." Hu therefore sought Chao's help in perpetuating his parents' legacies.[31] In his epitaph for Mr. Lü's stepmother, Mao Pang (1050s–1120s) used Lü's own words to illustrate Lü's filial piety: "My mother died when I was eight. My stepmother treated me as her own. It was she who looked after me [when my father was away pursuing his studies]. She taught me everything that I know. . . . Now that she has passed away, I am afraid that her virtue might be forgotten. If I could get a sentence or two from you, she would be remembered by her descendants."[32] Just like his fellow epitaph writers, Mao remarked in the mother's epitaph that he was impressed by the woman's virtue. More important, he wanted to celebrate Lü as a filial son, who treated his stepmother as his real mother.

In all of the above cases, the epitaph writer quoted the son's letter in the epitaph to contextualize the circumstances under which the request had been communicated, the son's efforts to convince him, and his response to the son's emotional plea, leaving us to wonder to what extent an author would modify a letter to fit his narrative. Fortunately, some epitaph-requesting letters and the resulting epitaphs have survived, offering tangible evidence of the length to which sons went to persuade the potential writer. Let us now turn to a letter from Chao Buzhi to Huang Tingjian, dated 1084.

> I am unfilial! When my father died in the capital in the Xining reign [1068–1077], I was living in Wu [Suzhou, Jiangsu] and was too poor to have him buried in a timely manner. I have since felt most guilty for dragging out an ignoble existence. I am planning on burying him in Yushan of Juye [in Shandong] in the tenth month. My late father cherished the Way and upheld the ideal when [other people in] the world were unprincipled. He died before reaching fifty, so he was not known to the world, but he must be remembered by posterity. Weeping, I request that you show me sympathy [and agree to compose an epitaph for him].[33]

Chao Buzhi's father, Chao Juncheng, died in 1075 and was not buried until 1084. To prepare for this burial, Buzhi turned to his close friend, Huang Tingjian, a literary giant and highly productive epitaph writer.[34] To Chao, Huang was the ideal choice. Not only had Huang known Chao's uncles well, but he was also aware of "all of Buzhi's unfilial deeds." Thus there would have been no reason for Chao to doubt that Huang would agree to his request. Chao nonetheless wrote in the most formal manner: "No one would be more capable than you in elevating my father from obscurity and pleasing him in death. Therefore, I have disregarded my failings and taken the liberty of writing you. If you could generously agree to write an epitaph for my father, I would feel most fortunate."[35] "With tears in his eyes," Chao Buzhi completed the letter and attached his father's record of conduct by Du Chun.

Chao Buzhi's letter, about six hundred characters long, was one of the lengthiest epitaph-requesting letters to have survived from the Northern Song. The goals of the letter were twofold, both having to do with fulfilling Buzhi's filial duty. First, Chao Buzhi declared that his father had died rather young and had not had the chance to establish himself. Buzhi was determined that "he must be remembered" and made sure that Huang Tingjian understood the intentions of the filial son. Second, Chao composed such a long letter because he was not completely satisfied with his father's record of conduct. He therefore provided what he knew about his father "lest his deeds be forgotten." These included several episodes that showed Chao Juncheng as a generous, filial, and uncorrupted person. Especially highlighted was the senior Chao's talent as a poet.

Not only did Huang Tingjian agree to write Chao Juncheng's epitaph, but he also incorporated half of Chao Buzhi's letter into Juncheng's funerary biography, with only minor modifications.[36] That was not all. Huang went on to praise

Chao Buzhi, his good friend and the requester of the epitaph. Specifically, Huang emphasized, "Buzhi loves learning and is dedicated to important things. His writing captures the style of the Qin and Han times. There is hope that he will become an influential writer. Given Buzhi's talent, is it not time for Juncheng's posterity to prosper?" By referring to Buzhi's role in securing his father's epitaph and his potential to become a well-known writer, Huang implied that Buzhi was realizing his father's unfulfilled aspirations. In this way, Huang Tingjian made Chao Buzhi a filial son and worthy descendant.

Huang's epitaph for Chao Juncheng did not touch on the long delay in the deceased's burial. Sons, however, routinely used this uncomfortable truth as a vehicle of persuasion. It is interesting that in this process, this gravely unfilial act was transformed into a gesture of filiality. In his letter to Yuwen Gan (n.d.), Li Xin (1062–?) wrote the following:

My father has been dead for years, and my family has been too poor to have him buried. I am weak and sick; should I die suddenly, the world would not know of my father's integrity and righteousness. I am what the world calls an unfilial son. Between having an unfilial son and no son at all, I would rather not have a son. After all, what is the use of having an unfilial son? In the early Yuanyou reign [1086–1093], I was a magistrate in Nanzheng [in Shaanxi]. When I heard that my father was ill, I traveled home alone without submitting a request to the court for a leave of absence. I arrived at Ling after walking nonstop for ten days so that I would be able to wait on my father at his bedside. When I reached home, my father ordered me to move closer to him and said: "You have shown your sincerity [by traveling home from your office to see me before I die]. My time is coming to an end, and I have been looking forward to your return. I do not have anything else to ask of you. My only request is that you seek out a person with superior writing and credible words [to compose my aboveground inscription] so that people from later times will not question [what is written on it]. If you could inscribe my conduct on a pillar and place it to the south of my grave, then you would have done everything I would want from a son." I have four younger brothers. . . . For ten years, we have been trying to seek out a person with superior writing and conduct. We now have found that person in you. As you know that we are poor, [I hope that] you will not reject our request.[37]

In this letter, Li Xin called himself an unfilial son, on the one hand, and took pains to show that he had never forgotten his filial obligations, on the other.

What especially stands out is the significance that Li and his father gave to epitaph writing and the son's enduring effort to locate a funerary biographer for his father. In this respect, Li and Chao Buzhi shared similar concerns. Both condemned their negligence of their parents' burials. Both humbled themselves to appeal to the potential epitaph writer. Li Xin went much further than Chao by stating that there was no difference between having an unfilial son and no son at all, yet Li's description of his rushing to his father's deathbed without notifying the government was meant to show that he was anything but unfilial.

In detailing his father's dying wish and demonstrating his persistence in its realization, Li Xin effectively shifted the burden to Yuwen, who held the power of making Li a filial son. The same can be said about Chao Buzhi's request to Huang Tingjian. The only difference in these two instances is that in Chao's case, there was little doubt that Huang would honor Chao's request. Li Xin was less sure. We do not know the outcome of his petition. If Yuwen accepted the request, it might not be a stretch to suppose that he would cite from Li Xin's moving letter, especially Li's violation of government policies in order to reach his father's deathbed and his perseverance in fulfilling his father's dying wish.

SONS TRAVELING LONG DISTANCES TO SECURE EPITAPHS FOR PARENTS

In addition to seeking an epitaph through written correspondence, many a son traveled a long distance to personally appeal to a potential author. Such an effort was duly noted as an extraordinary filial gesture. In two epitaphs, Su Song narrated the circumstances under which he had agreed to compose them. In the first case, Mr. Shi traveled from Fujian to Runzhou twice to implore Su Song to author his father's epitaph. Su specifically remarked in the completed biography that he had agreed to the request to "commend the diligence of the filial son for making such long trips."[38] In the epitaph for Sun Yong, Su Song recounted that Sun's son had come to him from far away. With Sun Yong's record of conduct in hand and tears in his eyes, the son explained that now that he had completed a year of mourning, it was time to make arrangements for his father's funerary biographies. He had already secured an epitaph for his father and now turned to Su Song for a spirit path stele, which would be placed next to the grave. This way, "I can die with no regrets."[39] Another Sun traveled a thousand *li* in mourning clothes to the capital to beg Xu Han (?–1133) to write his father's epitaph. Xu recorded, "At first, I declined firmly. His pleas became sadder. How could I not have changed my mind? I therefore agreed to write the funerary inscription."[40]

In all three epitaphs, the authors highlighted the mourning sons' arduous efforts, in the form of long journeys, to obtain funerary biographies for their parents. Inspired by the sons' dedication and resolution, the authors were left with no alternative but to agree to the requests. In the epitaph for Mr. Hu, Wang Anshi provides us with even more vivid details about a son's resolve to honor his father:

> Three months after I was appointed to Yin [Ningbo, Zhejiang], my old acquaintance Hu Shunyuan stood at my door in mourning clothes. After exchanging greetings, I invited him in. I then asked why he was wearing mourning clothes. It turned out that he had lost his father five months earlier. I arranged for him to stay at the government inn but secretly thought it strange that he had come to visit me so soon [after his father's passing]. After staying for several months, Hu said to my younger brother: "I left behind my father's funeral-related matters, climbed mountains and crossed the Yangzi River, and arrived at your older brother's post at the seaside. [I have yet to have a meeting with him since.] I have been meaning to call on him but did not dare request what I have come here for. My parents gave birth to me. Although I studied at many places, I was not able to support them the way I wished [i.e., Hu failed to pass the examinations]. Now that my father has passed away, I would like to ask your older brother to author my father's epitaph to be placed in the tomb so that my father will become distinguished and his name will be remembered in later times. Even though his son is insignificant, if he would be able to enjoy posthumous fame, I would have no regrets. I am not sure if your older brother would agree to my request." My younger brother related their conversation to me. I sighed and said: "If this is the case, he can be considered a filial person. A gentleman would want to assist a son's filial wish. Besides, I have known Hu. Why would I decline his request?" I took what I have learned [about Hu's father] and completed the epitaph.[41]

Wang Anshi went on to record the most basic information about the senior Hu and his family. Compared to the above account, however, the epitaph is disproportionately brief. Aside from the deceased's native place, his death date, the number of sons he had, and the fact that he had sent Shunyuan to school, we learn nothing about the deceased. Instead, it was Shunyuan's epitaph-requesting performance that took up the most space.

Wang Anshi made it clear that he did not see Hu as a filial son at first. In fact, he was originally bothered by Hu's visit. After all, mourning sons should stay home and concentrate on grieving and funeral preparations. As soon as he learned about Hu's intentions, however, Wang was impressed. To Wang, what Hu had done was an outstanding act. There was the travel from Anhui to northeastern Zhejiang, which, under the most auspicious conditions, would have taken a few dozen days. This was followed by several months' stay at an inn while waiting to call on Wang. Hu's dedication eventually moved Wang Anshi. Besides, as Wang reasoned, it was a gentleman's obligation to help fulfill a filial son's wish. In this sense, Wang's work was a celebration of Hu Shunyuan's filial piety more than of the senior Hu's life. From a different perspective, not only did Hu succeed in getting his father an epitaph, but his epitaph-seeking experience also distinguished him as a son. In fact, of the senior Hu's seven sons, Shunyuan was the only one whose name was mentioned in the epitaph.

The Problems of Commemorating

So far, we have looked at the various ways sons used epitaphs to demonstrate their filial piety and the role that funerary biographers played in promoting the epitaph seekers. Often enough, the epitaph-writing process was messier and less straightforward. My recent study of Fan Zhongyan's epitaphs, for example, reveals the way literati politics shaped the commemoration of one of the most distinguished personalities in Chinese history and how a disagreement between Fan's biographers and his sons regarding his legacy greatly complicated the outcome.[42] For the majority of Northern Song scholar-official families, politics did not occupy as prominent a place in the epitaph-writing process. This section discusses more "mundane" challenges that sons and epitaph authors faced.

THE SON'S DILEMMA I: PROCRASTINATING WRITERS

The majority of Northern Song epitaphs did not provide a clear timeline for us to gauge the time that it took to arrange for an epitaph. Given that most requests involved letter writing or long-distance travel, the process could have easily taken months or even a few years. For example, sometime in 1044, Zeng Gong wrote from Jiangxi to Ouyang Xiu in the capital, asking for a funerary biography for his grandfather. Ouyang did not deliver the biography to Zeng until the fall of 1045, to which Zeng responded with a thank-you note in 1046.[43] This means that the writing process alone took at least several months. Many writers subsequently caused anxiety for the epitaph-requesting sons when they were slow in responding to inquiries. Such delays were true of both prominent literary figures and writers of modest backgrounds. Two years after Chen Shunyü requested an epitaph for his father from Ouyang Xiu, Chen wrote to remind Ouyang.[44] The letter began with a recollection of a meeting between the two during which "You pitied my sincerity [in commemorating my father] and agreed to my request." If Ouyang did not honor his promise, Chen continued, that would be disastrous:

> Even if I bridged mountains to be by my father's grave, melted gold to make his coffin, used a thousand people to hold the cord leading to the hearse, and prepared hundreds of urns of tomb goods, it would not be a proper funeral. . . . Only if you compose an epitaph for my father will I get to complete his burial. The virtues of my late father will be forever preserved, and I will feel no shame facing people in my native place. This way, I will be able to redeem my crime of having delayed his burial for fifteen years.[45]

From this letter, we learn that Chen Shunyü did not begin planning for his father's burial for thirteen years after his death, and waiting for Ouyang's response had taken two more years. Chen, however, was willing to wait longer based on the belief that an epitaph by Ouyang would not only make his father immortal, but also give him the "credentials" to face his clansmen and fellow villagers. In Chen's view, having put off his father's burial for so long, Ouyang's epitaph had become the only way to spare him of feeling or appearing unfilial.

Many others found themselves "stuck" in a similar situation. In a letter to Mr. Fu, Mao Pang recounted traveling to the capital to ask Fu for an epitaph for a parent. Since then, Mao remarked, seven years had passed, during which he had sent several reminders but had never heard back from Fu. Mao might have acted humble and gentle earlier, but his attitude had changed in the extant letter. Mao especially referred to an episode about the Tang scholar Han Yu (768–824), who authored the epitaph for an obscure official simply because the deceased's wife and son had begged him to do so. Mao implied that by not honoring his promise, Fu was a lesser man than Han Yu and might have acted as a snob. Most important, Fu's failure to keep his promise would have made Mao "an unfilial son."[46]

Seven years was certainly an abnormally long time to wait for an epitaph, and families could justifiably get impatient. Mao's assumption that Fu had been ignoring him because of his obscurity might have explained Fu's unresponsiveness. However, the reality was that even prominent figures suffered from procrastinating authors. Ouyang Xiu, one of the most respected writers in the Northern Song, experienced his share of anxiety when it came to the delay of a relative's epitaph by a colleague. Ouyang grew so irritated that he instructed his nephew (presumably the deceased's son) to give the author a gentle nudge.[47] At the same time, he took over two years to finish Fan Zhongyan's funerary biography, and his delay put Fan's sons' patience to the test.[48]

THE SON'S DILEMMA II: EPITAPH WRITERS DECLINING REQUESTS

Considering Ouyang Xiu's and Fan Zhongyan's standings in the political, social, and literary circles, it should not come as a surprise that epitaph writers procrastinated when dealing with people of more modest backgrounds. From a son's perspective, a worse situation would be a polite rejection.

In personal correspondence, quite a few Northern Song writers explained their unwillingness or inability to agree to certain requests. One person said that he could not write because he was in mourning.[49] Another had stopped writing epitaphs simply because he was old and sick.[50] A voluminous writer in every other literary genre, Su Shi only authored twelve epitaphs. In more than one letter, he explained that due to earlier complications, he no longer composed epitaphs, asking the requestors not to take his rejection personally.[51]

Both such implicit and explicit refusals give us a sense of the challenges that sons faced. While some who continued to pester, as Mao Pang had with Fu, might not get what they wanted, others were rewarded for their persistence. After hearing that Yang Wei (1044–1112) had stopped writing epitaphs, a man named Yin penned his mother's epitaph and had it delivered to Yang. Yin's wish was simple. He asked Yang to append a few lines at the end of the biography so that he could justifiably inscribe Yang's name on the stele. Surprisingly, Yang Wei was not offended by the request and happily complied. Yang's writing did not refer to Yin's mother at all. Instead, Yang remarked: "Yin is thoughtful and trustworthy in his personal conduct. He waited on his mother with filiality and dedication. People in the coming times should trust his words. Mine are not important."[52] Although these were only a few lines, Yin eventually got what he had sought: he could use Yang's name in his mother's inscription and take pride in Yang's recognizing him as a filial son.

Most of Yang Wei's peers were less flexible. Of all the Song writers, Sima Guang was probably the most outspoken about declining epitaph-writing requests. In a 1084 letter to Mr. Zhao, Sima mentioned that he had not composed an epitaph in more than ten years. Over those years, he had declined dozens of families. When Sun Ling (n.d.) made a request,

> I answered by detailing the reasons why I could not oblige. Since then, I have declined the requests of Wang Ledao [n.d.], Zeng Zigu [Gong], and others by sending them the same letter. When Mr. Fu Bi passed away last year, I went to offer my condolences. His son, kneeling on grass and dirt, wailed and threw himself onto the ground, insisting that I author his father's epitaph. He later sent a messenger over to my residence three or

four times, but I told him exactly what I had told Sun Ling and was able to reject his request in the end. Now if I write an epitaph for your late father, I will end up treating people differently. Please consider this matter from my perspective.[53]

Sima was able to stand firm in the face of frequent demands due to his belief that if one's reputation were not enough to impress everyone under Heaven or his writing were not enough to last into latter generations, even if an epitaph were written for the person, posterity would surely discard it. In a different letter, Sima commented as follows:

Filial sons and grandsons wish to write about the virtue their fathers and grandparents possessed so that their reputations will last forever. As ignorant as I was, I previously had the vanity to take this as my duty; what I had accomplished in the end was to bring disgrace to one's fathers and grandfathers and cover up their virtues and achievements. How great is my crime! I therefore stopped writing funerary biographies. It has been six or seven years since I made the decision and I have declined the requests from dozens of families. . . . Everyone in the capital and Luoyang knows about this.[54]

Sima made it clear that what concerned him was the filial descendants' and epitaph writers' earnest, but futile, efforts to promote a person's life. Since Zhao's father was known for his honesty and incorruptibility, Sima reasoned, he would be adequately recorded in the state history and achieve immortality even without an epitaph:

Why would you need my shallow essay to promote his name? Besides, nowadays there are countless people whose prose is of higher quality and whose comments are more convincing than mine. You did not ask them but dispatched a messenger, who traveled for thousands of *li* from Quzhou [in Zhejiang] to Luoyang, specifically for this matter. There is no greater offense than knowing that your expectations were so high but that your request was still declined.[55]

Sima's letter is sufficient evidence that he was serious about not writing any more epitaphs. The same text also allows us to appreciate the challenges that sons faced in the acquisition of epitaphs. While a variety of strenuous efforts, including long-distance travel, public displays of grief, and perseverance, did help many to succeed, not all had the good fortune to obtain an epitaph for their parents. The following numbers further demonstrate the obstacles that sons faced. As noted above, the two thousand or so Northern Song epitaphs contained in *The Complete Prose of the Song Dynasty* were written by about 370 authors. Twenty percent of them, or seventy-five men, were responsible for about 80 percent of the work. For the tens of thousands of elite men who set out to acquire an epitaph for parents or other family members, their chances of successfully approaching one of these leading writers were slim, to say the least.

The Writer's Dilemma I: Between Satisfying the Filial Son and Writing Objectively

Other issues further complicated a son's chances of obtaining an epitaph from the writer of his choice. Despite a funerary biographer's eagerness to elevate the epitaph-seeking son in the epitaph, the interests of the two sides differed greatly. The most important concern of the filial child and his family was to glorify the ancestor. This meant they would be more than willing to overlook what they considered to be "unworthy" deeds or "inconvenient" truths, a trend that caught the attention of many epitaph writers. The biographer's position varied significantly. On the one hand, he was obligated to promote the deceased as well as the son. After all, this was the task for which he had been commissioned. On the other hand, Northern Song authors agreed that they were also responsible to write truthfully. More than anything, this tension manifested the inherent conflict between the epitaph author's interest in controlling his work and reputation and the deceased family's commitment to shaping their ancestor's image and family memory.

Of all the Northern Song epitaph writers, Zeng Gong discussed the biographer's dilemma most systematically. In a long letter to Ouyang Xiu, dated 1046, Zeng compared the differences between epitaph and history writing. On the one hand, Zeng wrote, both had as one of their primary goals to perpetuate the words and deeds of the ancients and enlighten later generations. In this sense, epitaphs were just like historical works. Zeng's focus, however, was on the differences between these two types of work. While history recorded all objective information, including the deeds of the evil, not everyone deserved an epitaph. To Zeng, ancients used epitaphs lest "the outstanding deeds of the accomplished, virtuous, talented, and righteous be forgotten by posterity. These deeds must be inscribed, circulated, and subsequently enshrined in temples or deposited in tombs." This way, "The deceased will have no regrets. The living would learn to discipline themselves. The good would be happy to see these records and would be motivated to establish themselves."[56]

In a way, Zeng Gong saw epitaphs as a mechanism to curb evil people, as they would be ashamed and afraid that if they did not deserve an epitaph, they would be forgotten by later generations. Zeng's general comparison of epitaph and history writing was followed by his criticism of contemporary practice: sons and grandsons, even those of evil people, went to great lengths to brag about and exaggerate their ancestors' accomplishments. Zeng wrote: "[One sign that] the world is in decline is when sons and grandsons disregard principle and focus only on lauding their parents and grandparents. As a result, even though their parents and grandparents were evil, they strive to acquire stele inscriptions for them so that their deeds can be boasted about to posterity."[57]

The problem, according to Zeng, was not created by the filial children alone. The epitaph writers added fuel to the fire. Potential writers, in being sensitive to the feelings of posterity, often hesitated to decline requests or include negative qualities of the deceased. "In addition, due to the supplications from sons and grandsons, it would be inconsiderate if writers wrote about the deceased's bad deeds. For this reason, epitaphs have become unreliable." Thus, Zeng stated, "For hundreds of years, from dukes, ministers, and scholar-officials to common people, all had epitaphs written for them, but few have survived."[58] Zeng urged families of the worthy to be extremely careful when selecting an epitaph writer; he should be virtuous and have exceptional writing skills. If one failed in this respect, no matter how glorifying a funerary biography was, it was not going to help preserve the deceased's reputation.

While Zeng claimed that only the good deserved an epitaph, written by a virtuous and capable writer, he also acknowledged the age-old problem of sons and grandsons trying to elevate their ancestors at any cost. Indeed, as he put it, "Among sons and grandsons, who would not want to exalt their ancestors?"[59] In the face of families sparing no costs in doing so and epitaph writers going along with their requests, Zeng Gong did not have a solution. At most he suggested that time would have its way of sifting through all the records. In the end only very few epitaphs, written by and for the worthiest individuals, would survive.

Many of Zeng's contemporaries shared his views. Su Shi, for example, observed the following:

> Recently, scholar-officials have all become greedy, indulgent, and self-aggrandizing. They often want others to liken them to the Duke of Zhou [eleventh century BCE] or Confucius and would be upset if they were compared to Mencius or other lesser figures. This trend should not continue. I have carefully thought about the origin of this problem and feel that it has grown out of [the emphasis on] promoting an undeserved reputation. . . .

This is especially true of those who would not bury [their parents] if they have not secured an epitaph from a famous scholar. I am afraid this is not in accordance with the rites.[60]

In their pursuit of fame for themselves and their ancestors, Su Shi felt that his fellow scholar-officials had neglected to follow the true spirit of ritual propriety. To illustrate his point, Su went on to give two examples, the case of Situ Wenzi (n.d.) and Zisi (fifth century BCE) and that of Wen Jiao (288–329) in the Jin (266–420).[61]

The gentlemen in the past would not change their mourning clothes [in the case of Situ Wenzi and Zisi] or assume an official position if they had not buried their parents [in the case of Wen Jiao]. Now that you have not completed the burial, [which is the most important task at hand], what other matters do you have to attend to? Someday if you find a famous person in the world after you have completed the burial, you can still ask him to write an aboveground stele. Why worry about it now?[62]

This piece should be read together with Zeng Gong's criticism of sons and grandsons who went out of their way to get a funerary biography to elevate their ancestors and acquire personal fame. More specifically, Su Shi identified two problems: first, epitaphs tended to exaggerate the virtues of the deceased. Second, families were keen on finding a famous person for a funerary biography. This goal further explains the long delays in burial. To Su Shi, this tendency caused a larger problem: on the one hand, a parent's burial was held up due to the lack of a funerary biography; on the other hand, the son had already completed mourning and taken off his mourning clothes, leaving unfinished business for later. What especially bothered Su Shi was one particular case: he was asked to write an aboveground stele for someone whose burial had not been completed. To Su, this emphasis on form (elevating a parent's fame) rather than substance (observing proper mourning and burial rituals) was especially troubling, a sign that for Zeng Gong meant "a world in decline."

The Writer's Dilemma II: Commemorating a Complete Stranger

In their funerary biographical works, Northern Song authors often highlighted the importance of their having an intimate knowledge of their subjects as a precondition for producing high-quality epitaphs. Many writers explicitly remarked that because they had known or had been admirers of the deceased or their families for years, they felt both honored and obligated to take on the task. This emphasis on a close relationship between the two parties posed an additional obstacle for sons who lacked the necessary social connections in ancestral commemoration. Su Xun's (1009–1066) experience in preparing the funerary biography for Yang Meiqiu's (n.d.) father illustrates this scenario in the most straightforward way.

Let us begin with Su's letter to Yang in its entirety, as it contains key information about Yang's epitaph request and Su's main concern in taking on the task.

> Previously you entrusted me with writing your father's epitaph and showed me his record of conduct, prepared by Mr. Cheng. I never had the opportunity of meeting your late father or the pleasure of chatting and sharing a laugh with him. In ancient times, epitaph writers were familiar with the deceased's entire life. They composed funerary biographies for the deceased because they were sorry about their passing and worried that the dead might be forgotten. Even if the epitaph writer did not know the deceased, if he was given detailed, reliable facts, the writer would still have to oblige. This is what it means to write an epitaph based on reliable information contained in the record of conduct.
>
> Since I did not have the good fortune of knowing your late father, the only thing I could have relied on was his record of conduct, but it was anything but reliable! How difficult my task was! I understood your fear that your late father might be forgotten by posterity. For this reason, you sought an epitaph from me [to commemorate him]. After agreeing to your request, my conscience did not allow me to decline [despite the deficiencies of the record of conduct]. I therefore did not give up and eventually completed your father's epitaph. The biography, which I have attached with this letter, should not disappoint a son who wishes for the immortality of his father.
>
> I nevertheless worried that you might not believe the uselessness of the record of conduct. I have therefore listed my reasons below. I will not discuss every superficial or untruthful detail but will only give some inadequate examples that it has provided. Your father's record of conduct says, "Mr. Yang had a son named Meilin [n.d.]. Mr. Yang died from the devastation caused by Meilin's demise." When Zixia [507–? BCE] lost his sight from mourning his son, Zengzi ridiculed him.[63] How could one attribute a father's death to the mourning of his own son? For this reason, I have left this item out lest it damage your father's reputation. The record of conduct also says, "Mr. Yang warned his sons against acting like their fellow villagers, who divided up family properties while their parents were still alive."

Were the fellow villagers not your clansmen and affines? How could one bear to talk about them this way? Moreover, [surely] not everyone in the village acted the same way. How could one dare to talk about them [as if they were all unfilial children]? These are the reasons that your father's epitaph is not based on his record of conduct. I hope that you will not blame me [for acting in this way].[64]

Su Xun's letter begins with a personal dilemma: Su did not know Yang Meiqiu's father. He nonetheless managed to complete the senior Yang's epitaph and reasoned that he did this because he sympathized with and admired Yang Meiqiu's filial wish. More important, the letter meant to clarify Su's frustration with the senior Yang's record of conduct. Su was critical of it for two reasons: first, it contained "false and superficial" information. Although Su did not substantiate this statement with specific examples, it might not be too far a stretch for us to imagine commendations of the deceased as a highly virtuous person and a beloved figure in the community, standard tropes used for members of the local gentry. Second, the record of conduct included information that would actually have damaged the reputation of the deceased and his family. Su Xun included two examples: that the deceased had died from grieving a son and that he had warned his sons against the popular practice of family property division. As far as Su Xun was concerned, both incidents might have been true but should not have been incorporated into the record of conduct or epitaph. Setting in stone statements that attributed a father's demise to a son's death or insinuated that members of a community were negligent of their parents' welfare would in no way elevate the deceased. On the contrary, the anecdotes would have a corrosive effect. Su Xun simply refused to compromise his principles or be an "accomplice" to such possibilities.

The primary goal of Su Xun's letter was to justify why he had written a very brief epitaph, even though he might have been given a detailed record of conduct. Without a reliable and useful record of conduct, here is what Su Xun was able to accomplish:

Mr. Yang's name is such-and-such and his informal name such-and-such. His family has lived in Danling of Meizhou [in Sichuan] for generations. His great-grandfather's name is such-and-such, his grandfather's such-and-such, and his father's such-and-such. None of them held office. Mr. Yang married the daughter of the [such-and-such] clan. The couple had four sons. The eldest son is Meiqi, followed by Meilin [n.d.], Meixun [n.d.], and Meiqiu. Meiqiu once served in the Anjing Commandary. At the time,

I happened to be traveling in Badong [in Sichuan] and got to know him. In the second year of the Jiayou reign [1057], Mr. Yang died at such-and-such an age. In the eleventh month of the fourth year [1059], he was buried in such-and-such ward of such-and-such village. Before the burial, Meiqiu asked me [to write an epitaph for his father] so that Mr. Yang would not be forgotten in later times. I could not bear to decline his request. Meilin died a month before his father. Meiqi and Meixun both aspire to become learned people. Meiqiu serves the court.[65]

This epitaph strikes us for its brevity and its lack of specific information. Su Xun included only the most basic information about the deceased: his genealogy, sons, marriage, and burial place. The absence of the names of the deceased's wife and ancestors was a general indication that the writer was not familiar with the Yangs. Note also that throughout the entire epitaph, Su Xun did not commend the senior Yang in any way. What Su did not neglect to specify was who had arranged for the epitaph and his relationship with the requester.

Su Xun's epitaph for the senior Yang is among a fair number of what I call "perfunctory" epitaph works. This characterization does not necessarily mean that the authors did not take their work seriously. Rather, time constraints, geographical barriers, inadequate records of conduct, and unfamiliarity with the deceased and their family all contributed to these terse and "token" biographies.

Above all, Su's biography for Mr. Yang reveals the challenges that sons with limited social and literary connections faced in securing epitaphs for parents. In all likelihood, Su was the most established writer Yang had ever known and represented Yang's only hope to elevate his father and himself. On his end, Su kept his promise, even when he was provided with an unusable record of conduct. Was Yang Meiqiu happy with Su's writing? We do not know. He certainly might have wished for extensive descriptions of his father and himself. Given his obscurity, however, he might have considered himself lucky. After all, of the senior Yang's four sons, he was the one that secured his father's epitaph, and, as brief as it was, Su Xun's words confirmed Yang Meiqiu as a filial son.

Inflexible Writers and Overly Demanding Sons

Eager to glorify parents and promote their own filial image, some Song men were overly demanding in the epitaph-acquisition process. This led to unfriendly, even hostile, exchanges between the epitaph author and the deceased's family. It is understandable that such confrontations were not widespread. After all, it would not have been in the interest of the deceased's son or family to offend the writer. At the same time, many authors had the option of simply ignoring what they considered inadequate information or unreasonable requests. With these considerations in mind, let us turn to the experience of Ouyang Xiu, the epitaph writer.

Ouyang was the author of about 110 funerary biographies. Given his reputation as a literary giant, most epitaph seekers would have been gratified if Ouyang agreed to their requests. This does not necessarily mean that the deceased's families did not make changes to or have concrete concerns about Ouyang's writing. As a result, Ouyang left abundant records about his dealings with the deceased's sons and families.

The earliest case involved Ouyang's epitaph for Yin Zhu. When Yin, an established writer and close friend of Ouyang, died in 1047, Ouyang was entrusted with Yin's epitaph. The completed biography, about nine hundred characters in length, was seen by Yin's family as too short and inadequate to perpetuate Yin Zhu's outstanding accomplishments and explain the political setbacks that he had suffered.[66] The Yins' reaction was so strong that Ouyang Xiu responded with an essay that was longer than the epitaph. In the essay, Ouyang explained, "The intention of my epitaph for Shilu [Yin Zhu] is deep and its language succinct because Shilu's writing is succinct in style and deep in meaning." He then went on to contradict Yin's sons' assessment of his work: "If the deceased were here, he would certainly accept this biography. This is what I have done to commemorate my lost friend. Why would I care about [the accusation from] his sons?"[67]

In addressing the Yins' complaint about the brevity of Yin Zhu's epitaph, Ouyang showed little flexibility, refusing to make any concessions. Seeing that Ouyang was not amenable, the family turned to Yin Zhu's other friends for more commemorative writings. Fan Zhongyan agreed to write the preface to Yin's collected works.[68] Han Qi composed an aboveground stele that was almost three times as long as Ouyang's epitaph at the time of Yin Zhu's burial in 1054.[69]

The Yins' disagreement with Ouyang and the involvement of Han Qi became widely known. Rumors subsequently spread. In a letter dated two years after Yin Zhu's death, we find Ouyang making another attempt to justify his biography of Yin: "About Mr. Yin's epitaph, my prior explanation [i.e., the long essay] is very detailed. Given my relationship with Shilu, why would I be stingy [with words of praise] and subsequently endure frequent questioning from his disciples, friends, and family? Please have no doubt [about my intentions]. We can talk about this [in more detail] when we meet. I do not want to ramble here."[70]

Ouyang's encounters with the Yins was the first major clash between him and a deceased's family. He had an even more difficult time composing Fan Zhongyan's funerary biography several years later due to differing views between him and Fan's sons and friends about Fan's political legacy and the principle of epitaph writing. The disagreement led to a long delay on Ouyang's part, resulting in his account of Fan's life being used as an aboveground stele inscription rather than the epitaph, which was needed at the time of the burial. Even so, Ouyang's work was altered by Fan's sons, forcing Ouyang to denounce that particular version and pointing his readers to the one compiled in his collected works.[71]

The above experience taught Ouyang to be more cautious when dealing with a deceased's family. After agreeing to compose Du Yan's (978–1057) epitaph in 1057, Ouyang Xiu wrote two long letters to Du Xin (n.d.), Du Yan's son. In the first letter, Ouyang apologized for not finishing the epitaph more promptly, suggesting that the Dus might want to use Du Yan's record of conduct, authored by Han Qi, as the epitaph. The main reason for his proposal was that "my writing is succinct. I record only important matters in order for them to be preserved for a long time. I am afraid this might not satisfy the intentions of the filial son [who would want every detail of a parent's life preserved], but I consider myself an intimate friend [of Du Yan] and will do my best. Please let me know of your decision."[72]

Did Ouyang really mean it when he suggested that the Dus simply use Han Qi's record of conduct? It is not very likely, as he quickly added that he would certainly do his best with Du's biography. Instead, the letter served to remind Du Xin of Ouyang's writing style so that Du would not expect a lengthy biography with every detail of Du Yan's life.[73] The same letter was also a warning for Du Xin not to become the kind of filial son Ouyang disapproved of. In fact, Ouyang did not shy away from naming names, as he continued: "Mr. Fan [Zhongyan]'s aboveground stele was modified by his sons without my permission. They could not help but make further changes [to my writing]. After Yin Zhu died [and his sons asked me to write his epitaph], they also asked Han Qi to write an aboveground stele separately [because they thought my epitaph was too laconic]."[74] Ouyang then adds the following:

> From this, it is clear that friends, disciples, and former colleagues and filial sons often have different purposes [when it comes to commemorating the deceased]. How could I ever turn my back on an intimate friend? The [incidents with the] Fans and Yins can be used as mirrors. Please think twice. If one intends [for a person's memory] to be preserved for a long time, he must record only the great deeds and omit the trivial ones. This is something that can be discussed with sensible and knowledgeable scholars. You must have a deep understanding of this.[75]

Ouyang's letter confirms that years after his confrontations with Yin Zhu's and Fan Zhongyan's sons, he was still irritated about the way the two families had treated him, accusing them of being short-sighted and ignorant. At the same time, he had become more aware of the inherent differences in the perspectives of the biographer and the deceased's family; while the biographer had a moral obligation to write responsibly and truthfully, that was not always a primary concern of the filial sons. What especially separated the biographer and the deceased's family was their understanding of the deceased's character compared to his minor accomplishments. In the long term, Ouyang declared, only one's character mattered. And it would be up to him, the biographer, to make the call.

Tensions between the biographer and the deceased's family frustrated other Northern Song writers as well. The exchange between Wang Anshi and Qian Gongfu (1023–1074) provides vivid details about what funerary biographers would call a fastidious son. In his letter to Qian, Wang wrote the following:

> Previously you entrusted me with writing an epitaph [for your mother]. As a prominent person, you are in the position to seek any famous writer. That you chose me must not have been an easy decision. For this reason, I did not reject your request and composed the epitaph. I did not anticipate that this would not satisfy your wishes. Now you want me to add something to the completed work. My work has its own logic and cannot be changed. You should have foreseen this and asked someone who might be willing to accommodate your wishes.[76]

This case is similar to that of Ouyang Xiu: the epitaph requester wrote the author after the completion of the text and demanded that more content be added. Wang replied that any change would upset the integrity of his writing. He was most likely annoyed because Qian had focused on two minor details. The first was related to some poems that Qian had written. Wang reasoned, "There are ponds, towers, and bamboos in all office complexes [and abundant poems have been written about them]. Why would adding your work on them make your late mother proud?" In addition, Wang noted, nowadays even a commoner could compose a poem or two, not to mention a degree holder like Qian. Instead, "It is what distinguishes her from a petty person in the marketplace that deserves to be recorded."

If the first request appeared unreasonable, the second was even more trivial to Wang. Obviously, Wang's original biography had left out the fact that the deceased had seven grandchildren. To Qian's request to insert that information, Wang replied, "Who has five sons but not seven grandchildren? If the seven children had worthy accomplishments, of course they should not be omitted. If they are still young and there is no way of knowing whether they are going to be virtuous or not, what is the point of listing them?" Wang ended, "I would not elaborate on other things. Please consult those who are knowledgeable [and see if they agree with me]."[77]

Should we blame Qian, as Wang did, for wanting to include these two pieces of information in his mother's epitaph? While the first request has more to do with Qian's attempt at self-promotion, we can probably sympathize with Qian on the importance of including the number of the deceased's grandchildren. It turned out that Wang did reconsider Qian's requests after writing his strongly worded letter. Wang's epitaph for Qian's mother has survived. The epitaph, about four hundred characters, did mention the seven grandsons. That Qian once wrote poems about a certain government complex, however, was not included.[78]

One Funerary Biography Was Not Enough

In a letter addressed to Shen Gou (1025–1067), a man named Jiang wrote the following:

> When my father was buried, Zhang Wangzhi (informal name Biaomin) wrote an epitaph that included my father's genealogical information, the times of his death and burial, and the planning of his funeral from the beginning to the end, but nobody knew my father better than you did. Now a stele has been established beside his tomb but has no inscriptions on it. I hope that you will write him a biography for this purpose. This way, my father will be remembered, and I will have no regrets when I die.[79]

Jiang's letter reveals that his father's burial had been completed with an epitaph. Since then, an aboveground stele had been erected, and it needed a biographical sketch. Jiang hoped that Shen would agree to author the inscription to help perpetuate his father's reputation.

This section focuses on a phenomenon that had parallels to and connections with excessive mourning and long-term graveyard repair and maintenance, discussed in the previous chapters: the growing popularity of ancestral commemoration through the composition of multiple funerary biographies. These often took the form of aboveground steles or addenda to existing ones. In addition to supplementing the epitaphs in perpetuating family memory, these writings served to validate sons', grandsons', and even great-grandsons' continual performance of filial devotion and their images as filial paragons. This development has to be considered in the following context: given the challenges that sons faced in securing epitaphs for parents, that some descendants were willing to go through the process not once but two or even more times attests to the central place of stele inscriptions in elite representations of filial performance.

Song commemorative literature is replete with references to the erection of tombside steles and requests for aboveground inscriptions. For example, Liu Zhi, whose burial of his father opened the previous chapter, wrote an inscription himself and employed three others for this purpose. Zeng Gong had an epitaph and an aboveground stele prepared for his father and grandfather decades after their deaths.[80] Four years after the passing of his maternal grandmother, Miss Huang, Wang Anshi wrote her aboveground stele, when his uncle had already prepared her epitaph.[81] Thirty-two years after Ouyang Xiu's death, his son requested his stele inscription from Su Che.[82]

Below I present three examples to contextualize descendants' considerations as they embarked on the mission of seeking additional funerary biographies.

The first case concerns a request from Zhang Tangmin (*jinshi* 1042) to Yu Jing for an aboveground stele for his father long after Zhang's parents, older brother, and several other senior family members had been buried. A total of five people, including Han Qi and Ouyang Xiu, had written epitaphs for the deceased. Zhang's commemorative activities, however, did not stop there. Due to his father's having received an honorary title, Zhang planned to "install a stele inscription for my father and older brother so that they will be forever remembered. I would like to ask for your words [to be inscribed on the stele]."[83] For Zhang, the new official emolument necessitated an update to his father's biography. Since the entombed inscription could not be changed, the most feasible option was to record the latest development on an aboveground stele. For this purpose, Yu Jing ended up writing a rather substantial commemorative piece.[84]

The second example involves Bi Shi'an's great-grandson, Bi Zhongyou (1047–1124), who asked Liu Xinlao (n.d.) for an aboveground stele for Bi Shi'an eighty-six years after Bi's death. The intention of Bi's great-grandson differed from that of Zhang Tangmin. Bi Zhongyou decided to erect a stele for his great-grandfather because Bi Shi'an's record of conduct (by Chen Pengnian [961–1017]) and epitaph (by Yang Yi) had missed many details in his great-grandfather's life—especially a mention of Emperor Zhenzong's generosity toward Bi and Bi's recommendations of advancement for Wang Yucheng and Kou Zhun (961–1023) to the emperor. Since both Wang and Kou had risen in prominence in the literary and political worlds and the entire realm was praising them for their virtue and accomplishments, Bi Zhongyou felt that people should be made aware of Bi's role in their ascendancy.[85] Liu Xinlao therefore was charged with adding both details and possibly more to elevate Bi's reputation in the stele.

The third and last eager commemorator was the great-grandson of a Huang family who, on the occasion of re-inscribing the epitaph of his ancestor by Ouyang Xiu, asked Wang Tinggui (1080–1172) to write a postscript to mark the occasion. Wang's addendum did not add any new information about Huang's ancestor, indicating that this, unlike the first two cases, involved neither title granting nor the restoration of any outstanding deed. Except for reiterating Huang's position as a disciple of Ouyang Xiu and Ouyang's praise of Huang's literary talent, Wang Tinggui focused on the great-grandson, who was said to be "capable of managing this project [because he was] extremely knowledgeable [and] bears a resemblance to his great-grandfather in their aspirations."[86]

Despite the diversity in circumstances, the goals of the above new initiatives were similar: to perpetuate one's ancestral legacy. The continual addition to and remembrance of one's ancestors was also meant to confirm a son's or grandson's whole-hearted dedication to his family. In a long letter to Liu Xinlao, Bi Zhongyou justified writing to Liu while he was still mourning his mother. Calling himself unfilial, Bi proceeded to show that the omission of his great-grandfather's deeds in the epitaph nonetheless deserved his urgent attention.[87] In other words, Bi Zhongyou, at the risk of acting unfilial toward his mother, was performing a greater filial deed: restoring his great-grandfather's reputation to its fullest. Epitaph writers such as Yu Jing, Liu Xinlao, and Wang Tinggui were happy to highlight this point. In the stele inscription for Zhang Tangmin's father, Yu Jing included much praise for Tangmin's filial piety: Zhang had demonstrated extraordinary dedication in mourning his mother; he had traveled thousands of *li* to collect multiple bodies of family members and had them returned home; he had moved Yu with his sincerity to acquire epitaphs for his parents and brother. Yu acclaimed, "The Zhangs indeed have a son!"[88]

In the second half of the Northern Song, addenda to existing epitaphs and additional funerary biographies grew in popularity. The stakes subsequently became higher for sons. In his request to Qiang Zhi for a supplement to his father's epitaph in 1073, Li Gao (n.d.) wrote, "My late father was buried with an epitaph authored by Mr. Wang. At the time, several things that were worthy of being recorded were left out. [Because of this], I have been unable to eat [well] for a year. I have now written down everything [that is missing from the epitaph] and plan to inscribe it on a stele next to the grave. This way, my ancestors will not be forgotten by posterity, and I will feel no qualms for my performance as a son."[89] Qiang, moved by Li, agreed to write the inscription.

Li's claim—that he had not been able to eat for a whole year due to the omission of his father's deeds in the epitaph—was certainly hyperbolic. The expression of his strong feelings and the way he had chosen to impress Qiang reveal the great lengths to which sons would go in seeking even a brief, addendum-type text in their displays of commitment to the memory of parents and other ancestors. This obsession generated much criticism from Northern Song biography writers. Sima Guang, for example, expressed his strong disapproval to this tendency on several occasions.

One of these occasions was when Tian Xi's (940–1104) great-grandson, Tian Yan (n.d.), approached Sima for Tian Xi's stele inscription. In a long response, Sima first acknowledged that he had admired Tian Xi greatly, but since Fan Zhongyan had already written Tian Xi's epitaph, in which he had called Tian "the most upright person under Heaven," Sima explained that he could not imagine himself capable of a more celebratory biography. The larger point Sima tried to convey was that he was against the practice of descendants asking two or even more authors to write funerary biographies for the same person.

> A person's virtues and accomplishments remain the same. How could the epitaph and stele inscription be different? Why do you not simply take the words of the virtuous [in this case, Fan Zhongyan] and both put them in the grave and inscribe them on a stele to place on the spirit path. How could there be doubt that your family's reputation would remain memorable? Please consider my suggestion. If my words are worth it, you can inscribe them on the back of the stele.[90]

Sima felt that since a person's epitaph and stele inscription contained practically the same information, what was the point of having several biographies written? In this particular case, if Fan Zhongyan had already praised Tian Xi profusely, why would the great-grandson want more validation from anyone else? The deceased's family obviously did not share Sima's sentiment. From the family's perspective, more funerary biographies meant more praise for both the ancestors and their descendants. In the end, Sima's words were inscribed in the back of Tian Xi's stele.

It should be noted that Sima did not object to using multiple stone inscriptions as a form of commemoration. What was problematic to him was the deceased's family going out of the way to include "unnecessary" information in the funerary biographies. Sima explained on a different occasion:

> Nowadays people will ask someone to write an epitaph [of the deceased] to be placed in the grave. They then will get another to author an inscription to be erected next to the tomb. The one in the tomb is called [mu]zhi

and the one outside, *[mu]bei*. The *zhi* is [placed in the grave] so that when there are changes in the mountains and valleys, the names of one's ancestors will not be forgotten, but the deceased is the same person. Even if the exact words [in the *zhi* and the *bei*] are different, the information about the person's native place, titles, virtues, and achievements is the same. Why would one want two people to write for them? I do not understand.[91]

Sima was more outspoken in this letter than in the previous one. Here he was asked to write a stele inscription for a deceased individual who had already been featured in an epitaph by Ouyang Xiu. Sima's logic remained the same: why not just use Ouyang's wording in the epitaph, inscribe it on a stele, and erect it next to the tomb? In this case, Sima did not offer that his writing be appended. Moreover, he noted the increasingly earnest pursuit on the part of descendants to perpetuate their ancestors' memory and his thoughts as a funerary biographer. Sima mused, "Filial sons and grandsons want to record the good deeds of their fathers and ancestors for them to be remembered forever"; to that he was sympathetic. However, he went on to offer a sober assessment to eager descendants:

Earlier, I often wrote epitaphs and stele inscriptions for people. I later blamed myself for this. My reason is this: For those who wish to have their deeds inscribed on metal and stone, if their reputation is not strong enough to earn people's respect or their writing is not good enough to circulate in later ages, even if I force myself to record their lives, people in the later generations will surely discard my words carelessly; how could their fame last forever?[92]

Here, Sima reminded us of Zeng Gong's thoughts on epitaph writing. If Zeng Gong advocated that the most competent epitaph writer should be found to commemorate a deceased, Sima Guang argued that what mattered the most in the end was how the deceased had lived his life. If the person had not developed a good reputation or his literary work was not of high quality, it would not matter who his biographer was or how much the biographer praised him. Elsewhere, Sima further downplayed the importance of stone inscriptions in general. He believed that if someone was of great virtue, he would be recorded in history. If he was not worthy but compared himself to those who were, he would only become a laughingstock. Given that most people could not avoid following popular practices, steles should list only objective information about one's family and rank.[93]

Sima's criticism did not seem to have stopped filial sons from undertaking extraordinary efforts. Let us end this discussion with some observations from

Wang Yang (1087–1153), who lived in the late Northern and early Southern Song:

> One's ancestors have long departed. Their virtuous descendants would not want them to be forgotten, but the bones cannot last forever. What can be done? The only option is to immortalize their ancestors' reputations. Is there a way to realize this goal? It is said that the way to do so is to find a person whose work will surely last to record one's ancestor's good deeds, have the record inscribed, placed in the tomb, and have copies made and circulated in the four directions. This should ensure that the fame of the ancestor will endure. Nowadays people do not think this is enough. They take the epitaphs of their ancestors and recite them every day. When they meet a writer, they beg him to bestow a favor on their ancestors by expanding the original funerary biographies. They approach those who have not heard about their ancestors and say: "Everything in the epitaph is truthful. This biography is different from those commissioned hyperbolic ones. You can therefore learn more from reading this than the others." Only when people accede to their pleas do they stop. Is this not too much, to go to these lengths to immortalize one's ancestors?[94]

The inappropriate practices criticized by Sima Guang and Wang Anshi paled in comparison with Wang Yang's description of overzealous descendants. Sons not only got epitaphs for parents and supplemented them with additional information, but they also made rubbings solely in an effort to spread their ancestors' reputations. They did this on top of the common practice of offering handsome commissions in exchange for highly flattering epitaphs. Wang seemed to have stopped short at asking, "Is this really the proper way of filial children?"

In the Northern Song, epitaphs were increasingly identified as a tool and literary genre that celebrated not only a deceased's life, but also a son's devotion. This development can be clearly seen from three angles. First, epitaphs were emphatically labeled an integral ritual of commemoration. Second, sons became a strong presence in their parents' funerary biographies and were often praised for their filial devotion and extraordinary efforts in pursuing a potential biographer. Third, many scholars, including leading literary figures, became active and prolific epitaph writers. Not only did they readily identify themselves and their relationship with the deceased and the deceased's family, but these writers also fashioned themselves as strong advocates of the filial child, often claiming that it was the son's outstanding deeds that had moved them to write for the parent.

The above developments had important implications. The representation of epitaphs as an exceptional filial practice tremendously empowered the scholarly and office-holding son, who had ready access to the pool of epitaph writers and who was routinely commended for his efforts at seeking the epitaphs. It was most significant that filial performance of this nature could be fulfilled without a son's having to leave officialdom or be physically available for his parents. In the end, due to his association with the epitaph writer and his epitaph-seeking efforts, the official son became *the* filial child and was recorded as such in his parents' funerary inscriptions. However, the understanding shared by the epitaph-requesting son and the epitaph writer in promoting both the deceased and his filial offspring had its limits due to fundamental differences in the interests of the two parties. Above all, this discussion shows that, just as in the case of reverent care, mourning, and burial practices, preparing an epitaph for one's parents was far from a straightforward filial obligation. On the contrary, it required the alignment of many elements to make the task successful.

Filial Piety and the Elite

Family, State, and Native Place in the Northern Song

In an undated letter, Liu Yizhong (act. 1090s–1110s), son of the renowned scholar-historian Liu Shu (1032–1078), wrote to his kinsmen in Yunzhou (Gao'an, Jiangxi) to explain why he had been out of touch with them for years.[1] Liu recollected that in the 1080s, after the death of his uncle and younger brother (who had presumably been the primary caretaker of his mother, Miss Cai), Liu went home to move Miss Cai to his official post. Unfortunately, Miss Cai died in transit. "Due to poverty, I was unable to return her body [back home at the time]." It was not until years later, in 1093, that Liu laid his parents and brother to rest in Jiangzhou (Jiujiang, Jiangxi). Around the same time, he had eight other Liu men and women entombed in the family's ancestral graveyard in Nankang (in Jiangxi). After the completion of the burials, Liu added, he was appointed to a position in Shandong. "It was a remote place and the roads were hard to travel, so I have not sent you my greetings for a long time." Liu assured his relatives that he had never forgotten about them and asked for their forgiveness.

Liu Yizhong's letter reveals several things. First, after his father passed away in 1078, his mother, Miss Cai, returned to their hometown to live with his younger brother. The brother's death left Yizhong with no alternative but to bring his mother to his local office. Second, Liu's parents died about a decade apart and far from home. Their interments were held up for years due to Yizhong's career and the time he needed to accumulate sufficient funds. The event was especially expensive because the 1093 burial was actually a reburial for his father, who had been temporarily entombed in the family's ancestral graveyard. Third, Liu Yizhong's self-acknowledged long absence from his native region is proof that he did not personally tend to the exhumation and movement of his father's remains from Nankang to Jiangzhou. Fourth, even with the establishment of a new graveyard in Jiangzhou, Liu Yizhong did not completely "desert" his ancestral home and burial ground; he took steps to have multiple extended family members buried there.

Luyang and Northern Song Literati

Liu Yizhong's letter offers intimate details about the challenges that he faced in performing reverent care, his negligence regarding his parents' burial, his long absence from home, and his decision to construct a new graveyard far away from the Lius' established burial complex. Liu's experience with these filial-piety-related duties would not have struck his fellow scholar-officials as particularly unusual. The diversity in these men's personal and family circumstances aside, many shared with Liu the all-too-familiar struggle to balance their official and scholarly careers; their absence from their parents and native places was directly responsible for their failure to carry out a son's most sacred domestic responsibilities. Northern Song literati were unusually outspoken about the various dimensions of this dilemma in their court memorials, literary writing, and personal correspondence. The predicament in which they found themselves, however, in no way diminished the importance of filial piety in elite life. Rather, as this study has shown, the Northern Song witnessed unprecedented literati activism and state involvement in redefining the meaning of *xiao* and its adequate performance. The result was the promotion and establishment of a new filial ideal, *luyang*. By labeling highly coveted honors and privileges that could be attained solely through a man's serving in office as the highest form of filial conduct, *luyang* elevated the earners of official emoluments (*lu*) as the most filial of sons. Consequently, *xiao* became more central than ever in Song scholar-officials' collective self-identification, as well as their sense of morality and masculinity.

Nowhere was the *luyang* model more vigorously supported than in epitaph writing. Contemporary funerary biographies consistently portrayed the ideal elite man as a successful degree holder, dedicated court official, and talented writer and scholar. The same accounts dutifully commended the same person for requesting close-to-home appointments, performing reverent care at his local posts, and obtaining honorary titles and emoluments for his parents and ancestors. By directly connecting hard-earned official credentials and privileges with the well-being of the parents and family, epitaph writing, just like the *luyang*-related official policies and court pronouncements, deliberately obscured the inherent conflicts between elite men's public pursuits and domestic obligations. As a result, the popular genre ceased to be "private" literature at its core. Instead, it became an important vehicle for the country's social and cultural elites to publicize their most cherished aspirations and achievements.

Exactly because of the role that they played in elevating the *luyang* model and circulating *luyang* exemplars, epitaphs evolved into a highly acclaimed form of filial expression. This development further confirmed the value of *lu* earning to elite men and their families, as, more often than not, it was the literati sons who were responsible for securing their parents' epitaphs. Consequently, the completed epitaphs not only assured the immortality of the parents, but they also provided the writers with a platform to showcase the unwavering devotion of the epitaph-requesting sons. To a large extent, social and cultural connections, established in the pursuit of official careers, became elite men's most important assets in the fashioning of their filial image.

Filial Piety, Literati, and the State

The *luyang* model, by allowing elite men to be "absent yet filial" sons, tremendously elevated the prestige of civil service and legitimized its practitioners' commitment to it. In this way, political success and filial devotion, two key aspects of elite identity and self-representation, ceased to be incompatible. This process was a long time in the making. In the first several decades of its existence, the Song court scrambled to achieve some degree of local and regional administrative continuity. The private needs of its civil servants were not the central government's top priorities. As a result, office-holding men were not granted full mourning leaves. Nor did they regularly receive *luyang*-related benefits. It was not until Emperor Renzong's reign that the state began to act more systematically regarding its civil servants' reverent care duties and mourning obligations. The *luyang* model, just like the gradual expansion of the examination system, the enactment of systematic personnel policies, and the generous implementation of special examinations and the protection privilege (*yin*), was part of the institutional changes that aimed to define a proper state-literati relationship. All these measures sought to sustain the appeal of civil service to the educated and social elites, as well as bolster the state's ability to control this prominent segment of the population.[2]

Two specific *luyang*-related policies, dated to Renzong's reign, merit mention in this context. The first, issued in 1041, granted high-ranking officials the privilege of building family shrines (*jiamiao*) and tombside cloisters (*fenmiao* or *fensi*).[3] The second was a government initiative that ordered civil servants to compile family- and lineage-based anthologies (*jiaji*), a collection of works by and records about their recent and more remote ancestors.[4] The history of the building of family shrines and graveyard cloisters is too complex a story to be told here. We do know that while Tang family shrines were privately sponsored ancestral worship structures, most Song shrines were "granted by emperors and funded by government resources."[5] For the purpose of political recognition and in the name of filial piety and family perpetuation, Northern Song scholar-officials engaged in extensive debates about the proper configuration of a family shrine. They likewise turned in substantial records of their forefathers' writings and biographical information for record keeping at the court.[6] In fact, responses to the call were so overwhelming that an edict was issued to suspend additional submissions.[7]

The above examples and the abundant evidence contained in the previous chapters demonstrate the close relationship between Northern Song literati and the state. With the tangible and intangible benefits bestowed by the state occupying an increasingly important place in the definition of personal achievement and family status, the *luyang* model caused ever more enthusiastic elite participation in examination preparation and civil service. This trend subsequently put office-holding men and their families at the mercy of the imperial state. For the first time in Chinese history, the state implemented systematic policies that aimed to regulate every aspect of its civil servants' domestic duties. "Private" matters such as when, where, and under what circumstances sons lived with their parents; the place and length of mourning for the deaths of parents; and the time frame for funeral and burial planning all became subject to political decree. To put it another way, at the same time that the *luyang* model legitimized elite men's public accomplishments as the most significant filial act, the new convention permanently tied the fortunes of elite families to those of the state.

The deepening intervention of the state in elite life, however, did not create a withdrawal of its members from their public pursuits. To the contrary, throughout the Northern Song, no other aspiration had the same appeal to the country's upper-class households as holding office. This was the case because political influence remained the foundation of other literati-oriented interests.[8] *Lu* earning was key to their claim of social and cultural leadership on both the national and local levels.[9]

Filial Piety and Elite Family Life

The rise of the *luyang* ideal impacted elite family life in important ways. First of all, the equation of scholarly and bureaucratic success with filial piety marked a reconfiguration not only of elite male filiality, but also that of non-official men and women. In recognizing *lu* earning as the most valued filial act, the *luyang* ideal and the practices that it endorsed effectively placed *lu* above *yang* (reverent care). In order to realize *luyang*, ambitious young men in elite households left their homes for the country's political and cultural centers in the pursuit of examination degrees and government service. Imperial personnel policies, time constraints, and geographical distance subsequently made it impossible for the *lu* seekers to maintain regular and tangible connections with their parents, not to mention the inability to personally wait on them. In the end, it was the non-office-holding men and women left behind who took on the bulk of the parental care.

This transfer of the filial duties of the politically successful men to those who did not hold office in the family seemed unavoidable. Of even greater consequence was the negligence and marginalization of the actual caretakers and their contributions in contemporary discourse. Liu Yizhong implied that his younger brother served as their mother's principal caretaker while Liu continued his career, but he made no reference to the role of his wife or sister-in-law. Mei Rang, discussed in chapter 1, spoke up about fulfilling his filial duties and acting as a substitute for his official brother, but he did not bring his wives and other family members into the picture. More broadly, Northern Song funerary biographers routinely portrayed an official son as if he were his parents' only son and had singlehandedly managed his parents' welfare, burials, and commemorations. Often absent from these records are the voices of non-official sons and their wives, who very likely were equally involved caretakers. In this sense, the *luyang* model created a status- and gender-based structure within elite households. By consigning the filial duties of official sons to the non-office-holding family members, the new arrangement did not give the true caretakers proper credit where it was due.

This divided-and-unequal system had serious effects on family relationships. By stressing sons' responsibility to honor and elevate their parents, the *luyang* discourse failed to take into account the long separation of the official sons and their parents. This made the cultivation and maintenance of any tangible parent-son relationship problematic. Hyperbolic though they are, letters, personal accounts, and epitaphs frequently refer to sons missing their parents simply because they had not seen each other for years. Parents must have had similar feelings. Most had no other option but to accept the fragility of the relationship. The lengthy times apart between parents and sons would understandably undermine the way parental authority was exercised. When aged parents did join their sons at the latter's official posts, the reunion was universally lauded as the highest form of *luyang*. Yet the parents' departure from their own homes and their entrance into their sons' homes must have weakened their power, potentially changing the dynamics between parents and sons, in-laws, and even grandparents and grandchildren. Widows, with less leverage at their disposal, would have had a harder time adjusting. The praise for mothers willingly accompanying their sons on official trips implicitly proves the hardships that older women had to overcome and their vulnerable positions in the family.

The popularity of *luyang* also had important implications for another key relationship, that between husband and wife. Northern Song epitaph writers routinely described elite women as dedicated daughters-in-law and the only ones who could please especially demanding mothers-in-law. Many were praised for serving as the husbands' filial surrogates, diligently waiting on their parents-in-law, even going so far as to take charge of their burials while their husbands pursued their careers in faraway places. Just as in the case of the parent-child relationship, the fact that husbands and wives did not see each other for years at a time must have taken a heavy emotional toll on their relationships. Equally important, other matters of key concern, such as the education of children, betrothals, marriages, and family finances would have to be delayed or discussed over long distances. In this context, we may be able to better appreciate the abundant references to female literacy, the role of the mother in early childhood education, and elite women proving themselves as capable household manager.[10] Unable to count on their husbands, many women might simply have taken on these tasks and in time tried to prepare their daughters for comparable burdens. The absence of wives likewise necessitated changes in the lives of their husbands. This opened the door for concubines to gain more importance, as both elite men's companions and "managers" of their daily lives. In a way, while wives were increasingly seen as their husbands' filial substitutes, concubines became the wives' replacements. The "domestication" of concubines in the Song and late imperial times has to be understood in light of the larger political, cultural, and intellectual currents of the time.[11] The glorification of elite women as filial caretakers of their in-laws, rather than helpmates of their husbands, reflects this shift.

The prominence of the *luyang* rhetoric suggests a need to rethink the relationship between the office-holding men and their non-official brothers. Office-holding men and their local-based brothers, for example, might very likely have had a different approach to important family matters, such as parental care, the maintenance of graveyards, and estate management. More research is needed before we can gain a fuller understanding of this aspect of elite family life.[12] Northern Song funerary biographers did imply that some movement of graveyards that was said to have been based on divination results was actually due to discord among brothers who had grown apart. Widows being bullied by their brothers-in-law explains why some Song scholar-officials grew up in their maternal grandparents' households. Moreover, numerous legal cases in the *Qingming ji* (Enlightened Judgments) have shown that property disputes were a major cause for parent-child conflict and sibling rivalry in the Southern Song. More often than not, the roots of the problem lay in the unequal distribution of parental-care responsibilities among sons and occasionally daughters. If members of wealthy local elite families took legal action against each other on these grounds, it would not be too far-fetched to assume that Northern Song elite families might have had similar experiences but chose to remain silent for the sake of the family reputation.

The issues brought up here do not begin to exhaust the relationship between filial performance and other family matters, but they are sufficient to remind us of the centrality of filial piety in family life and family relationships. Above all, this examination of people's experiences has confirmed that there never was a neat, universal model of filiality, not even for the political and social elites. In other words, the paradigm of sons making unconditional sacrifices, which were then taken for granted by parents as the ultimate symbols of their children's devotion, existed only in ritual prescriptions and was never the norm in Song elite households. In reality, parents were not all happy recipients of their children's kindness and sacrifice, nor were sons and daughters-in-law all pious followers of classical prescriptions and filial tales. To be sure, many parents had a significant say in their own care and posthumous arrangements, but just as often they were subject to the will of sons and other family members. Filial expression was also conditioned by a variety of real-life scenarios. Parents died at all ages, relieving children of reverent care duties. Others had no son or survived all their sons, even grandsons, and ended up depending on their daughters or other family members. Some families had the good fortune to produce officials in consecutive generations, causing the absence of both parents and sons from their native place. Other reasons, such as adoption, remarriage, and concubinage, could result in a son's having two, three, or even four mothers, further complicating filial performance and family relationships. Filial piety to concubine mothers continued to generate controversy and remained a political, family, and ritual concern throughout the second half of the Northern Song. It was precisely these personal and human stories, as well as the emotional and calculated responses of the individuals and their families, that enable us to see filial piety as both an enduring cultural value and a concrete, prevalent practice.

Filial Piety, Home, and Native Place

Outside of the family setting, the *luyang* ideal and its associated practices exerted a profound impact on the relationship between elite men and their native places. Several phenomena, including long delays in burials, graveyard construction away from ancestral tomb complexes, and the emergence of new patterns of commemoration, complicated the meanings and significance of home and native place. In his study of Su Shi's letters, Ronald Egan has observed that "Song literati were surprisingly unattached to their native place. It was not unusual for a man to stay away from his ancestral home and the all-important graves for decades at a time, or even to end up settling down in retirement in another part of the empire."[13] After the completion of their parents' burials in the late 1050s and 1060s respectively, Su Shi and Su Che never again returned to their native place of Meizhou in Sichuan. Both were buried in the capital region. More important, out of necessity or for the sake of convenience, Song office-holding families frequently set up new graveyards, irrevocably distancing themselves and their descendants from their native regions and ancestral burial grounds. Wang Yi, Li Yin, Ouyang Xiu, and Liu Zhi, whose stories open the introduction and the first three chapters of this study, all were laid to rest in new burial grounds far away from their ancestral graveyards. Su Song's father and many others specifically instructed their sons not to return their bodies to their native places. This readiness on the part of office-holding men to remove themselves permanently from their places of origin led to large-scale and frequent segmentation of elite families across the country.

This trend dictates that we be cautious when dealing with standard statements about a person's or family's geographical origins or affiliations. In the Northern Song, labeling someone as a "native of such-and-such prefecture" did not necessarily indicate that he was born, resided for substantial periods of time, or wished to be or actually was buried there. Rather, while office holding and extensive travel took Song literati away from their homes and native places, the same engagements provided them with abundant opportunities to become attached to other places. This commonplace occurrence partly explains the ubiquity of new graveyard construction and temporary burials and reburials. In the process, a man's ancestral home and native place receded in importance in his life.

This phenomenon created great anxieties in the minds of Northern Song scholar-officials, leading to sobering musings about the relationship between *lu* and *yang*. Written at the end of the Northern Song, Wang Zishen's (1050–1128) "Rhapsody on Longing to Return Home" (*Sigui fu*) is representative of this genre both for its attention to personal experience and the "generic-ness" of its content. Wang opens with a deliberation on the relationship between earning *lu* and practicing *yang*:

Earning *lu* is enviable under some circumstances. Under other circumstances one should interrupt his pursuit of *lu*. Why is this? When a man intends to express his filial devotion [to his parents] through entering officialdom, if he does not have domestic worries, then the *lu* he achieves is enviable, and he should continue along this path; if a man has old parents, he should stop concentrating on seeking *lu*.[14]

By no means attempting to repudiate the value of *lu* as a filial act, Wang nonetheless made it conditional on a man's domestic situation. It was fine for scholarly men to stay in office as long as their parents had passed away or were relatively young and healthy. Those who had aged parents, however, should temporarily suspend their professional careers for the sake of the seniors' well-being. Turning to his own circumstances, Wang Zishen lamented, "Alas, my father is eighty and my mother's hair has also turned white. Yet I continue to serve as an official and remain busy on the road. Even hungry [mother] birds have their chicks to feed them in the morning. Am I not even as good as a chick?"[15] Wang's reference to young chicks feeding their mother every morning made his sense of shame and remorse especially palpable.

Wang Zishen's emotional distress was further exacerbated by the physical barrier between him and his parents. Far from home at the time of this composition, Wang proceeded to list a variety of local delicacies that both he and his parents enjoyed. This nostalgic reminiscence is followed by a description of the ideal life that he would have liked to lead.

> With servants staying quiet and a book in hand, I could either remain silent for a whole day or enjoy lively conversations with friends. I believe that my parents would be pleased if I remained in my hometown [*lüli*] for long periods of time. This is also my wish. I therefore intend to resign from office. I do this not to imitate [Tao] Yuanming's [365–427] narrow-minded grudge [against his failure in officialdom] or because I am ashamed of having succumbed to the appeal of official emoluments. I have this intention because, ever since reaching adulthood, I have never waited at my parents' sides and contributed to their well-being. If I do not make a commitment now, will I not regret it later?[16]

Wang's portrayal of his profound sense of longing for his parents and hometown is representative of a broad development. While civil service remained the top priority of Song educated men, the late eleventh century witnessed the growing prominence of the notions of *juanyou* and *sigui*.[17] Practically every major Northern Song official-writer composed something with reference to these concepts. Literally meaning "tired of travel" and "longing to return [home]" respectively, these two expressions regularly appeared in poetry, personal correspondence, and official memorials in which officialdom was contrasted with native place and extensive physical mobility with prosaic home life. In other words, several decades after the triumph of the *luyang* ideal, its drawbacks came to the attention of its practitioners.

Few gave up their careers and returned home to practice parental care, manage the ancestral graveyard, or enjoy the romanticized lifestyle that was the opposite of enduring "hardships on the road." The *luyang* ideal and its approved practices, however, were directly responsible for elite reflections on and changing ideas about family life, social status, and cultural values. Many turned to strengthening family hierarchies through family rituals and the establishment of kinship organizations.[18] Moreover, efforts to search for, recover, and correct ancestral information for official purposes made elite men acutely aware of the vulnerability of the family due to their frequent physical absences, unreliable memories, and inadequate textual records. This realization, along with factional struggles and a growing competition for status, generated a strong interest in family preservation as a filial performance. Exasperated with clan members who did not even remember their recent ancestors' names, Su Xun evoked children's filial responsibilities to justify his genealogy-writing endeavor.[19] Scrutinizing his family history led Han Qi onto a similar path. Following his extensive investigative effort, Han's sixty-chapter collection of family writings contained works by and about five generations of ancestors. Han specifically marked his compilation and its preservation as a unique filial act. "I ordered that my sons and nephews each keep a copy at home. If those who are in charge in later generations lose it out of negligence, Almighty Heaven and the ancestral spirits will bring down calamities on the unfilial. Be warned! Be warned!"[20]

The revived interest in family history, ancestral shrines, and sacrificial rites symbolized shared efforts among Northern Song literati to fashion themselves as both filial sons and family men. This development in turn contributed to new staple components in epitaph works in the late Northern Song. In addition to having achieved *luyang*, observed proper mourning, and taken pains to secure parents' funerary biographies, office-holding men were increasingly portrayed as extremely generous to brothers, especially at times of property division. They were similarly praised for being attentive to the marriages of nephews and nieces and for undertaking massive burials of men and women of multiple generations. Many were especially credited with composing or obtaining epitaphs for family members who had stayed behind. In other words, by the end of the Northern Song, the ideal elite man did not stop at being a *lu* earner and a *luyang* performer; he also went to great lengths to preserve and elevate his clan, often at a heavy financial cost to him and his nuclear family. These efforts were not "filial performances" in and of themselves. Many elite men in earlier times had certainly behaved in similar ways. That these deeds were detailed in standard-ized language in commemorative works added a new element in elite self-iden-tification: by being brotherly and helping out their relatives, the office holders saw their actions as a substitute for or extension of their allotted shares of filial responsibilities.

Other, more ambitious family- and native-place-oriented activities recon-nected office-holding men with their kinsmen and ancestral places in concrete ways. Dissatisfied with the way family fortunes had become so closely depen-dent on the good fortune of a small number of politically successful men, Fan Zhongyan began a movement to set aside property to fund ancestral worship and provide for the welfare of relatives.[21] This was followed by the emergence of fully developed kin groups, with common graveyards, ancestral sacrifices, and shared assets, such as tomb land and lineage schools, as methods of elite perpetuation in the Song and later.[22] As many scholars have shown, these developments grew out of regional roots and diverse intellectual commitments.[23] In the context of this study, what is especially notable is the "long-distance collaboration" between the national literati and their local relatives. Fan Zhongyan and his sons set foot in the Suzhou area only occasionally, so the daily management of the charitable estate was handled by their kinsmen. Su Xun and Ouyang Xiu completed the genealogies of their families while far away from their native places of Sichuan and Jiangxi respectively. This left the actual construction of the inscriptions and related work to Su's and Ouyang's clansmen in Meizhou and Jizhou. In this sense, the creation and survival of kinship organizations was made possible by a col-lection of agents and forces. These included the central and local governments, which recognized and supported the politically and socially influential families; the scholar-officials, who created and propagated the ancestral rituals, family instructions, genealogies, clan rules, and village covenants; and the clan and lin-eage heads who ran the descent groups at the local level. In more than one way, a reconfiguration of their relationships with family, ancestors, and native place effectively established the Song literati's dominance of culture and society. These family-based, ground-level initiatives linked their moral and cultural visions with those of the leading scholar-intellectuals, providing the social and familial foundation for the ascendancy of Neo-Confucianism, as well as new social and cultural norms that transformed Chinese society in the Song and beyond.[24]

NOTES

Abbreviations

QSW: Quan Song wen

QSS: Quan Song Shi

SHY: Song huiyao jigao (see under Xu Song)

SS: Songshi (see under Tuo Tuo)

Introduction

1. The *jinshi* (presented scholar) degree was the most prominent and competitive examination degree in the Song Dynasty. For major studies of the Song examination system, see Chaffee, *The Thorny Gates of Learning in Sung China*; de Weerdt, *Competition over Content*; T. H. C. Lee, *Government Education and Examination in Sung China*.

2. This narrative about the Wang family is based on an account by Wang Anshi of his life, Zeng Gong's epitaphs for Wang Yi and Wang Yi's wife and mother, and three of Wang Anshi's chronological biographies by Cai Shangxiang, Gu Donggao, and Zhan Dahe in *Wang Anshi nianpu sanzhong*. Wang Anshi in *Quan Song wen* (hereafter *QSW*), 65:1409.70–71; Zeng Gong in *QSW*, 58:1268.242–243, 1269.254–255, 1269.258–259.

3. Since ancient times, ritual guidelines stipulated that sons mourn their parents for three years. This aspect of the filial performance will be discussed in chapter 2 below.

4. Wang Anshi in *Quan Song shi* (hereafter *QSS*), 550.6574–6575. Zhongshan was the name of a hill near Jiangning.

5. Wang Zhi, *Moji*, xia.48; Ding Chuanjing, *Songren yishi huibian*, 10.481.

6. *Songshi* (hereafter *SS*), by Tuo Tuo et al., 327.10557. Wang Anshi in *QSW*, 65:1413.131, 65:1416.184.

7. For some important studies on Wang Anshi's political career in English, see Levine, *Divided by a Common Language*; J. T. C. Liu, *Reform in Sung China*; Smith: *Taxing Heaven's Storehouse*; "Shen-tsung's Reign and the New Policies of Wang An-shih"; and "Anatomies of Reform." For Chinese scholarship on Wang Anshi, see Zhang Baojian and Gao Qingqing, *Wang Anshi yanjiu lunzhu mulu suoyin*. For two recent book-length studies in Chinese, see Li Huarui, *Wang Anshi bianfa yanjiu shi*, and Shen Qinsong, *Beisong wenren yu dangzheng*.

8. For the significance of travel in the life of Song literati, see C. E. Zhang, *Transformative Journeys*.

9. For some general surveys of the centrality of *xiao* in Chinese thought and culture, see

Chan and Tan, "Introduction," 1–11; Holzman, "The Place of Filial Piety in Ancient China"; Wu Chongshu and Li Shouyi, *Xiao wenhua yanjiu*; Xiao Qunzhong, *Xiao yu zhongguo wenhua*; Zhu Lan, *Zhongguo chuantong xiaodao sixiang fazhanshi* and *Zhongguo chuantong xiaodao de lishi kaocha*. Filial piety was also incorporated into political and intellectual discourses as well as family life in Korea and Japan. See Haboush, "Filial Emotions and Filial Values"; Sugano, "State Indoctrination of Filial Piety in Tokugawa Japan"; and the multiple articles in Ikels, *Filial Piety*.

10. K. Chang, *The Archeology of Ancient China*; Keightley: "Art, Ancestor, and the Origins of Writing in China" and "The Making of the Ancestors"; Pu: "Ideas Concerning Death and Burial in pre-Han and Han China" and *In Search of Personal Welfare*; Puett, "The Offering of Food and the Creation of Order."

11. Brashier, *Ancestral Memory in Early China*; Chen Lai, *Gudai zongjiao yu lunli*; Huang Kaiguo, "Lun Rujia de xiao xueshuo"; Knapp, "The *Ru* Reinterpretation of *Xiao*"; Lin Anhong, *Rujia xiaodao sixiang yanjiu*; Olberding, "I Know Not 'Seems'; Radice: "The Ways of Filial Piety in Early China" and "Confucius and Filial Piety." For a useful summary of the Confucian discourse on family rituals, ancestral rites, and imperial ritual codes, see Ebrey, *Confucianism and Family Rituals in Imperial China*, 14–44.

12. See Mozi, *Mozi*, especially chapters 16 ("Impartial Caring") and 25 ("For Moderation in Funerals"); Han Feizi, *Han Feizi*, especially his treatise on *zhongxiao* (loyalty and filial piety); Kang, *Xianqin xiaodao yanjiu*.

13. The *Classic of Filial Piety* was promoted by all the major dynasties throughout Chinese history. For a study of the commentaries on the text, see Chen Yifeng, *Xiaojing zhushu yanjiu*. For a summary of Chinese scholarship on the study of *Xiaojing*, see Du, "1978 nian yilai *Xiaojing* yanjiu." For a recent comprehensive study in Chinese of the text, see Zang, *Renlun benyuan*. Emperor Xuanzong of the Tang was the first ruler who penned a commentary. See Zhu Hai: "Tang Xuanzong yuzhu *Xiaojing* fawei" and "Tang Xuanzong yuzhu *Xiaojing* kao." *Xiaojing* has been translated into all major world languages. For a recent study and translation in English, see Rosemont and Ames, *The Chinese Classic of Family Reverence*.

14. Zhao Dingxin, "The Han Bureaucracy," 69.

15. Ji Naili, *Sangang liuji yu shehui zhenghe*.

16. Wu Fanming, *Cong renlun zhixu dao falu zhixu*, 75–178.

17. Liu Houqin and Tian Yun, "Handai buxiao rulü yanji."

18. Unfiliality was formally listed as one of the ten abominations in the legal codes of all major dynasties starting from the Tang. For a translation of a list of these crimes, see de Bary and Bloom, *Sources of Chinese Tradition*, 549–552. The article on unfiliality in the *Song Penal Code* can be found in Dou, *Song xing tong*, 1.6.

19. Zhangsun, *Tanglü shuyi*, 1.12. Dou, *Song xing tong*, 1.7. These general guidelines were further expanded in many imperial edicts. See Zhou Mi, *Songdai xingfa shi*, 192–194, 209–210, 314–318; Lau: "Yang'er fanglao" and "Songdai tongju zhidu xia de suowei gongcai."

20. Buoye, "Filial Felons"; Chen Dengwu, "Fuchou xinshi"; Epstein, "Making a Case"; Huang Chunyi, "Tang Song shiqi de fuchou"; Liu Sha, "Handai weixiao qufa xianxiang de fali fenxi"; Zhu Lan, *Zhongguo chuantong xiaodao sixiang fazhanshi*, 249–267. For a study of earlier literary representations of filial avengers, see M. Luo, "Gender, Genre, and Discourse."

21. For the most comprehensive compilation of these materials, see *Zhongguo gudai xiaodao ziliao xuanbian*. See also Eicher, "Early Representations of Filial Piety in Dynastic Historiography"; Murray, "The '*Ladies' Classic of Filial Piety*' and Sung Textual Illustration."

22. Choo, "That 'Fatty Lump'"; Cline, *Families of Virtue*; Kinney, "Dyed Silk"; Wu Hung, "Private Love and Public Duty"; P. Wu: "Education of Children in the Sung" and "Childhood Remembered"; Y. Zhou, "The Child in Confucianism."

23. R. L. Davis, "Chaste and Filial Women in Chinese Historical Writing of the Eleventh Century"; Knapp: *Selfless Offspring* and "Reverent Caring"; Mather, "Filial Paragons and Spoiled Brats"; Wang Sanqing, *"Dunhuang bianwen ji zhong de Xiaozi zhuan* xintan."

24. Choi, *Death Rituals and Politics in Northern Song China*.

25. Ebrey: *Chu Hsi's Family Rituals, Confucianism and Family Rituals in Imperial China* and "Liturgies for Ancestral Rites in Successive Versions of the *Family Rituals*"; Lu Yilong, *Zhongguo lidai jiali*.

26. Dien, "Instructions for the Grave"; Ebrey, *Family and Property in Sung China*; Fei, *Zhongguo de jiafa zugui*; Furth, "The Patriarch's Legacy"; Niu, *Zhongguo lidai xiangyue*; Übelhör, "The Community Compact (*hsiang yüeh*) of the Sung and Its Educational Significance"; Xu Shaojin and Chen Yanbin, *Zhongguo jiaxun shi*; Yang Kaidao, *Zhongguo xiangyue zhidu*.

27. Barnhart, "The *Classic of Filial Piety* in Chinese Art History"; Chen Dengwu, "Falü yu jiaohua"; Fu, "The Cultural Fashioning of Filial Piety"; Idema: *Personal Salvation and Filial Piety* and *Filial Piety and Its Divine Rewards*. For an in-depth study of the printing industry in the Song, see Chia, *Printing for Profit*.

28. C. E. Zhang, "Negative Role Models." For a study of unfilial stories from earlier times, see Knapp, "There Are Maggots in My Soup!"

29. Lai Guolong, *Excavating the Afterlife*; Wu Hung: *The Wu Liang Shrine* and *The Art of the Yellow Springs*; Pu, "Preparation for the Afterlife"; and Zheng Yan, *Weijin Nanbeichao bihuamu yanjiu*.

30. T. M. Davis, *Entombed Epigraphy and Commemorative Culture in Early Medieval China*.

31. Chen Lüsheng and Lu Zhihong, *Gansu de Song Yuan huaxiangzhuan*; Cheng Yi, "Songdai mushi bihua yanjiu zongshu"; Deng Fei: "Guanyu Song Jin muzang zhong xiaoxing tu de sikao"; "Song Jin shiqi zhuandiao bihuamu de tuxiang ticai tanxi"; and *Zhongyuan beifang diqu Song Jin muzang yishu yanjiu*, 205–255; Jiang, "Songdai muzang chutu de ershisi xiao tuxiang bushi"; Laing, "Auspicious Motifs in Ninth- to Thirteenth-Century Chinese Tombs"; Wei, Shi, and Tang, "Gansu Song Jin mu 'Ershisi xiao' tu yu Dunhuang yishu *Xiaozi zhuan*"; Zou, *Beiwei xiaozi huaxiang yanjiu*. For a study on the design and production of filial exemplars in Song tombs, see Deng Fei, "Modular Design of Tombs in Song and Jin North China." Jeehee Hong's recent study, *Theater for the Dead*, shows that local elite families did not necessarily follow the orthodox Confucian ideology but still practiced ancestral protection and filial piety in burials. See also Hong, "Changing Roles of the Tomb Portrait."

32. Asim, "Status Symbol and Insurance Policy"; Hansen: *Negotiating Daily Life in Traditional China* and "Why Bury Contracts in Tombs?," 59–66.

33. Pu, "Handai bozang lun de lishi beijing jiqi yiyi"; Xu Jijun, *Zhongguo sangzang shi*, 105–116, 212–217, 321–330, 345–356, 420–424, 440–452.

34. M. Xu, *Crossing the Gate*, 47.

35. Chan, "Does *Xiao* Come before *Ren*?"; Li Chenyang, "Shifting Perspectives"; Raphals, "Reflections on Filial Piety, Nature, and Nurture."

36. A. Cheng, "Filial Piety with a Vengeance"; Kutcher, *Mourning in Late Imperial China*; Tang, "Wei Jin Nanchao de junfu xianhou lun."

37. Zhu Rui, "What If the Father Commits a Crime?"

38. Brown: *The Politics of Mourning in Early China* and "Mothers and Sons in Warring States and Han China."

39. Ebrey, "Imperial Filial Piety as a Political Problem"; Kahn, "The Politics of Filiality"; Li Shuyuan, *Zhengcai jingchan*; Tan, "Filial Daughters-in-Law."

40. There is a large literature on this topic. See Bokenkamp, *Ancestors and Anxiety*; K. Chen, "Filial Piety in Chinese Buddhism"; Dudbridge, *The Legend of Miaoshan*; Teiser, *The Ghost Festival in Medieval China.*

41. Kieschnick, *The Impact of Buddhism on Chinese Material Culture.*

42. Kyan: *The Body and the Family* and "Family Space"; Y. K. Lo, "Filial Devotion for Women"; Yao, "Good Karmic Connections."

43. Cole, *Mothers and Sons in Chinese Buddhism.*

44. Fang, "Songdai nüxing gegu liaoqin wenti shixi"; Knapp, "Chinese Filial Cannibalism"; T. Lu, *Accidental Incest, Filial Cannibalism, and Other Peculiar Encounters in Late Imperial Chinese Literature*; Qiu, "Buxiao zhi xiao"; Yu Gengzhe, "Gegu fengqin yuanqi de shehui beijing kaocha"; J. Yu, *Sanctity and Self-Inflicted Violence in Chinese Religions.*

45. Ebrey, "Cremation in Sung China."

46. Idema, *Personal Salvation and Filial Piety.*

47. E. L. Davis, *Society and the Supernatural in Song China*, 171–199.

48. For several early Song imperial edits, see Song Taizu in *QSW*, 1:6.126, 1:8.185–186; Song Taizong in *QSW*, 4:76.356; Song Zhenzong in *QSW*, 11:217.15. For Song government policies on "caring for the old," see Jin, "Songdai jizhong shehui fuli zhidu"; Wang Deyi, "Songdai de yanglao yu ciyou."

49. Zhou Mi, *Songdai xingfa shi*, 46–47, 209–210.

50. See the "Ritual (*Li*)" sections in *SS*, especially chapters 115, 124, and 125.

51. Yang Shiwen, "Songdai *Xiaojing* xue shulun." See also the multiple articles in Barnhart, *Li Kung-lin's Classic of Filial Piety.*

52. For a sample of these essays, see the following in *QSW*: Liu Kai, 6:122.317–318, 125.361–363; Wang Yucheng, 8:156.58; Song Xiang, 21:431.9–12; Song Qi, 23:488.206–208; Zhang Fangping, 38:811.89–91; Cai Xiang, 47:1015.148; Liu Chang, 59:1286.228–229; Wei Xiang, 82:1777.7–8; Xie Mai, 136:2945.360–361; Zhou Xingji, 137:2952.103–104.

53. For two major studies, see Ebrey: *Confucianism and Family Rituals in Imperial China* and *Chu Hsi's Family Rituals.*

54. Choi, *Death Rituals and Politics in Northern Song China.*

55. Archeological excavations continue to yield large numbers of *muzhiming* for elite members and ordinary people. For some discussion of recent findings, see Huai, "Beisong Shaanzhou Louzeyuan shibing muzhiwen yanjiu"; M. Xu, "China's Local Elites in Transition."

56. Charles Hartman has found that the literati government of the Song was "more socially diverse, but more culturally and intellectually cohesive" than its earlier counterparts. Hartman, "Song Government and Politics," 35.

57. There is a large literature on these topics, too much to list here. To gain a general understanding of the scholarly trends, see S. Chen, "The State, the Gentry, and Local Institutions,"141–182; R. L. Davis, "Review of *Negotiated Power*"; Ebrey, "The Dynamics of Elite Domination in Sung China"; Lau, "Hewei Tang Song biange"; John Lee, "Recent Studies in English on the Tang-Song Transition"; Li Huarui, *Tang Song biange lun de youlai yu fazhan*; Luo Yinan, "A Study of the Changes in the Tang-Song Transition Model"; Smith and von Glahn, "Introduction."

58. For several major studies of the medieval aristocratic families, see R. Chen, *Tangdai wenshi yu Zhongguo sixiang de zhuanxing*; Ebrey, *The Aristocratic Families of Early Imperial China*; Johnson, *The Medieval Chinese Oligarchy*; Tackett, *The Destruction of the Medieval Chinese Aristocracy*.

59. In addition to works mentioned above, see also Bol, "The Sung Examination System and the Shih"; R. L. Davis, *Court and Family in Sung China*; He Zhongli, *Keju yu Songdai shehui*; Jin, "Songdai keju zhidu yanjiu" (two parts); W. W. Lo, *An Introduction to the Civil Service of Sung China*; Miao Chunde, *Songdai jiaoyu*.

60. Bol: *This Culture of Ours* and *Neo-Confucianism in History*; Bossler, *Powerful Relations*; R. L. Davis, "Political Success and the Growth of Descent Groups"; Hartwell, "Demographic, Political, and Social Transformations in China"; Hymes, *Statesmen and Gentlemen*.

61. Egan, *The Problem of Beauty*; Halperin, *Out of the Cloister*; Hargett, "Song Dynasty Local Gazetteers and Their Place in the History of *Difangzhi* Writing"; Walton, *Academies and Society in Southern Sung China*; C. E. Zhang: "To Be 'Erudite in Miscellaneous Knowledge'"; "Of Revelers and Witty Conversationalists"; and "Things Heard in the Past, Material for Future Use."

62. Hartman, "Poetry and Politics in 1079"; Ji Xiao-bin, *Politics and Conservatism in Northern Song China*; Levine: *Divided by a Common Language*; "Faction Theory and the Political Imagination of the Northern Song"; "Che-tsung's Reign (1085–1100) and the Age of Faction"; and "The Reigns of Hui-tsung (1100–1126) and Ch'in-tsung (1126–1127) and the Fall of the Northern Sung."

63. Bol, "The Rise of Local History"; Clark, *Portrait of a Community*; Gerritsen, *Ji'an Literati and the Local in Song-Yuan-Ming China*; Huang Kuanchong: "Renji wangluo, shehui wen-hua huodong yu lingxiu diwei de jianli" and "Songdai Siming shizu renji wangluo yu shehui wenhua huodong"; Hymes: *Statesmen and Gentlemen*; "Marriage, Descent Groups, and the Localist Strategy"; and "Sung Society and Social Change"; Tao, *Beisong shizu*.

64. In a recent study of non-mourning related weeping and wailing, Ya Zuo argues that "emotional tears could bear significant moral and political meanings and might even be a sign of manliness." Zuo, "It's OK to Cry," 1. For some recent studies on the construction and negotiation of masculinity in imperial China, see M. W. Huang, *Negotiating Masculinities in Late Imperial China*.

65. For general surveys, see Xing, *Songdai jiating yanjiu*, and the multi-volume *Zhongguo jiating shi* which has the following: Xing (Song, Liao, Jin, and Yuan periods); Yu Xinzhong (Ming Qing period), and Zhang Guogang (Sui, Tang, and Five Dynasties).

66. For some book-length studies, see Bossler, *Powerful Relations*; Ebrey, *The Inner Quarters*; Kinney, *Exemplary Women of Early China*; W. Lu, *True to Her Word*; Mann, *Precious Records*; M. Xu, *Crossing the Gate*; Yao, *Tangdai funü de shengming licheng*; Zhang Bangwei, *Songdai hunyin jiazu shilun*.

67. Bernhardt: *Women and Property in China* and "The Inheritance Rights of Daughters"; Birge, *Women, Property, and Confucian Reaction in Sung and Yüan China*; Ebrey, "Conceptions of the Family in Song Times"; Lau, "Songdai de jiating jiufen yu zhongcai"; Li Shuyuan, *Zhengcai jingchan*; McDermott: "Family Financial Plans of the Southern Sung" and "Women of Property in China, 960–1368"; McKnight, "Who Gets It When You Go"; Wang Shanjun, "Jiafa yu gongcai"; Xing, *Jiachan jicheng shilun*.

68. In addition to the many book-length studies in Chinese and English mentioned above, see also Lau, "Cong Zhao Ding *Jiaxun bilu* kan Nansong Zhedong de yige shidafu jiazu" and

the multiple essays in Lau, *Songdai de jiating yu falü*; Li Guilu, *Beisong Sanhuai Wangshi jiazu yanjiu*; Liang Gengyao, "Jiazu hezuo, shehui shengwang yu difang gongyi"; Wang Deyi: "Songdai de Henei Xiangshi jiqi zuxi"; "Songdai de Chengdu Fanshi jiqi shixi"; and "Songdai de Shangcai Zushi jiqi shixi"; Xu Yangjie, *Song Ming jiazu zhidu shilun*.

69. Clark: "The Fu of Minnan"; "Reinventing the Genealogy"; and *Portrait of a Community*; Ebrey, "The Early Stages in the Development of Descent Group Organization," 16–61; Ebrey and Watson, introduction to *Kinship Organization in Late Imperial China*, 1–15; Walton, "Charitable Estates as an Aspect of Statecraft in the Southern Sung"; Wang Shanjun, *Songdai zongzu he zongzu zhidu yanjiu*. For a list of recent scholarly works on family and kinship organizations in Chinese, see Su Pinxiao: "Songdai jiazu yanjiu lunzhu mulu" and "Songdai jiazu yanjiu lunzhu mulu xuyi."

70. For some earlier studies on the parent-child relationship, see Birdwhistell, "Cultural Patterns and the Way of Mother and Son"; Bossler, "A Daughter Is a Daughter All Her Life"; Fong, "Inscribing a Sense of Self in Mother's Family"; Lewis, "Mothers and Sons in Early Imperial China"; Liao Yifang, *Tangdai de muzi guanxi*; Zheng Yaru, *Qinggan yu zhidu*.

71. For some book-length studies on remarriage, concubinage, and adoption, see Ebrey, *The Inner Quarters*; Bossler, *Courtesans, Concubines, and the Cult of Female Fidelity*; Waltner, *Getting an Heir*; Wolf and Huang, *Marriage and Adoption in China*.

72. My earlier work on Song travel culture highlights the key role this engagement played in scholar-official identity formation and the evolution of China's cultural geography. C. E. Zhang, *Transformative Journeys*.

73. For some book-length studies of Song Neo-Confucianism, see Bol, *Neo-Confucianism in History*; Tillman: *Confucian Discourse and Chu Hsi's Ascendancy* and *Utilitarian Confucianism*; Wyatt, *The Recluse of Loyang*.

Chapter 1: The Triumph of a New Filial Ideal

1. This introduction of the Li family is based on Li Xuzhou's *muzhiming*, Li Xuji's official biography, and the father's and sons' biographies in a Ming gazetteer of Hongzhou. Yu Jing in *QSW*, 27:574.126–130; *SS*, 300.9973–9975; *Wanli xinxiu Nanchang fuzhi*, 12.21b; 15.20b–21a.

2. The *yin* privilege allowed sons and other male relatives of high-ranking officials to enter officialdom based on the merit of said officials, a measure that was responsible for decreasing social mobility in the Song period. For a systematic study, see Chaffee, *The Thorny Gates of Learning*, 22–30.

3. Yu Jing in *QSW*, 27:574.126.

4. Confucius, *Lunyu*, 2.7. The translation is by Burton Watson, *The Analects of Confucius*, 21.

5. Confucius, *Lunyu*, 2.8. The translation is by Burton Watson, *The Analects of Confucius*, 21.

6. Mengzi (Mencius), *Mengzi*, 4A:12, 4A:19, 4A:27. The translation is by D. C. Lau, *Mencius: A Bilingual Edition*, 161, 165, 169.

7. Li Xueqin, *Liji zhengyi*, 426. References to these expectations appeared occasionally in early medieval records; for some examples, see Fang Xuanling, *Jinshu*, 50.1398, 55.1504; Shen Yue, *Songshu*, 51.2257.

8. The translation is by Ebrey, *The Classic of Filial Piety*, 374, 377.

9. Knapp, *Selfless Offspring*. For studies on the role women played in caring for family

members, see Jen-der Lee: "Han Tang zhijian jiating zhong de jiankang zhaogu yu xingbie" and "Tangdai de xingbie yu yiliao."

10. Wang Sanqing, "*Dunhuang bianwen ji* zhong de *Xiaozi zhuan* xintan."

11. While most *gegu* practitioners were men, Fang Yan has found one reference to women practicing *gegu* in the Han and Tang, respectively, and eighteen instances in the Song. Fang Yan, "Songdai nüxing gegu liaoqin wenti shixi." For more studies on the practice, see Kyan, "The Body and the Family"; T. Lu, *Accidental Incest, Filial Cannibalism, and Other Peculiar Encounters in Late Imperial Chinese Literature*; J. Yu, *Sanctity and Self-Inflicted Violence in Chinese Religions*.

12. Zheng Yaru, *Qin'en nanbao*, 10–14, 26–39.

13. For some examples, see Zheng Xie in *QSW*, 67:1456.332–336.

14. Zhang Yong in *QSW*, 6:108.68.

15. Ouyang Xiu in *QSW*, 31:664.167.

16. Su Song in *QSW*, 62:1342.28.

17. Ibid., 62:1344.58.

18. Li Zhaoqi in *QSW*, 121:2616.257.

19. Wang Yucheng in *QSW*, 8:161.177.

20. For a discussion of the representation of filial devotion in Tang poetry, see Zhao Xiaohua, "Tangren de xiaoqin guannian yu xiaoqin shi."

21. Xu Xuan in *QSS*, 1:7.95.

22. Mei Xun in *QSS*, 2:99.1117.

23. Li Zhiyi in *QSS*, 17:963.11225.

24. Shen Gua in *QSW*, 78:1694.19.

25. Ge Shengzhong in *QSW*, 143:3077.89.

26. Lü Tao in *QSW*, 74:125. For more similar references, see Song Qi in *QSW*, 25:528.141; Qiang Zhi in *QSW*, 67:1455.171; Liu Zhi in *QSW*, 77:1681.160.

27. Bossler, *Powerful Relations*, 16–24.

28. Yu Jing in *QSW*, 27:574.139.

29. Ibid., 27:575.143.

30. For more examples on degree earning as a form of *luyang*, see Sima Guang in *QSW*, 56:1225.276; Zheng Xie in *QSW*, 68:1480.172; Lü Tao in *QSW*, 74:1613.104.

31. For official guidelines on title bestowal, see *SS*, 170.4083–4086.

32. The earliest precedent for this practice was found in 748. *Tang da zhaoling ji*, 9.49.

33. Hu Su in *QSW*, 21:449.330–342; Yu Jing in *QSW*, 26:556.218–234; Zeng Gong in *QSW*, 57:1232.17–22; Wang Anshi in *QSW*, 63:1371.174–184; Wang Anli in *QSW*, 83:1799.21–32; Su Shi in *QSW*, 85:1852.194–203; Su Che in *QSW*, 94:2044.101–110; Zou Hao in *QSW*, 131:2827.87–88.

34. Li Fang, for example, earned titles for both his natural and adopted parents. *SS*, 265.9139.

35. Han Qi in *QSW*, 40:856.66. For a recent study of the Song-Tangut war, see Smith, "A Crisis in the Literati State."

36. For a sample of such requests, see Xiong Wenya in *QSW*, 17:364.394; Xu Shi in *QSW*, 16:327.139; Huang Tingjian in *QSW*, 104:2280.277; Song Shenzong in *QSW*, 115:2480.108–109, 115:2488.254–255.

37. Duan Shaolian in *QSW*, 20:312.67.

38. Fan Zhongyan in *QSW*, 18:379.256.

39. *SS*, 318.10364.

40. For some examples, see Cai Xiang in *QSW*, 46:998.277, 46:998.281; Wang Gui in *QSW*, 52:1140.338–339; Liu Chang in *QSW*, 59:1278.56; Zheng Xie in *QSW*, 67:1465.330–331.

41. Zheng Xie in *QSW*, 67:1466.335.

42. For a sample of these memorials, see Diao Zhan in *QSW*, 13:274.412; Li Di in *QSW*, 14:275.27; Lu Cha in *QSW*, 16:332.258; Xie Jiang in *QSW*, 20:411.51; Duan Shaolian in *QSW*, 20:412.67; Hu Su in *QSW*, 22:459.80; Wu Kui in *QSW*, 46:985.33.

43. Yu Jing in *QSW*, 27:574.125.

44. Wang Yucheng in *QSW*, 8:161.177.

45. Lü Tao in *QSW*, 73:1590.102–116.

46. Zheng Xie in *QSW*, 67:1465.330–336.

47. For some examples, see Yang Yi in *QSW*, 15:299.300.37, 15:300.54; Hu Su in *QSW*, 21:449.332; Zheng Xie in *QSW*, 67:1465.331.

48. Cai Xiang in *QSW*, 46:998.284. For similar references, see Wang Gui in *QSW*, 52:1137.287, 52:1137.289; Zheng Xie in *QSW*, 68:1477.122.

49. Patricia Ebrey has found that more wives outlived their husbands as first marriage partners than vice versa. Moreover, when men outlived their wives and remarried, their second wives were generally considerably younger. As a result, these marriages not only did not last as long, but also left many younger widows than those who remained unmarried after the deaths of their first partners. Ebrey, *The Inner Quarters*, 188–216.

50. For a sample of Northern Song officials with multiple mothers, see the following in *QSW*: Guo Jun, 3:53.284; Hu Su, 21:449.332, 22:467.212; Cai Xiang, 46:998.282–293; Wang Gui, 52:1140.342; Wang Anshi, 63:1371.181; Zheng Xie, 67:1466.333, 67:1466.336; Lü Tao, 73:1590.104, 73:1590.106, 73:1590.110–111; Liu Zhi, 77:1678.107; Wang Anli, 83:1799.28, 83:1799.34; Su Shi, 85:1852.202; Su Che, 94:2044.102–103, 94:2044.109.

51. Hu Su in *QSW*, 21:449.337–342.

52. Ibid., 21:449.334–336.

53. Ibid., 21:449.332.

54. Ebrey, *The Inner Quarters*, 216.

55. Sima, *Jiafan*, 7.643.

56. Chao Jiong in *QSW*, 7:137.143.

57. Han Qi in *QSW*, 40:856.66.

58. Durrant, Li, and Schaberg, *Zuozhuan*, 1:594–595 (Lord Xuan, 2.3b).

59. For an Eastern Han case concerning a mother encouraging her son to fulfill his official duty, leaving her home while sick, see Brown, "Mothers and Sons in Warring States and Han China," 157.

60. For an English translation of Ban Zhao's "Dongzheng fu," see Knechtges, *Wen Xuan or Selections of Refined Literature*, 2:173–179. One *li* equaled about one-third of a mile.

61. Hu, "Qianli huanyou cheng dishi, meinian fengjing shi taxiang," 65–107. Zheng Yaru, *Qin'en nanbao*, 41–46.

62. Earlier dynasties from the Jin to the Tang had allowed individual officials to take leave to care for parents who were over eighty or seriously ill. Zheng Yaru, *Qin'en nanbao*, 54–64.

63. Song Zhenzong in *QSW*, 11:217.15.

64. Ibid., 11:218.20. An official petitioned to return home to care for his father, aged ninety, based on this or an earlier policy. Sun Shi in *QSW*, 9:193.363.

65. Song Renzong in *QSW*, 44:942.19.

66. Ibid., 45:963.2.

67. Ibid., 45:963.20, 45:966.72, 45:978.323.

68. Deng Xiaonan, *Songdai wenguan xuanren zhidu zhu cengmian*, 201. Mr. Jiang, for example, was praised for trading an appointment with a colleague, Zhu, so that Zhu could serve much closer to home. Li Xian in *QSW*, 27:578.203.

69. For a comprehensive study of the Song personnel system, including the implementation of the Principle of Avoidance, see W. W. Lo, *An Introduction to the Civil Service of Sung China*, and Miao Shumei, *Songdai guanyuan xueren he guanli zhidu*. For the implementation of the Principle of Avoidance, see Miao Shumei, "Songdai guanyuan huibi fa shulun," 24–30.

70. For a sample of these records, see Li Zi in *QSW*, 16:329.175; Wen Tong in *QSW*, 51:1102.71; Sima Guang in *QSW*, 54:1176.181; Han Zongshi in *QSW*, 84:1831.204; Wang Liangcai in *QSW*, 128:2773.204.

71. For some examples, see *SHY, zhiguan*, 46.2b, 46.2b–3a, 77.23b–26b, 77.34b, 77.45b, 77.51b, 77.60a–b, 78.23b–24a; *SS*, 298.9899, 298.9918, 304.10075–10076, 311.10202, 318.10362, 331.10643.

72. Song Qi in *QSW*, 25:527.124.

73. Zheng Xie in *QSW*, 68:1481.187.

74. Cai Xiang in *QSW*, 46:1005.404.

75. Ibid., 46:1005.405.

76. Lü Tao in *QSW*, 74:1611.70–72.

77. Ibid., 74:1611.71. In 1020, an imperial edict allowed natives of Sichuan and Shaanxi to serve three hundred *li* away from their home regions once every three terms. *Song da zhaoling ji*, 161.610–611.

78. Yang Yi in *QSW*, 15:302.82; *SS*, 281.9517.

79. Shen Gua in *QSW*, 78:1686.45–46.

80. Ge Shengzhong in *QSW*, 143:3076.69.

81. Based on Thomas H. C. Lee's calculation, the number of civil servants in the Northern Song fluctuated between ten thousand and forty thousand, with the early decades having the smallest bureaucracy. Starting from the mid-eleventh century, the number of officials surpassed twenty thousand, when rhetoric on redundant officials appeared frequently. T. H. C. Lee, "Songdai guanyuan shu de tongji."

82. In one case, an official was demoted for making a detour to visit his mother while on a business trip. Du Chun in *QSW*, 79:1722.151.

83. Wang Yucheng in *QSW*, 8:161.183.

84. Su Shunqin in *QSW*, 41:880.125.

85. Shen Gua, in *QSW*, 78:1696.41–42.

86. Huang Tingjian in *QSW*, 104:2282.322–323.

87. Song Zhenzong in *QSW*, 12:239.50.

88. Song Renzong in *QSW*, 44:955.295.

89. Yang Yi in *QSW*, 15:299.37.

90. Song Qi in *QSW*, 25:528.138.

91. Lü Tao in *QSW*, 74:1613.95–96. For another example of similar filial acts, see Liu Zhi in *QSW*, 77:1678.99–100.

92. Su Shunqin in *QSW*, 41:882.135.

93. Li Zhiyi in *QSW*, 112:2429.258–259.

94. *SHY, zhiguan*, 77.24a–b.

95. *SS*, 301.10005.

96. *SHY, zhiguan*, 68.17a.

97. *SHY, zhiguan*, 68.20a.

98. Li Xin in *QSW*, 134:2890.75–76.

99. Shen Gua in *QSW*, 78:1696.42.

100. Zhang Yong in *QSW*, 6:108.68.

101. *SHY, zhiguan*, 65.6b.

102. Zhang Fangping in *QSW*, 37:796.223; Lü Tao in *QSW*, 74:1615.127.

103. Fan Zhongyan in *QSW*, 19:389.42–43.

104. Su Shunqin in *QSW*, 41:880.115.

105. Su Song in *QSW*, 62:1352.171–172.

106. Bi Zhongyou in *QSW*, 111:2405.170.

107. A translation by Patricia Ebrey can be found in Wang, *Images of Women in Chinese Thought and Culture*, 380–390.

108. Knapp, *Selfless Offspring*, 164–165.

109. Fan Zhongyan in *QSW*, 19:389.43.

110. Bossler, *Courtesans, Concubines, and the Cult of Female Fidelity*. A parallel can be seen in abundant records about merchants leaving wives at home and living with *chang* women, who combined concubines and courtesans. Tian, *Songdai Shangren jiating*, 93–102.

111. Su Shunqin in *QSW*, 41:880.115.

112. Xiao Su in *QSW*, 78:1701.136.

113. Wang Yucheng in *QSW*, 8:161.167.

114. Ibid., 8:161.185; Su Shunqin in *QSW*, 41:881.129.

115. *SS*, 287.9660.

116. For a discussion of the Bao family and the Baos as filial exemplars, see C. E. Zhang: "The Rise and Fall of a Northern Song Family" and "A Family of Filial Exemplars."

117. Bao Zheng, *Bao Zheng ji jiaozhu*, 265.

118. Ibid., 265–267.

119. *SS*, 314.10282.

120. Tang Weixi in *QSW*, 65:1426.360; Yang Jie in *QSW*, 75:1646.284; Liu Zhi in *QSW*, 77:1680.133; Zou Hao in *QSW*, 131:2829.133.

121. Ge Shengzhong in *QSW*, 143:3075.50; *SS*, 333.10705.

122. Yang Jie in *QSW*, 75:1645.265.

123. Knapp, "Creeping Absolutism," 65–91.

124. In my study of dozens of unfilial stories contained in Song *biji* I found genuine concern on the part of the authors to reform minds and behaviors by prescribing severe punishments for the offenders. See C. E. Zhang, "Negative Role Models," 39–55.

125. Ouyang Xiu in *QSW*, 35:750.290.

126. Ibid., 35:750.289–291, 753.338–339, 755.361–362. Mei Xun and Mei Yaochen's official biographies can be found in *SS*, 301.9984–9985, 413.13091–13092. For some thorough studies of Mei Yaochen and Ouyang, see Chaves, *Mei Yao-ch'en and the Development of Early Sung Poetry*; Egan, *The Literary Works of Ou-yang Hsiu*.

127. Ouyang Xiu in *QSW*, 35:750.291, 755.362.

128. Yang Jie in *QSW*, 75:1646.276–278.

129. Ouyang Xiu in *QSW*, 35:753.338.

130. Ibid., 35:753.338.

131. We can almost be certain that Rang's sons were protected into officialdom by Xun, as no extant evidence points to any of them having passed the examinations.

132. Ouyang Xiu in *QSW*, 35:753.339.

133. Yang Jie in *QSW*, 75:1646.276–278.

134. Ibid., 75:1646.277.

135. Ouyang Xiu in *QSW*, 35:753.339.

136. References to office-holding sons standing next to or behind parents, especially in front of guests, appeared often in Song writing. For more examples, see Ding Chuanjing, *Songren yishi huibian*, 4.121, 5.207.

137. We do know that Mei Yaochen engaged in other filial activities, one of them being a commemorative hall erected in his father's and uncle's honor in 1055. Mei Yaochen in *QSW*, 28:593.165–166.

138. The separation of Miss Zhu and her sons was well documented by Zeng Gong in multiple memorials. See, for example, Zeng in *QSW*, 57:1243.201, 1243.203, 1243.204–5, 1246.264.

139. Bossler, *Courtesans, Concubines, and the Cult of Female Fidelity*, 128.

140. Han Qi in *QSW*, 40:856.66.

141. Yin Zhu in *QSW*, 28:590.104; Wang Gui in *QSW*, 53:1163.342; Chen Jian in *QSW*, 48:1052.334–335.

142. Li Qingchen in *QSW*, 79:1715.3.

143. Han Qi in *QSW*, 40:856.66.

144. Ibid., 40:856.67–68.

145. Ding Chuanjing, *Songren yishi huibian*, 4.127, 10.468. *SS*, 255.8913, 8918.

146. *SS*, 255.8913, 8918; Wang Yong, *Yan yi yi mou lu*, 2.17; Ding Chuanjing, *Songren yishi huibian*, 4.127.

147. *SS*, 255.8918.

148. Liu Ban in *QSW*, 69:1504.204.

149. Ding Chuanjing, *Songren yishi huibian*, 10.468; *SS*, 302.10018.

150. Su Shi in *QSW*, 91:1977.107.

151. Qian Mingyi in *QSW*, 48:1046.253; Wen Tong in *QSS*, 435.5331; Wang Anshi in *QSS*, 568.6716; Lü Dafang in *QSS*, 620.7395; Su Shi in *QSS*, 791.9163.

152. *SS*, 456.13404–13405.

153. One of the most famous stories involved Huang Xiangjian, who left Suzhou to look for his parents during the Ming-Qing transition. Lü Miaofen, "Ming Qing Zhongguo wanli xun-qin de wenhua shijian"; Kindall: "The Paintings of Huang Xiangjian's Filial Journey to the Southwest" and *Geo-Narratives of a Filial Son*.

Chapter 2: Mourning and Filial Piety

1. This narrative is based on Yan Jie, *Ouyang Xiu nianpu*.

2. Wu Chong in *QSW*, 78:1698.80.

3. For four major studies on mourning in imperial China, see Brown, *The Politics of Mourning in Early China*; Choi, *Death Rituals and Politics in Northern Song China*; Knapp, *Selfless Offspring*; and Kutcher, *Mourning in Late Imperial China*.

4. Confucius, *The Analects*, 17.21, 3.4. In Ivanhoe and Van Norden, *Readings in Classical Chinese Philosophy*, 46, 7. Olberding, "I Know Not 'Seems.'"

5. Mengzi, *Mengzi*, 3A.2.

6. "Discourse on Ritual," *Xunzi*; in Ivanhoe and Van Norden, *Readings in Classical Chinese Philosophy*, 271. Also see Radice, *The Ways of Filial Piety in Early China*.

7. For comprehensive treatments of this topic, see Chen Huawen, *Sangzang shi*; Ding Linghua, *Zhongguo sangfu zhidu shi*; Xu Jijun, *Zhongguo sangzang shi*; Zhang Jingming, *Xianqin sangfu zhidu kao*.

8. For a thorough discussion of mourning for mothers, see Y. Zhou, "The Status of Mothers in the Early Chinese Mourning System."

9. Wu Zhao in *Quan Tang wen xinbian*, 2:97.1132. For a similar edict issued several decades later, see Tang Xuanzong, *Quan Tang wen xinbian*, 1:34.415.

10. Ding Linghua, *Zhongguo sangfu zhidu shi*, 236.

11. Brown, *The Politics of Mourning in Early China*; Brown and Fodde-Reguer, "Rituals Without Rules."

12. Knapp, "Borrowing Legitimacy from the Dead," 192.

13. Knapp, *Selfless Offspring*, 145–163; Ding Linghua, *Zhongguo sangfu zhidu shi*, 242–244.

14. Ding Linghua, *Zhongguo sangfu zhidu shi*, 251–258.

15. Zhangsun, *Tanglü shuyi*, 2.35; 12.236–237; 13.257–259; 22.414–416; 23.432–433; 24.435–438

16. *Datang kaiyuan li*, chapters 138–149.

17. Ding Linghua, *Zhongguo sangfu zhidu shi*, 269–270; Zheng Yaru, *Qin'en nanbao*, 82–93.

18. Ding Linghua, *Zhongguo sangfu zhidu shi*, 270–273; Xu Jijun, *Zhongguo sangzang shi*, 354.

19. Dou, *Song xing tong*, 2.23, 10.183–186, 13.242.

20. This discussion is limited to policies regarding civil servants. Military personnel were not allowed to wear mourning for three years throughout the entire Northern Song period. In 1041, an imperial edict stipulated that low-ranking military officers be given a month's leave upon a parent's death. Song Renzong in *QSW*, 45:964.35. For a general summary of mourning policies for military personnel, see Zheng Xia in *QSW*, 100:2176.2–3.

21. Song Zhenzong in *QSW*, 10:213.364, 11:220.88.

22. For a set of such documents, see Zhang Gang in *QSW*, 168:3666.195–196, 168:3667.206, 168:3673.315, 168:3673.320.

23. Most of these policies can be found in *SS*, 125.2922–2925.

24. Song Taizong in *QSW*, 4:69.181.

25. Ibid., 4:71.242.

26. *SHY, zhiguan*, 77.1b–2a.

27. Song Zhenzong in *QSW*, 10:214.376.

28. Zhang Yong in *QSW*, 6:110.99.

29. Song Zhenzong in *QSW*, 12:241.116.

30. Song Taizong in *QSW*, 4:76.356. *SS*, 125.2922.

31. *SS*, 125.2924.

32. Zhang Guo in *QSW*, 14:280.108; *SHY, zhiguan*, 71.2b–3b.

33. Liu Ye in *QSW*, 8:169.333.

34. Lorge, *The Unification of China*.

35. W. W. Lo, *An Introduction to the Civil Service of Sung China*.

36. For a general history of Emperor Renzong's reign, see McGrath, "The Reigns of Jen-tsung (1022–1063) and Ying-tsung (1063–1067)," 279–346.

37. Song Renzong in *QSW*, 44:959.369.

38. *SS*, 125.2922.

39. Ibid.

40. Shi Yu in *QSW*, 8:173.408. In fact, so many people wore mourning clothes to work that in 1035, an official proposed that mourners be allowed to participate in all but a few court activities. Zhang Dexiang in *QSW*, 15:320.401. A 1047 memorial added that officials in mourning should not be allowed to participate in sacrifices to Heaven and Earth, revealing how many officials in active service were wearing mourning. Shao Bi in *QSW*, 29:617.169–170.

41. Yang Yi, Wang Sui, and Dong Xiyan were recalled within a few months to half a year after the death of a parent. *SHY, zhiguan*, 71.3b, 77.4a–b. For more examples, see Yang Tingmei in *QSW*, 3:41.39; Teng Zongliang in *QSW*, 19:396.189–190; Song Qi in *QSW*, 25:528.128. *SS*, 256.8932, 262.9072, 262.9081, 263.9112, 263.9113, 265.9161, 267.9203, 287.9643.

42. Song Qi in *QSW*, 25:528.134.

43. Liu Chang in *QSW*, 59:1281.112–113.

44. Song Renzong in *QSW*, 45:978.317.

45. *SS*, 313.10254.

46. See multiple examples in *SHY, zhiguan*, 77.5b–7b.

47. Ibid., 11.6b

48. Ibid., 11.2b.

49. Ding Jianjun and Jia Yafang, "Jianlun Songdai dingyou zhidu dui guanyuan shitu de yingxiang," and Zu Hui, "Songdai rongli yiyuan wenti yanjiu." By the Southern Song, court officials were known to have kept parents' deaths secret to avoid taking mourning leave. Emperor Gaozong almost executed someone for doing this, but he eventually had the man's face tattooed and sent him into exile. Zhang Duanyi, *Gui er ji*, 3.57–58.

50. Liu Ban in *QSW*, 69:1496.201.

51. Zhao Tingzhi in *QSW*, 97:2107.8; Fan Dang in *QSW*, 101:2216.342.

52. *SS*, 320.10410.

53. *SS*, 329.10602.

54. Miranda Brown has found that members of the Eastern Han political elite went out of their way to make public demonstrations of their personal devotion to mothers, while playing down their mourning of lords and fathers. The ratio of mourning mothers to fathers is more than two to one. Brown, *The Politics of Mourning in Early China*, 67. Of the filial tales that Keith Knapp studies, 63 percent feature filial sons taking care of mothers, and only 25 percent mention fathers. Knapp, *Selfless Offspring*, 134–135.

55. Knapp, *Selfless Offspring*, 137–151.

56. Wang Yucheng in *QSW*, 8:161.186; Su Shunqin in *QSW*, 41:880.111.

57. *SS*, 263.9107.

58. Shen Liao in *QSW*, 79:1728.243.

59. Fan Chunren in *QSW*, 71:1555.306; *SS*, 330.10623.

60. Lü Tao in *QSW*, 74:1614.107. For more similar references, see Yang Tingmei in *QSW*, 3:41.39; Yang Yi in *QSW*, 15:299.35, 15:300.51; Fan Zhongyan in *QSW*, 19:388.19; Fan Zhen in *QSW*, 40:872.296–297; Zhang Gang in *QSW*, 168:3678.396; *SS*, 257.8948. 267.9203, 270.9244, 270.9254, 287.9643, 305.10083, 316.10326, 320.10413, 333.10699, 333.10705, 336.10757, 336.10770.

61. Knapp, *Selfless Offspring*, 147–153.

62. Song Qi in *QSW*, 25:528.143.

63. Fan Zhongyan in *QSW*, 19:387.17.

64. Su Song in *QSW*, 62:1346.86.

65. Knapp, *Selfless Offspring*, 144–146.

66. Zheng Xie in *QSW*, 68:1480.182.

67. Liu Ban in *QSW*, 69:1506.231.

68. Song Qi in *QSW*, 25:528.132.

69. Han Qi in *QSW*, 40:859.127.

70. Yang Jie in *QSW*, 75:1645.265.

71. Huang Tingjian in *QSW*, 105:2291.175–184.

72. Ibid., 105:2291.175.

73. Ibid., 105:2291.176–177, 105:2291.183–184, 105:2291.187.

74. Ibid., 105:2292.194.

75. *Lumu* appeared early in Chinese history, and the Tang even witnessed women practicing *lumu*. Ding Linghua, *Zhongguo sangfu zhidu shi*, 269–270.

76. *SS*, 327.10557.

77. Su Song in *QSW*, 62:1351.158.

78. *SS*, 318.10369. For similar references, see Su Shunqin in *QSW*, 41:880.123; Liu Ban in *QSW*, 69:1506.225, 69:1506.231. "Not entering the inner quarter" was a euphemism for the mourner's not having sex.

79. Yu Jing in *QSW*, 27:575.150.

80. For a sample of this activity, see Fan Zhongyan in *QSW*, 19:389.41, 19:390.67; Su Song in *QSW*, 62:1344.59, 62:1351.158; Liu Ban in *QSW*, 69:1506.225; Lü Tao in *QSW*, 74:1611.70; Shen Gua in *QSW*, 78:1694.13; Xu Jingheng in *QSW*, 144:3098.96.

81. Yu Jing in *QSW*, 27:575.151.

82. The close bonds between parents and sons were even known to move outlaws as well as emperors and transform bad men and the natural realm. Brown, "Mothers and Sons in Warring States and Han China"; Knapp, "Reverent Caring."

83. Hu Su in *QSW*, 22:476.216.

84. Fan Zuyu in *QSW*, 98:2140.188–189.

85. Fan Zhongyan in *QSW*, 19:389.41.

86. Lü Tao in *QSW*, 74:1612.88–90.

87. Ge Shengzhong in *QSW*, 143:3075.58.

88. Ibid.

89. Knapp, *Selfless Offspring*, 59.

90. Kinney, "The Theme of the Precocious Child in Early Chinese Literature," and Wu Hung, "Private Love and Public Duty."

91. *SS*, 262.9067.

92. Liu Chang in *QSW*, 59:1295.386.

93. Yang Shi in *QSW*, 125:2698.73.

94. Ge Shengzhong in *QSW*, 143:3075.52.

95. Ouyang Xiu in *QSW*, 35:757.388.

96. Shen Gou in *QSW*, 74:1628.350.

97. Song Qi in *QSW*, 25:528.133.

98. Ibid., 25:527.118.

99. Sima Guang in *QSW*, 56:1225.269.

100. Zheng Xie in *QSW*, 68:1479.167. For more references, see Hu Su in *QSW*, 22:469.244; Lü Tao in *QSW*, 74:1614.116; Fan Chunren in *QSW*, 71:1555.309, 71:1557.336; Li Zhaoqi in *QSW*, 121:2615.234, 121:2615.238; Yang Shi in *QSW*, 125:2696.51, 125:2698.73.

101. For an epitaph for a boy from the Tang, see Shields, "Grieving for a Married Daughter and a Grandson."

102. Han Qi in *QSW*, 40:856.70–72, 856.75–77, 858.105–106.

103. Ibid., 40:856.75–76.

104. For a sample of these requests, see Wang Yucheng in *QSW*, 8:161.186; Yang Yi in *QSW*, 15:300.51; Fan Zhongyan in *QSW*, 19:390.56, 19:390.59; Song Qi in *QSW*, 25:528.128, 25:528.134; Fan Zhen in *QSW*, 40:872.301; Su Song in *QSW*, 62:1344.55.

105. Su Shunqin in *QSW*, 41:880.110; Liu Ban in *QSW*, 69:1506.230–231.

106. Wang Yucheng in *QSW*, 8:161.186.

107. Song Qi in *QSW*, 25:529.145.

108. Lü Tao in *QSW*, 74:1611.84.

109. Ibid., 74:1613.98.

110. This phenomenon is seen in frequent references to property acquisition, often in or near the capital or an area where an official had previously served. Su Song once remarked that from the Qingli reign period (1041–1048) onward, Ruyin (in Henan) became a favorite destination for retirement or a home away from home due to its convenient location, fertile land, and high living standards. "No one who has decided to settle down would deny it as the most desirable location." Su Song in *QSW*, 62:1351.159. In fact, so many purchased properties away from their native places that when Zhang Jiang (1009–1084) approached retirement and planned on returning to his native region in Qiantang, the emperor was puzzled and even offered to subsidize him to buy a house in the capital. Su Song in *QSW*, 62:1342.30.

111. Ouyang Xiu in *QSW*, 36:759.20–21.

112. Su Shi wrote five letters to Fan Yuanchang about the passing of Fan's father. Su Shi in *QSW*, 87:1895.387–389. Su wrote in one letter, "The grief and hardship you will experience will be indescribable when you accompany [your father's body] home from ten thousand *li* away in this summer heat." Su Shi in *QSW*, 87:1895.388.

113. Fan Zhongyan in *QSW*, 19:388.35.

114. Su Shunqin in *QSW*, 41:880.123.

115. Su Song in *QSW*, 62:1352.178–179.

116. Sima Guang in *QSW*, 56:1226.270.

117. Shen Gua in *QSW*, 78:1696.50.

118. Yu Jing in *QSW*, 27:576.156.

119. Ebrey, *Chu Hsi's Family Rituals*, 66–67, 115.

120. Sima continued to describe the customs of the vulgar and uneducated, who indulged in all sorts of activities that were in strict violation of the ritual codes. Sima, *Simashi shuyi*, 6.65.

121. Yang Yi in *QSW*, 15:300.62.

122. Song Qi in *QSW*, 25:528.135.

123. Su Shunqin in *QSW*, 41:881.136–138.

124. *SS*, 294.9822.

125. Ibid., 316.10320.

126. Su Song in *QSW*, 62:1348.119.

127. *SS*, 336.10770.

128. Ibid., 340.10847.

129. E. L. Davis, *Society and the Supernatural in Song China*, 171–199.

130. Ebrey: *Confucianism and Family Rituals in Imperial China*, 77–80, 85–101, and "The Response of the Sung State to Popular Funeral Practices."

131. Xu Jingheng in *QSW*, 144:3098.95–96.

132. Xu Jingheng in *QSW*, 144:3098.101.

133. Ibid., *QSW*, 144:3099.110.

134. Ge Shengzhong in *QSW*, 143:3075.50–52.

135. For a survey of ritual stipulations on the mourning of mothers, see Y. Zhou, "The Status of Mothers in the Early Chinese Mourning System."

136. The status of sons with concubine mothers varied as well. Tang Changru has found that in the Han, men born to concubine mothers were not severely scorned. It was in the Period of Disunity that sons of main wives and concubine mothers became more clearly defined as to their parentage; this was especially true in the north. Tang, "Du Yanshi jiaxun, houqu pian lun nanbei dishu shenfen de chayi."

137. For several major studies about concubines and courtesans, see the following: Bossler: *Courtesans, Concubines, and the Cult of Female Fidelity*; "Shifting Identities"; and "Men, Women, and Gossip in Song China"; Ebrey: "Concubines in Sung China" and *The Inner Quarters*.

138. *SS*, 125.2929.

139. Ibid.

140. Han Qi in *QSW*, 40:856.68.

141. Li Qingchen in *QSW*, 79:1717.39.

142. Ding Chuanjing, *Songren yishi huibian*, 8.352.

143. Han Qi in *QSS*, 320.3984.

144. Fu Bi in *QSW*, 29:609.47–51.

145. Han Qi in *QSW*, 40:856.65.

146. Ibid.

147. Yin Zhu in *QSW*, 28:590.102–105; Fu Bi in *QSW*, 29:609.47–51. Nor did Han Guohua's official biography mention Miss Hu. *SS*, 277.9442–9444.

148. Xue Shen in *QSW*, 20:409.2.

149. Liu Ban in *QSW*, 69:1507.245

150. Su Song in *QSW*, 62:1340.3.

151. Ibid.

152. Yang Jie in *QSW*, 75:1646.281.

153. Su Song in *QSW*, 62:1349.136.

154. Ge Shengzhong in *QSW*, 143:3077.84. Bossler, *Courtesans, Concubines, and the Cult of Female Fidelity*, 114–115.

155. Ebrey, *The Inner Quarters*, 231; Bossler, *Courtesans, Concubines, and the Cult of Female Fidelity*, 121–127; Smith, "Shen-tsung's Reign and the New Policies of Wang An-shih," 365.

156. Song Shenzong in *QSW*, 113:2443.135, 113:2445.158.

157. *SS*, 125.2929.

158. See the following in *QSW*: Xie Jingwen, 65:1424.318; Fan Bailu, 76:1655.41–42; Fan Yu, 76:1658.81; Zhang Kan, 76:1663.173; Xue Changchao, 76:1664.197; Su Shi, 91:1977.107; Lin Dan, 92:2006.289–291; Wang Yansou, 102:2222.3–5; Song Shenzong, 113:2443.135; Song Shenzong, 113:2445.158.

159. Xue Changchao in *QSW*, 76:1664.197.

160. Bossler, *Courtesans, Concubines, and the Cult of Female Fidelity*, 124–128.

161. Li Ding's notoriety was further propagated in at least four Song *biji*, collected in Ding Chuanjing, *Songren yishi huibian*, 13.707–708.

162. Su Shi in *QSW*, 91:1977.107.

163. Ebrey, *The Inner Quarters*, 228.

164. Ibid.

Chapter 3: When and Where?

1. This narrative is based on Su Song's *shendaobei* for Liu Juzheng, Liu Zhi's account of his father's death and burial, and Liu Zhi's official biography in *Songshi*. Su Song in *QSW*, 62:1344.60–64; Liu Zhi in *QSW*, 77:1678.103–106; *SS*, 340.10849–10858.

2. For in-depth studies of factionalism in the Northern Song, see Levine, *Divided by a Common Language*; Luo Jiaxiang, *Pengdang zhizheng yu Beisong zhengzhi*; Shen Qinsong, *Beisong wenren yu dangzheng*; Smith: *Taxing Heaven's Storehouse* and "Anatomies of Reform."

3. Edward L. Davis has found that "Since the beginning of the Song, the use of merit cloisters (*gongde si*) had become a necessary staple of filial expression and a much sought-after privilege of China's super-elite." E. L. Davis, *Society and the Supernatural in Song China*, 172.

4. For a detailed case study of another equally time-consuming burial event, see C. E. Zhang, "How Long Did It Take to Plan a Funeral?"

5. Wang Yucheng in *QSW*, 8:160–161.155–186; Yu Jing in *QSW*, 27:573–576.116–160; Zheng Xie in *QSW*, 68:1480–1482.176–213. I have included in this calculation only the epitaphs that specified both the place of death and place of burial of the deceased.

6. Su Song in *QSW*, 62:1350.153, 62:1352.171–181; Shen Gua in *QSW*, 78:1694.14–15, 1694.17–18, 1696.41–42.

7. Yang Shuda, *Handai hunsang lisu kao*, 129–138; Pu, "Ideas Concerning Death and Burial in Pre-Han and Han China," 25–62.

8. *Jinshu*, 82.2138.

9. Crowell, "Northern Emigres and the Problems of Census Registration under the Eastern Jin and Southern Dynasties," and T. M. Davis, *Entombed Epigraphy and Commemorative Culture in Early Medieval China*.

10. Tackett, *The Destruction of the Medieval Chinese Aristocracy*; Zheng Yaru, *Qin'en nanbao*, 126–146.

11. Shi Jie in *QSW*, 29:621.227–229, 29:624.261–262, 30:634.17–21; Ouyang Xiu in *QSW*, 35:755.368.

12. Yin Zhu in *QSW*, 28:588.59.

13. Wu Songdi, *Zhongguo yimin shi*, 232–268.

14. Fan Chunren in *QSW*, 71:1559.360.

15. Ibid., 71:1694.3.

16. Yin Zhu in *QSW*, 28:588.63, 28:589.75, 28:589.77, 28:589.92, 28:589.94, 28:590.100, 28:590.121, 28:590.124.

17. Fan Zhongyan in *QSW*, 19:390.57–61.

18. Su Song in *QSW*, 62:1343.41.

19. Ibid., 62:1346.84–87.

20. Fan Chunren in *QSW*, 71:1559.360.

21. Su Song in *QSW*, 62:1346.90.

22. Teng Zongliang himself died in Suzhou and was buried in the same graveyard. Fan Zhongyan in *QSW*, 19:388.32–33, 19:390.67.

23. Chao Buzhi in *QSW*, 127:2742.86–87.

24. Lü Tao in *QSW*, 74:1612.87.

25. Liu Zhi in *QSW*, 77:1681.160.

26. Ibid., 77:1681.164.

27. Liang Hongsheng's survey of 371 Jiangxi natives shows that a significant number of office-holding men and their families were not returned to Jiangxi in the Northern Song, especially those who died far away from Jiangxi. However, in the Southern Song, almost all were returned to Jiangxi. Liang Hongsheng, "Jiangxi Songdai muzhi jiqi sangqi kao." Han Guihua's study of nineteen cases has revealed that the majority of Song men were buried, within two to three years, in their ancestral graveyards. Han Guihua, "Muzhiming zhong suojian Songdai guanyuan guizang wenti." Han's findings do not correspond with the findings of this current study, which has a much larger sample.

28. Fan Zhongyan in *QSW*, 19:391.79.

29. Ouyang Xiu in *QSW*, 33:705.219.

30. Su Song was an influential political figure in the 1070s to 1090s. In addition to multiple posts in the capital, Su served in a dozen or so local positions but not once in Fujian. Based on extant material, he might never have visited his native place in adulthood. To learn more about Su's life, see his funerary inscription by Zeng Zhao, his record of conduct by Zou Hao, his and his father's official biographies in *Songshi*, and the epitaph that he authored for his uncle, Su Yi. Zeng Zhao in *QSW*, 110:2383.119–125; Zou Hao in *QSW*, 132:2843.1–17; *SS*, 340.10859–10869, 294.9808–9814; Su Song in *QSW*, 62:1352.168–171; Yan Zhongqi, "Su Song nianbiao," 1244–1280; Bai, *Zhongguo tongshi, di qi juan*, 1629–1645.

31. Zeng Zhao in *QSW*, 110:2383.119–125; Su Xiangxian, *Chengxiang Weigong tanxun*, 2.1127–1131.

32. Yan Zhongqi, "Su Song nianbiao," 1252. One plausible reason behind this arrangement was that the family owned properties in the Jiangnan region and that Su Shen felt more at home there than in Tong'an, where he had spent little of his adult life. This speculation is supported by a common practice of the time. Northern Song scholar-officials often purchased estates for retirement from the capital and their native place. In multiple documents, Su Shi refers to having purchased property in Changzhou (in Jiangsu) for retirement. Su Shi in *QSW*, 86:1863.130; 88:1901.34, 88:1921.436.

33. Su Song in *QSW*, 62:1352.168.

34. Ibid., 62:1352.168–171.

35. Su Xiangxian, *Chengxiang Weigong tanxun*, 3.1134.

36. Su Song in *QSS*, 523.6342.

37. Ibid.

38. These like-minded families were from Jiangxi, Sichuan, and Fujian. For a few examples, see ibid., 62:1352.171, 62:1352.179.

39. Su Xiangxian, *Chengxiang Weigong tanxun*, 3.1134.

40. Ibid., 6.1159.

41. Ibid., 6.1152.

42. Sima, *Simashi shuyi*, chapters 5–10.

43. Bi Zhongyou in *QSW*, 111:2405.168; Yin Zhu in *QSW*, 28:588.68. In the Han, most

burials occurred within a few months, with a broad range between 7 to 433 days. Yang Shuda, *Handai hunsang lisu kao*, 87–97.

44. Yin Zhu in *QSW*, 28:590.110; Su Song in *QSW*, 62:1343.49–53.

45. Liang Hongsheng's study of 371 Song epitaphs of Jiangxi natives shows that over half of the deceased (56 percent) were buried within a year, but quite a number of burials took one to three years (37 percent), and about 25 percent took more than two years. Liang Hongsheng, "Songdai Jiangxi muzhi jiqi sangqi kao."

46. Han Qi in *QSW*, 40:857.92–93.

47. Yu Jing in *QSW*, 27:573.116–160.

48. Chao Buzhi in *QSW*, 127:2742–2746.71–155.

49. Song Qi in *QSW*, 25:528.140.

50. Ibid., 25:528.140–142, 25:529.144–147.

51. In the Song, Buddhist temples and local officials were known to have built public grave-yards as alternatives for cremation or the public exposure of corpses. Jin Zhongshu, "Songdai jizhong shehui fuli zhidu"; von Eschenbach, "Public Graveyards of the Song Dynasty."

52. Shen Gua in *QSW*, 78:1696.50.

53. Ibid.; *SS*, 314.10289; Fan Zuyu in *QSW*, 98:2248.302; Song Shenzong in *QSW*, 115:2485.210.

54. Shi Jie in *QSW*, 29:621.228.

55. Sima Guang in *QSW*, 56:1219.157–158.

56. Ibid.

57. Lü Tao in *QSW*, 74:1613.103.

58. Cheng Yi in *QSW*, 80:1756.319–320.

59. Song Zhezong in *QSW*, 150:3240.287.

60. Sima Guang in *QSW*, 56:1219.157–158.

61. Northern Song tombs often took the form of simple coffin chambers designed for the burial of a single individual. Tomb goods were often items for daily use and mostly consisted of pottery and lacquer. Filial tales and bird and flower motifs were staples; so were land deeds. Asim, "Status Symbol and Insurance Policy"; Deng Fei, "Guanyu Song Jin muzang zhong xiaoxing tu de sikao"; Hansen: *Negotiating Daily Life in Traditional China* and "Why Bury Contracts in Tombs"; Kuhn, "Decoding Tombs of the Song Elite"; Laing, "Auspicious Motifs in Ninth- to Thirteenth-Century Chinese Tombs"; Lin, "Underground Wooden Architecture in Brick"; Zhu Xiaoli, *Chuannan Songmu shike tushi fenxi ji shuzi tapian yanjiu*. For a detailed study of a Song tomb, see Su Bai, *Baisha Songmu*; for some focused studies of the burials of some leading Northern Song figures, see Shaanxi sheng kaogu yanjiuyuan, "Lüshi jiazu mudi," and Stahl, "Su Shi's Orthodox Burial."

62. As early as 982, the government issued its first decree on simple funerals and burials. *Song da zhaoling ji*, 182.659. Also see *SS*, 125.2917–2919.

63. For a general history of *jianzang* (simple burial), see Xu Jijun, *Zhongguo sangzang shi*, 420–424, 440–450. For an introduction to the rhetoric and practice of simple burial in the Song, see Kuhn, "Decoding Tombs of the Song Elite," and Tsao, *Differences Preserved*. A number of Northern Song figures left specific instructions on planning simple funerals. See *SS*, 310.10192; Sima Guang in *QSW*, 56:1219.157–158; Cheng Yi in *QSW*, 80:1750.213–215; Fan Zuyu in *QSW*, 98:2128.37–39; Ge Shengzhong in *QSW*, 143:3075.52; Xu Han in *QSW*, 145:3135.6–7.

64. For a detailed discussion of funeral feasts, ruinous expenses, and the use of Buddhists,

see Ebrey, *Confucianism and Family Rituals in Imperial China*, especially the chapter on "Combating Heterodoxy and Vulgarity in Weddings and Funerals." For information on the participation of Buddhist and Daoist monks in death rituals, see E. L. Davis, *Society and the Supernatural in Song China*; and Morgan, "Inscribed Stones." The use of *mingqi* (spirit articles), tomb art, and architectural features could add to the burial costs. See Hong: *Theater for the Dead*; "Mechanism of Life for the Netherworld"; and "Changing Roles of the Tomb Portrait"; Lin, "Underground Wooden Architecture in Brick."

65. For a description of the cost of a Tang funeral, see Tackett, *The Destruction of the Medieval Chinese Aristocracy*, 17–25.

66. Cheng Minsheng, *Songdai wujia yanjiu*, 359–364, 454–465.

67. Ibid., 572–573.

68. Cai Xiang, for example, warned against the ruinous cost of funeral feasts at his local post in Fujian. Ebrey, *Confucianism and Family Rituals*, 70–71.

69. Han Qi in *QSW*, 40:856.70, 40:858.100–106.

70. Chen Shidao in *QSW*, 124:2670.8.

71. Wang Yucheng in *QSW*, 8:161.176–177.

72. Ouyang Xiu in *QSW*, 35:755.367–369; *SS*, 432.12833–12836.

73. Shi Jie in *QSW*, 29:625.270–271.

74. Lü Tao in *QSW*, 74:1611.69, 74:1612.85, 74:1613.100–105, 74:1614.108–118, 74:1615.128.

75. Ibid., 74:1613.104–105.

76. Sima Guang in *QSW*, 56:1227.292.

77. *SS*, 124.2902–2912.

78. The *Songshi* includes a summary of the detailed regulations specifying which funeral expenses the government would cover for high officials before 1068. *SS*, 124.2909–2910; Hansen, *Negotiating Daily Life in Traditional China*, 164–165. For a sample of references in epitaphs, see Hu Su in *QSW*, 22:466.217, 22:467.221, 22:468.223–233, 22:469.241–248; Su Song in *QSW*, 62:1340.9, 62:1341.15, 62:1341.21, 62:1344.56, 62:1352.178; Li Qingchen in *QSW*, 79:1718.55, 79:1718.59, 79:1718.62–63.

79. Song Zhenzong in *QSW*, 11:220.80.

80. Song Xiang in *QSW*, 21:433.43.

81. Su Song in *QSW*, 62:1346.91–94.

82. Wen Yanbo in *QSW*, 30:651.305.

83. Yang Shuda, *Handai hunsang lisu kao*, 150–151. *Datang kaiyuan li*, 138.13a–b, 142.13a–b.

84. Ouyang Xiu in *QSW*, 35:755.369.

85. Fan Zhen in *QSW*, 40:868.236–237.

86. Cheng Minsheng, *Songdai wujia yanjiu*, 465–466.

87. Sima Guang, *Simashi shuyi*, 7.85.

88. Liu Zhi in *QSW*, 77:1678.121.

89. Shen Gua in *QSW*, 78:1694.17–18.

90. Yin Zhu in *QSW*, 28:590.101.

91. Lü Tao in *QSW*, 74:1613.100.

92. Yin Zhu in *QSW*, 28:590.121–122.

93. Qiang Zhi in *QSW*, 67:1455.171–172.

94. Li Zhaoqi in *QSW*, 121:2615.242–245.

95. Su Song in *QSW*, 62:1347.103.

96. Lü Tao in *QSW*, 74:1614.110.

97. Yin Zhu in *QSW*, 28:589.94.

98. Chen Shunyu in *QSW*, 70:1535.334–5.

99. Ibid., 70:1535.337–338.

100. Chao Buzhi in *QSW*, 127:2744.118.

101. Yin Zhu in *QSW*, 28:590.123–124.

102. Ibid.

103. Ibid.

104. Sima Guang in *QSW*, 56:1226.273–276.

105. Ibid., 56:1226.274–275.

106. Ibid., 56:1226.275–276.

107. Ibid.

108. There were precedents from earlier periods. Yan Zhitui (531–590s), for example, left specific instructions about his own burial, including the items that he did and did not want in his tomb. Dien, "Instructions for the Grave."

109. Yang Yi in *QSW*, 15:300.59; Hu Su in *QSW*, 22:468.224, 22:468.231–232; Song Qi in *QSW*, 25:529.147, 25:529.149–150; Yu Jing in *QSW*, 27:574.139.

110. Fan Zhongyan in *QSW*, 19:388.35.

111. Song Qi in *QSW*, 25:529.149–150.

112. Shen Gua in *QSW*, 78:1696.42.

113. Su Song in *QSW*, 62:1345.76.

114. Song Qi in *QSW*, 25:528.129.

115. Ibid., 25:529.159.

116. Fan Zhen in *QSW*, 40:872.297–298.

117. Su Song in *QSW*, 62:1345.76.

118. Song Qi in *QSW*, 25:529.159.

119. Ebrey, *Confucianism and Family Rituals*, 89–92.

120. *Datang kaiyuan li*, chapters 141, 145, 149.

121. For some examples, see Su Shunqin in *QSW*, 41:880.119; Liu Ban in *QSW*, 69:1506.231; Li Zhaoqi in *QSW*, 121:2615.244–246, 121:2616.253, 121:2616.258, 121:2616.263–264.

122. Li Zhaoqi in *QSW*, 121:2615.244–246.

123. Ibid., 121:2616.263–264. For more similar cases, see Chao Buzhi in *QSW*, 127:2746.142–145, 127:2746.153.

124. Chao Buzhi in *QSW*, 127:2746.145–146.

125. For some legal disputes among local families, see *Minggong shupan qingming ji*.

126. Zhu Changwen in *QSW*, 93:2024.147.

127. For a sample of such references, see *SS*, 295.9847, 314.10276, 314.10293, 329.10603, 334.10736; Yu Jing in *QSW*, 27:574.132.

128. It is not surprising that one of the major concerns of the charitable estate that Fan Zhongyan established in his native place of Suzhou was burial- and ritual-related. Twitchett, "The Fan Clan's Charitable Estate."

129. Han Qi in *QSW*, 40:853.28–30, 860.128–131; Lü Tao in *QSW*, 74:1614.120–121.

130. Ouyang Xiu in *QSW*, 34:714.1.

131. Ibid., 32:674.3–16.

132. Ibid., 32:674.13.

133. Ibid., 32:674.14.

134. Ibid., 35:749.273–277.

135. Zeng Gong in *QSW*, 58:1272.307.

136. Li Shu in *QSW*, 28:597.238.

137. Su Shi in *QSW*, 88:1902.45, 88:1920.426–427, 88:1921.436. 89:1930.154.

138. Ibid., 88:1921.449, 89:1929.150, 89:1930.165.

139. Su Xiangxian, *Chengxiang Weigong tanxun*, 3.1136.

140. Hu Su in *QSW*, 22:466.217.

141. Ding Chuanjing, *Songren yishi huibian*, 10.497–498.

142. Chao Buzhi in *QSW*, 127:2747.170.

143. Liu Anshang in *QSW*, 138:2968.11–17.

144. Lü Tao in *QSW*, 74:1614.120–121.

145. Zhang Bangwei and Zhang Min, "Liangsong houzang heyi weiran chengfeng." Xu Jijun argues that families of different financial situations chose cremation for different reasons. The wealthy chose cremation due to their belief in Buddhism, while those who were less well off had loved ones cremated due to their inability to purchase burial plots and pay for mortuary rites. Xu Jijun, *Zhongguo sangzang shi*, 425–440.

146. Song Taizu in *QSW*, 1:2.27.

147. Liu Zhi in *QSW*, 77:1680.150; Li Zhaoqi in *QSW*, 121:2606.95–96.

148. Lü Tao in *QSW*, 74:1611.67; Bi Zhongyou in *QSW*, 110:2389.225–226.

149. Ebrey, "Cremation in Sung China," 408–409.

150. Jia Tong in *QSW*, 14:279.99–100.

151. Song Qi in *QSW*, 23:488.206–208.

152. Jia Tong in *QSW*, 14:279.99–100.

153. Cheng Yi in *QSW*, 80:1756.319–320.

154. Ebrey, "Cremation in Sung China," 421–425.

155. Sima Guang in *QSW*, 56:1225.270.

156. Ibid.

157. Zheng Yaru has noted cases in the Tang when burial or co-burial was delayed due to inauspicious divination. Zheng Yaru, *Qin'en nanbao*, 149–152, 168–175.

158. See *Datang kaiyuan li*, 138.14a–16a, 142.14a–17a, 146.10b–13a; Choo, "Shall We Profane the Service of the Dead?"

159. Liu Xiangguang, *Songdai richang shenghuo zhong de busuan yu guiguai*; Liao Hsien-huei: "Experiencing the 'Lesser Arts'"; "Exploring Weal and Woe"; and "Geomancy and Burial"; Xu Jijun, *Zhongguo sangzang shi*, 453–457.

160. Liao Hsien-huei, "Exploring Weal and Woe."

161. It should be noted that some Neo-Confucians, including Zhu Xi, found value in geomancy. Ebrey: "Sung Neo-Confucian Views on Geomancy" and "The Response of the Sung State to Popular Funeral Practices."

162. Liu Kai in *QSW*, 6:128.409–411.

163. Ebrey, "Sung Neo-Confucian Views on Geomancy."

164. Sima Guang in *QSW*, 56:1219.157.

165. Ibid., 56:1219.158.

166. Ibid.

167. Cheng Yi in *QSW*, 80:1756.319–320.

168. Ibid., 80:1756.322.

169. Ibid., 80:1756.319–320, 80:1757.332–333.

170. Xu Jingheng in *QSW*, 144:3094.30–32.

171. Ibid., 144:3094.30.

172. In a few cases, Song elite men specifically instructed descendants not to rely on divination to determine their burial places. A man surnamed Mu, for example, told his son, "Do not follow popular practices; do not go against the rites; do not adhere rigidly to geomancy; do not advocate luxurious funerals." Mu Si in *QSW*, 154:3319.277.

173. Sima Guang in *QSW*, 56:1219.158.

174. C. E. Zhang, "How Long Did It Take to Plan a Funeral?"

175. Yin Zhu in *QSW*, 28:588.63.

176. Liu Caishao in *QSW*, 176:3848.85–86.

177. Su Song in *QSW*, 62:1348.111–113.

178. Ibid., 62:1349.131.

179. Ibid., 62:1351.166–167.

Chapter 4: Remembering and Commemorating

1. Qiang Zhi in *QSW*, 67:1455.174–175.

2. Ibid., 67:1455.175.

3. This brief overview is a summary of a much lengthier introduction to Ebrey, Yao, and Zhang, *Chinese Funerary Biographies*. For two major studies of *muzhiming* writing, see T. M. Davis, *Entombed Epigraphy and Commemorative Culture in Early Medieval China*, and Zhao Chao, *Gudai muzhi tonglun*.

4. Ditter, "The Commerce of Commemoration." Cheng Minsheng's voluminous study of Song consumer prices has only a brief summary of the fees for all types of remuneration for writers and calligraphers. Cheng Minsheng, *Songdai wujia yanjiu*, 359–364. When we do learn about payments for epitaphs, they often involve high-profile cases. For example, Ouyang Xiu was paid ten pairs of gold cups and saucers and two pairs of gold chopsticks for writing Wang Zeng's (978–1038) epitaph (Ding Chuanjing, *Songren yishi huibian*, 8.384), and Liu Chang (1019–1068) received 500 ounces of silver for writing Mr. Cheng's *muzhiming* (Liu Ban in *QSW*, 69:1505.221).

5. For a discussion of Han inscriptions, see Ebrey, "Later Han Stone Inscriptions," 333–336, and Brown, *The Politics of Mourning in Early China*.

6. Zhao Chao, "Stone Inscriptions of the Wei Jin Nanbeichao Period." For a study of *muzhiming* as historical sources, see Lu Yang, "Cong muzhi de shiliao fenxi zouxiang muzhi de shixue fenxi."

7. For discussions of *muzhiming* writing in the Tang and Song, see the introduction to Bossler, *Powerful Relations*; Huang Kuanchong: "Songshi yanjiu de zhongyao ziliao" and "Muzhi ziliao de shiliao jiazhi yu xianzhi"; Liu Jingzhen, "Beisong qianqi muzhi shuxie chutan"; Schottenhammer, "Characteristics of Song Epitaphs"; Shields, *One Who Knows Me*; Tackett, *The Destruction of the Medieval Chinese Aristocracy*; Tong Xiangqing, *Beisong muzhi beiming zhuanxie yanjiu*; Wang Deyi, "Songren muzhiming de shiliao jiazhi"; M. Xu, "Ancestors, Spouses, and Descendants"; Yao: "Women in Portraits" and "Women's Epitaphs in Tang China."

8. For those who did not have official ranks, land deeds were used as epitaphs. Asim, "Status Symbol and Insurance Policy."

9. Some of the most illustrious literary names of the period, such as Han Yu (768–824), Ouyang Xiu, Wang Anshi, and Huang Tingjian, were among the most prolific and highly sought-after epitaph authors. For a comparison of Han Yu and Ouyang Xiu's epitaph writing,

see Egan, *The Literary Works of Ou-yang Hsiu*, 49–63. Also see Zhu Shangshu, "Chuan Shiqian zhi fengshen, neng chushen er ruhua."

10. In this sense, epitaphs adopted the characteristics of private historiography. Franke, "Some Aspects on Chinese Private Historiography in the Thirteenth and Fourteenth Centuries."

11. Fan Zhongyan in *QSW*, 19:388.32.

12. Liu Ban in *QSW*, 69:1507.235.

13. Lü Tao in *QSW*, 74:1614.121.

14. Fan Zhongyan in *QSW*, 19:389.39.

15. Liu Yan in *QSW*, 118:2554.322–323.

16. Su Shunqin in *QSW*, 41:880.112.

17. Shen Gou in *QSW*, 74:1628.350.

18. Fan Zhongyan in *QSW*, 19:389.39. The original text appears in Confucius' *Analects*, 9.10.

19. Many epitaphs apparently did not survive. A certain Li Zhongshi, for example, was said to have been a highly sought-after epitaph writer. "Filial sons would feel fortunate if they got him to write their ancestors' inscriptions." None of Li's epitaph writings have survived. Qiang Zhi in *QSW*, 67:1455.167.

20. Of these fourteen people, six wrote for their fathers and eight for their mothers.

21. In *Intimate Memory*, Martin Huang has shown the different ways that Ming literati approached the commemoration of their parents and other family members. For two additional studies, see Carlitz, "Mourning, Personality, Display," and W. Lu, "Personal Writings on Female Relatives in the Qing Collected Works."

22. For a thorough study of the place of eulogy writing among Tang social and cultural elites, see Shields, *One Who Knows Me*.

23. Wang Yucheng in *QSW*, 8:160.155–186.

24. Yang Yi in *QSW*, 15:299–302.46–87; Hu Su in *QSW*, 22:467–470.211–256.

25. Su Song in *QSW*, 62:1340–1352.2–181.

26. Ibid., 62:1346.87.

27. Ibid., 62:1341.25.

28. Ibid. For more similar references, see Fan Zhongyan in *QSW*, 19:390.61; Zheng Xie in *QSW*, 68:1480.182, 68:1480.183. Sun Yong's epitaph work was also very popular. "If they were not successful in getting him to write their parents' or grandparents' *muzhiming* or *shendaobei*, sons and grandsons would consider themselves inadequate." Su Song in *QSW*, 62:1344.47.

29. Yang Yi in *QSW*, 15:299.36.

30. Fan Zhongyan in *QSW*, 19:390.61.

31. Chao Buzhi in *QSW*, 127:2744.122.

32. Mao Pang in *QSW*, 132:2860.316.

33. Chao Buzhi in *QSW*, 126:2718.41–42.

34. Chao Juncheng's epitaph is translated in its entirety in C. E. Zhang, "Preserving a Father's Memory."

35. Chao Buzhi in *QSW*, 126:2718.41–42.

36. Huang Tingjian in *QSW*, 108:2335.70–71.

37. Li Xin in *QSW*, 134:2885.13.

38. Su Song in *QSW*, 62:1345.72.

39. Ibid., 62:1343.41–42.

40. Xu Han in *QSW*, 145:3135.10.

41. Wang Anshi in *QSW*, 65:1416.186–187.

42. C. E. Zhang, "Bureaucratic Politics and Commemorative Biography." When factionalism plagued court politics in the mid- and late Northern Song, epitaph writing became even more politicized. As a result, both potential writers and elite families became increasingly cautious. Many people ended up being buried without an epitaph. Liu Chengguo, "Bei Song dangzheng yu beizhi xiezuo."

43. Zeng Gong in *QSW*, 57:1245.231, 57:1246.246.

44. Chen Shunyu in *QSW*, 70:1535.334–335, 337–338.

45. Ibid., 70:1535.337–338.

46. Mao Pang in *QSW*, 132:2856.235–236.

47. Ouyang Xiu in *QSW*, 34:714.5.

48. C, E. Zhang, "Bureaucratic Politics and Commemorative Biography."

49. Cai Xiang in *QSW*, 47:1010.42.

50. Li Zhaoqi in *QSW*, 121:2607.106–107.

51. Su Shi in *QSW*, 87:1894.368–9, 88:1903.69–70, 88:1907.164–165.

52. Yang Wei in *QSW*, 104:2269.51.

53. Sima Guang in *QSW*, 56:1214.61. Despite literary hyperbole, Sima Guang was telling the truth. Zhang Shunmin recorded that after Sima Guang reached forty, he stopped writing epitaphs. There were two exceptions. Sima authored the epitaphs for Lü Xianke and Liu Shu. Zhang Shunmin in *QSW*, 83:1815.302.

54. Sima Guang in *QSW*, 56:1214.40–41.

55. Ibid., 56:1214.61–62.

56. Zeng Gong in *QSW*, 57:1246.246–247.

57. Ibid.

58. Ibid.

59. Ibid.

60. Su Shi in *QSW*, 87:1893.350–351.

61. In the conversation Situ Wenzi asked Zisi, "When burying [one's parents] after one has taken off the mourning clothes, what clothes would the mourning son wear?" Zisi answered, "One mourns for three years, and he does not take off the mourning clothes until the burial. How could one have taken off the mourning clothes?" Wen Jiao in the Jin was not reappointed because he had not buried his parent. Su Shi in *QSW*, 87:1893.351.

62. Su Shi in *QSW*, 87:1893.350–351.

63. Both Zixia and Zengzi were disciples of Confucius.

64. Su Xun in *QSW*, 43:920.42–43.

65. Ibid., 43:927.186.

66. Ouyang Xiu in *QSW*, 35:751.308–309.

67. Ibid., 34:718.82.

68. Fan Zhongyan in *QSW*, 18:385.392–393.

69. Han Qi in *QSW*, 40:856.78–80.

70. Ouyang Xiu in *QSW*, 33:711.355–356.

71. C. E. Zhang, "Bureaucratic Politics and Commemorative Biography."

72. Ouyang Xiu in *QSW*, 33:699.108–109.

73. Du Yan's epigraph, just like Fan Zhongyan's aboveground stele, was about two thousand words; these were among the longest funerary biographies that Ouyang had ever authored.

74. Ouyang Xiu in *QSW*, 33:699.108. Ouyang also discussed the Yins' case with Han Qi. Ouyang Xiu in *QSW*, 33:704.192–193.

75. Ibid., 33:699.108.

76. Wang Anshi in *QSW*, 64:1390.142.

77. Ibid., 64:1390.132.

78. Ibid., 65:1419.230.

79. Shen Gou in *QSW*, 74:1628.352.

80. Ouyang Xiu in *QSW*, 35:746.226–228; Li Qingchen in *QSW*, 79:1718.74–76; Wang Anshi in *QSW*, 65:1413.135–137, 65:1414.147–149.

81. Wang Anshi in *QSW*, 65:1419.227.

82. Su Che in *QSW*, 96:2101.263–264.

83. Yu Jing in *QSW*, 27:575.145.

84. Ibid., 27:575.145–146.

85. Bi Zhongyou in *QSW*, 110:2393.294–296.

86. Wang Tinggui in *QSW*, 158:3411.236.

87. Bi Zhongyou in *QSW*, 110:2393.296.

88. Yu Jing in *QSW*, 27:575.146.

89. Qiang Zhi in *QSW*, 67:1455.168–169.

90. Sima Guang in *QSW*, 56:1225.266.

91. Ibid., 56:1212.40–41.

92. Ibid.

93. Sima Guang, *Simashi shuyi*, 7.80.

94. Wang Yang in *QSW*, 177:3875.181.

Epilogue: Filial Piety and the Elite

1. Liu Yizhong in *QSW*, 133:2870.136–137.

2. Chaffee: *The Thorny Gates of Learning in Sung China* and "Sung Education"; W. W. Lo, *An Introduction to the Civil Service of Sung China*; Hartman, "Sung Government and Politics."

3. Song Xiang in *QSW*, 20:429.404–405.

4. Song Renzong in *QSW*, 45:964.28.

5. Cheung, "Inventing a New Tradition," 87. For some important anthropological and historical works on family shrines and ancestral halls, see Chang Jianhua: *Mingdai zongzu yanjiu* and *Zongzu zhi*; Faure, *Emperor and Ancestor*; Gan, *Tangdai jiamiao lizhi yanjiu*; Freedman, *Lineage Organization in Southeastern China*; You, "Clan, Ancestral Hall, and Clan Sacrifice in the Song Dynasty."

6. For a detailed narrative of such efforts, see Han Qi's preface to his collection of his ancestors' anthologies, dated sometime after 1045. Han Qi in *QSW*, 40.853.21–22.

7. Song Renzong in *QSW*, 45:964.28.

8. The term is Robert Hymes'. Hymes proposes that Song elites participated in both a "court-centered culture" and a literati (*shi*)-oriented culture. During the Southern Song, *shi*-oriented culture "grew in relative weight in elite lives, even for those who gained high office." Hymes, "Sung Society and Social Change," 627–634.

9. Bossler, *Powerful Relations*; R. L. Davis, *Court and Family in Sung China*; S. Lee, *Negotiated Power*; C. E. Zhang, *Transformative Journeys*.

10. Ebrey, *The Inner Quarters*.

11. Bossler, *Courtesans, Concubines, and the Cult of Female Fidelity*.

12. For a general discussion of family property issues in the Tang and Song, see Li Shuyuan, *Zhengcai jingchan*.

13. Egan, "Su Shih's 'Notes' as a Historical and Literary Source," 574–575.

14. Wang Zishen in *QSW*, 120:2594.270–271.

15. Ibid.

16. Ibid.

17. For some examples, see *QSS*, 56.626, 56.627, 58.650, 67.762, 67.768, 216.2485, 216.2490, 272.2466, 349.4324, 349.4330, 350.4356, 463.5618, 860.9988, 867.10090–10091.

18. Ebrey, *Confucianism and Family Rituals in Imperial China*.

19. Su Xun in *QSW*, 43:927.164–165, 927.174–185.

20. Han Qi in *QSW*, 40:853.22.

21. Twitchett, "The Fan Clan's Charitable Estate," 97–133.

22. For some major studies, see Brook, "Funerary Ritual and the Building of Lineages in Late Imperial China"; Chow, *The Rise of Confucian Ritualism in Late Imperial China*; Ebrey, "The Early Stages in the Development of Descent Group Organization"; Faure: *Emperor and Ancestor* and "The Lineage as a Cultural Invention"; Feng, *Zhongguo gudai de zongzu yu citing*; He Shuyi, *Xianghuo*; McDermott, *The Making of a New Rural Order in South China*; Szonya, *Practicing Kinship*; Xing: *Songdai jiating yanjiu* and "Songdai de mutian"; Xu Shaojin and Chen Yanbin, *Zhongguo jiaxun shi*; Xu Yangjie, *Song Ming jiazu zhidu shilun*; Zhu Ruixi, *Songdai shehui yanjiu*.

23. Hugh Clark finds that kin groups in the Mulan Valley in Fujian were compiling genealogies in the tenth century and setting up ancestral shrines of one sort or another in the same period. Clark: *Portrait of a Community* and "Reinventing the Genealogy."

24. For comprehensive treatments of the Confucian revival in the Tang and Song, see Bol, *Neo-Confucianism in History*; Hartman, *Han Yü and the T'ang Search for Unity*; Tillman, *Confucian Discourse and Chu Hsi's Ascendancy*.

BIBLIOGRAPHY

Primary Sources

Bao Zheng 包拯. *Bao Zheng ji jiaozhu* 包拯集校註. Hefei: Huangshan shushe, 1999.

Confucius 孔子. *Lunyu* 論語. Translated by Burton Watson. New York: Columbia University Press, 2007.

Datang kaiyuan li 大唐開元禮. Beijing: Minzu chubanshe, 2000.

de Bary, William, and Irene Bloom, eds. *Sources of Chinese Tradition*, vol. 1. New York: Columbia University Press, 1999.

Ding Chuanjing 丁傳靖. *Songren yishi huibian* 宋人軼事彙編. Beijing: Zhonghua shuju, 1981.

Dou Yi 竇儀. *Song xing tong* 宋刑統. Annotated by Xue Meiqing 薛梅卿. Beijing: Falu chubanshe, 1999.

Durrant, Stephen, Wai-yee Li, and David Schaberg, trans. *Zuozhuan* 左傳 (Zuo Tradition: Commentary on the *Spring and Autumn Annals*), vol. 1. Seattle: University of Washington Press, 2016.

Fang Xuanling 房玄齡. *Jinshu* 晉書. Beijing: Zhonghua shuju, 1974.

Han Feizi 韓非子. *Han Feizi* 韓非子. Annotated by Gao Huaping 高華平, Wang Qizhou 王齊洲, and Zhang Sanxi 張三夕. Beijing: Zhonghua shuju, 2010.

Ivanhoe, Philip J., and Bryan W. Van Norden, eds. *Readings in Classical Chinese Philosophy*. Cambridge, MA: Hackett Publishing, 2005.

Knechtges, David R., trans. *Wen Xuan* 文選 *or Selections of Refined Literature*. Princeton, NJ: Princeton University Press, 1996.

Liji Zhengyi 禮記正義. Annotated by Li Xueqin 李學勤. Beijing: Beijing daxue chubanshe, 1999.

Mengzi (Mencius) 孟子. *Mengzi* 孟子. Ttranslated by D. C. Lau as *Mencius, A Bilingual Edition*. Hong Kong: Hong Kong University Press, 2003.

Minggong shupan qingming ji 名公書判清明集. Beijing: Zhonghua shuju, 1987. For selected translations, see *Enlightened Judgments: The Ch'ing-ming Chi: The Sung Dynasty Collection* by Brian E. McKnight and James T. C. Liu. Albany: State University of New York Press, 1999.

Mozi 墨子. *Mozi* 墨子. Annotated by Fang Yong 方勇. Beijing: Zhonghua shuju, 2015.

Quan Song shi 全宋詩 (*QSS*). Edited by Beijing daxue guwenxian yanjiusuo. Beijing: Beijing daxue chubanshe, 1986–1998.

Quan Song wen 全宋文 (*QSW*). Edited by Zeng Zaozhuang 曾棗莊 and Liu Lin 劉琳.

Shanghai and Hefei: Shanghai shiji chuban youxian gongsi, Shanghai cishu chu-
    banshe, Anhui chuban jituan, Anhui jiaoyu chubanshe, 2006.
Quan Tang wen xinbian 全唐文新編. Edited by Zhou Shaoliang 周绍良. Changchun: Jilin
    wenshi chubanshe, 1999.
Shen Yue 沈约. *Songshu* 宋書. Beijing: Zhonghua shuju, 1974.
Sima Guang 司馬光. *Jiafan* 家範. *Siku quanshu* edition.
———. *Simashi shuyi* 司馬氏書儀. *Congshu jicheng* edition.
Song da zhaoling ji 宋大詔令集. Beijing: Zhonghua shuju, 1962.
Songshi (SS) 宋史, by Tuo Tuo 脫脫 et al. Beijing: Zhonghua shuju, 1977.
Su Xiangxian 蘇象先. *Chengxiang Weigong tanxun* 丞相魏公譚訓. In *Su Weigong wenji*
    蘇魏公文集. Beijing: Zhonghua shuju, 1988.
Song Minqiu 宋敏求. *Tang dazhaoling ji* 唐大詔令集. Beijing: Zhonghua shuju, 2008.
Wang Yong 王栐. *Yan yi yi mou lu* 燕翼詒謀錄. Beijing: Zhonghua shuju, 1981.
Wang Zhi 王铚. *Moji* 默記. Beijing: Zhonghua shuju, 1981.
Zhang Huang 章潢 and Fan Lai 範淶, comps. *Wanli xinxiu Nanchang fushi* 萬歷新修南
    昌府志. 1588.
Watson, Burton, trans. *The Analects of Confucius*. New York: Columbia University Press,
    2007.
Xiaojing 孝經. Translated by Patricia Ebrey. In *Images of Women in Chinese Thought and
    Culture*, edited by Robin R. Wang, 372–380. Cambridge, MA: Hackett Publishing,
    2003.
Xu Song 徐松. *Song huiyao jigao (SHY)* 宋會要輯稿. Beijing: Zhonghua shuju, 1957.
Xunxi 荀子. *Xunzi* 荀子. Annotated by Fang Yong 方勇 and Li Bo 李波. Beijing: Zhong-
    hua shuju, 2011.
Zhang Duanyi 張端義. *Gui er ji* 贵耳集. Beijing: Zhonghua shuju, 1958.
Zhangsun Wuji 長孫無忌. *Tanglü shuyi* 唐律疏議. Annotated by Liu Junwen 劉俊文.
    Beijing: Zhonghua shuju, 1983.
Zhongguo gudai xiaodao ziliao xuanbian 中國古代孝道資料選編. Compiled and edited
    by Luo Chenglie 駱承烈. Jinan: Shandong daxue chubanshe, 2003.
Zhu Xi 朱熹. *Jiali* 家禮. In *Zhuzi quanshu* 朱子全書 (27 volumes), vol. 7. Shanghai and
    Hefei: Shanghai guji chubanshe and Anhui jiaoyu chubanshe, 2000.

Secondary Sources

Asim, Ina. "Status Symbol and Insurance Policy: Song Land Deeds for the Afterlife." In
    Kuhn, *Burial in Song China*, 307–371.
Bai Shouyi 白壽彝. *Zhongguo tongshi, di qi juan, Wudai Liao Song Xia Jin shiqi* 中國通史,
    第七卷, 五代遼宋夏金時期. Shanghai: Shanghai renmin chubanshe, 1999.
———. *Zhongguo tongshi, di san juan, shanggu shiqi* 中國通史, 第三卷, 上古時期. Shang-
    hai: Shanghai renmin chubanshe, 1994.
Barnhart, Richard M. "The *Classic of Filial Piety* in Chinese Art History." In *Li Kung-lin's
    Classic of Filial Piety*, edited by Richard M. Barnhart, 73–155. New York: Metro-
    politan Museum of Art, 1993.

———, ed. *Li Kung-lin's Classic of Filial Piety*. New York: Metropolitan Museum of Art, 1993.

Bernhardt, Kathryn. "The Inheritance Rights of Daughters: The Song Anomaly?" *Modern China* 21, no. 3 (1995): 269–309.

———. *Women and Property in China, 960–1949*. Stanford, CA: Stanford University Press, 1999.

Birdwhistell, Anne D. "Cultural Patterns and the Way of Mother and Son: An Early Qing Case." *Philosophy East and West* 42, no. 3 (1992): 503–516.

Birge, Bettine. *Women, Property, and Confucian Reaction in Sung and Yüan China*. Cambridge: Cambridge University Press, 2004.

Bloom, Irene, and Joshua A. Fogel, eds. *Meetings of Mind: Festshrift for W. T. Chan and Wm. T. de Bary*. New York: Columbia University Press, 1997.

Bokenkamp, Stephen R. *Ancestors and Anxiety: Daoism and the Birth of Rebirth in China*. Berkeley: University of California Press, 2009.

Bol, Peter. *Neo-Confucianism in History*. Cambridge, MA: Harvard University Asia Center, 2010.

———. "The Rise of Local History: History, Geography, and Culture in Southern Song and Yuan Wuzhou." *Harvard Journal of Asiatic Studies* 61, no. 1 (2001): 37–76.

———. "The Sung Examination System and the Shih." *Asia Major* (series 3) 3, no. 2 (1990): 149–171.

———. *This Culture of Ours: Intellectual Tradition in T'ang and Sung China*. Stanford, CA: Stanford University Press, 1992.

Bossler, Beverly. *Courtesans, Concubines, and the Cult of Female Fidelity*. Cambridge, MA: Harvard University Asia Center, 2016.

———. "A Daughter Is a Daughter All Her Life: Affinal Relations and Women's Networks in Song and Late Imperial China." *Late Imperial China* 21, no. 1 (2000): 77–106.

———. *Powerful Relations: Kinship, Status, and the State in Sung China*. Cambridge, MA: Council on East Asian Studies, Harvard University, 1998.

———. "Men, Women, and Gossip in Song China." In *Idle Talk: Gossip and Anecdote in Traditional China*," edited by Jack W. Chen and David Schaberg, 154–177. Berkeley: University of California Press, 2014.

———. "Shifting Identities: Courtesans and Literati in Song China." *Harvard Journal of Asiatic Studies* 62, no. 1 (2002): 8–28.

Brashier, K. E. *Ancestral Memory in Early China*. Cambridge, MA: Harvard University Asia Center, 2011.

Brook, Timothy. "Funerary Ritual and the Building of Lineages in Late Imperial China." *Harvard Journal of Asiatic Studies* 49, no. 2 (1989): 465–499.

Brown, Miranda. "Mothers and Sons in Warring States and Han China, 453 B.C.–A.D. 220." *Nan Nü: Men, Women and Gender in Early and Imperial China* 5, no. 2 (2003): 137–169.

———. *The Politics of Mourning in Early China*. Albany: State University of New York Press, 2007.

Brown, Miranda, and Anna-Alexandra Fodde-Reguer. "Rituals without Rules: Han Dynasty Mourning Practices Revisited." In Rothschild and Wallace, *Behaving Badly in Early and Medieval China*, 91–105. Honolulu: University of Hawai'i Press, 2017.

Buoye, Thomas. "Filial Felons: Leniency and Legal Reasoning in Qing China." In *Writing and Law in Late Imperial China: Crime, Conflict, and Judgment*, edited by Robert Hegel and Katherine Carlitz, 109–124. Seattle: University of Washington Press, 2009.

Cai Shangxiang 蔡上翔. *Wang Jinggong nianpu kaolue* 王荊公年譜考略. In *Wang Anshi nianpu sanzhong* 王安石年譜三種. Shanghai: Shanghai renmin chubanshe, 1954.

Carlitz, Katherine. "Mourning, Personality, Display: Ming Literati Commemorate Their Mothers, Sisters, and Daughters." *Nan Nü: Men, Women and Gender in Early and Imperial China* 15, no. 1 (2013): 30–68.

Chaffee, John W. "Sung Education: Schools, Academies, and Examinations." In Chaffee and Twitchett, *The Cambridge History of China*, vol. 5, part 2: "Sung China, 960–1279," 286–320. Cambridge: Cambridge University Press, 2015.

———. *The Thorny Gates of Learning in Sung China: A Social History of Examinations*. Cambridge: Cambridge University Press, 1985.

Chaffee, John W., and Denis Twitchett, eds. *The Cambridge History of China*, vol. 5, part 2: "Sung China, 960–1279." Cambridge: Cambridge University Press, 2015.

Chan, Alan K. "Does *Xiao* Come before *Ren*?" In Chan and Tan, *Filial Piety in Chinese Thought and History*, 154–175. London: RoutledgeCurson, 2004.

Chan, Alan K., and Sor-hoon Tan, eds. *Filial Piety in Chinese Thought and History*. London: RoutledgeCurson, 2004.

———. "Introduction." In Chan and Tan, *Filial Piety in Chinese Thought and History*, 1–11. London: RoutledgeCurson, 2004.

Chang Jianhua 常建華. *Mingdai zongzu yanjiu* 明代宗族研究. Shanghai: Shanghai renmin chubanshe, 2005.

———. *Zongzu zhi* 宗族誌. Shanghai: Shanghai renmin chubanshe, 1998.

Chang Kuang-chih. *The Archeology of Ancient China*. New Haven: Yale University Press, 1968.

Chaves, Jonathan. *Mei Yao-ch'en and the Development of Early Sung Poetry*. New York: Columbia University Press, 1976.

Chen Dengwu 陳登武, ed. *Diyu, falu, renjian zhixu: Zhongguo zhonggu zongjiao, shehui yu guojia* 地獄, 法律, 人間秩序: 中國中古宗教, 社會與國家. Taipei: Wunan tushu, 2009.

———. "Falu yu jiaohua: Ershisi xiao gushi suojian jianei zhixu yu guojia tongzhi 法律與教化: 二十四孝故事所見家內秩序與國家統治." In Chen Dengwu, *Diyu, falu, renjian zhixu*, 171–225.

———. "Fuchou xinshi: Cong huangquan de jiaodu zailun Tang Song fuchou ge'an 復雠新釋: 從皇權的角度再論唐宋復雠個案." *Taiwan shida lishi xuebao* 31 (2003): 1–36.

Chen Huawen 陳華文. *Sangzang shi* 喪葬史. Shanghai: Shanghai wenyi chubanshe, 2007.

Chen, Kenneth. "Filial Piety in Chinese Buddhism." *Harvard Journal of Asiatic Studies* 28, no. 1 (1968): 81–97.

Chen Lai 陳來. *Gudai zongjiao yu lunli: Rujia sixiang de genyuan* 古代宗教与倫理: 儒家思想的根源. Beijing: Sanlian shudian, 1996.

Chen Lüsheng 陳履生 and Lu Zhihong 陸志宏. *Gansu de Song Yuan huaxiangzhuan* 甘肅的宋元畫像磚. Beijing: Renmin meishu chubanshe, 1996.

Chen Ruoshui 陳弱水. *Tangdai wenshi yu Zhongguo sixiang de zhuanxing* 唐代文士与中國思想的轉型. Guilin: Guangxi shifan daxue chubanshe, 2009.

Chen, Song. "The State, the Gentry, and Local Institutions: The Song Dynasty and Long-Term Trends from Tang to Qing." *Journal of Chinese History* 1, no. 1 (2017): 141–182.

Chen Yifeng 陳一風. *Xiaojing zhushu yanjiu* 《孝經注疏》研究. Chengdu: Sichuan daxue chubanshe, 2007.

Cheng, Anne. "Filial Piety with a Vengeance: The Tension between Rites and Law in the Han." In Chan and Tan, *Filial Piety in Chinese Thought and History*, 29–43.

Cheng Minsheng 程民生. *Songdai wujia yanjiu* 宋代物价研究. Beijing: Renmin chubanshe, 2008.

Cheng Yi 程義. "Songdai mushi bihua yanjiu zongshu 宋代墓室壁畫研究綜述." *Shaanxi lishi bowuguan guankan* 22 (2015): 211–222.

Cheung, Hiu Yu 程曉宇. "Inventing a New Tradition: The Revival of the Discourses of Family Shrines in the Northern Song." *Journal of Sung Yuan Studies* 47 (2017): 85–136.

Chia, Lucille. *Printing for Profit: The Commercial Publishers of Jianyang, Fujian (11th to 17th Centuries)*. Cambridge, MA: Harvard University Asia Center, 2002.

Choi, Mihwa. *Death Rituals and Politics in Northern Song China*. Oxford: Oxford University Press, 2017.

Choo, Jessey. "Shall We Profane the Service of the Dead? Burial Divination and Remembrance in Late Medieval *Muzhiming*." *Tang Studies* 33 (2015): 1–37.

———. "That 'Fatty Lump': Discourses on the Fetus, Fetal Development, and Filial Piety in Early Imperial China." *Nan Nü: Men, Women and Gender in Early and Imperial China* 14, no. 2 (2012): 177–221.

Chow, Kai-wing. *The Rise of Confucian Ritualism in Late Imperial China: Ethics, Classics, and Lineage Discourse*. Stanford, CA: Stanford University Press, 1994.

Clark, Hugh R. "The Fu of Minnan: A Local Clan in Late Tang and Song China (9th–13th Centuries)." *Journal of the Economic and Social History of the Orient* 38, no. 1 (1995): 1–74.

———. *Portrait of a Community: Society, Culture, and the Structures of Kinship in the Mulan River (Fujian) from the Late Tang through the Song*. Hong Kong: Chinese University Press, 2007.

———. "Reinventing the Genealogy: Innovation in Kinship Practice in the Tenth and Eleventh Centuries." In *The New and the Multiple: Sung Sense of the Past*, edited by Thomas H. C. Lee, 237–286. Hong Kong: Chinese University Press, 2004.

Cline, Erin M. *Families of Virtue: Confucian and Western Views on Childhood Development*. New York: Columbia University Press, 2015.

Cole, Alan. *Mothers and Sons in Chinese Buddhism*. Stanford, CA: Stanford University Press, 1998.

Crowell, William G. "Northern Emigres and the Problems of Census Registration under the Eastern Jin and Southern Dynasties." In Dien, *State and Society in Early Medieval China*, 171–209.

Davis, Edward L. *Society and the Supernatural in Song China*. Honolulu: University of Hawai'i Press, 2001.

Davis, Richard L. "Chaste and Filial Women in Chinese Historical Writing of the Eleventh Century." *Journal of the American Oriental Society* 121, no. 1 (2001): 204–218.

———. *Court and Family in Sung China, 960–1279: Bureaucratic Success and Kinship Fortunes for the Shih of Mingchou*. Durham, NC: Duke University Press, 1986.

———. "Political Success and the Growth of Descent Groups: The Shihs of Ming-chou during the Sung." In Ebrey and Watson, *Kinship Organization in Late Imperial China, 1000–1940*, 62–94.

———. "Review of *Negotiated Power: The State, Elites, and Local Governance in Twelfth-to Fourteenth-Century China*, by Sukhee Lee." *Harvard Journal of Asiatic Studies* 77, no. 1 (2017): 227–235.

Davis, Timothy M. *Entombed Epigraphy and Commemorative Culture in Early Medieval China: A History of Early Muzhiming*. Leiden: Brill, 2015.

De Bary, W. T., and John Chaffee, eds. *Neo-Confucian Education: The Formative Stage*. Berkeley: University of California Press, 1989.

De Weerdt, Hilde. *Competition over Content: Negotiating Standards for the Civil Service Examinations in Imperial China*. Cambridge, MA: Harvard University Asia Center, 2007.

Deng Fei 鄧菲. "Guanyu Song Jin muzang zhong xiaoxing tu de sikao 關於宋金墓葬中孝行圖的思考." *Zhongyuan wenwu* 4 (2009): 75–81.

———. "Modular Design of Tombs in Song and Jin North China." In Ebrey and Huang, *Visual and Material Cultures in Middle Period China*, 41–81.

———. "Song Jin shiqi zhuandiao bihuamu de tuxiang ticai tanxi 宋金時期磚雕壁画的圖像題材探析." In *Gudai muzang meishu yanjiu, di yi ji* 古代墓葬美術研究, 第一輯, edited by Wu Hung 巫鴻 and Zheng Yan 鄭巖, 285–312. Beijing: Wenwu chubanshe, 2011.

———. *Zhongyuan beifang diqu Song Jin muzang yishu yanjiu* 中原北方地區宋金墓葬藝術研究. Beijing: Wenwu chubanshe, 2019.

Deng Xiaonan 鄧小南. *Songdai wenguan xuanren zhidu zhu cengmian* 宋代文官選任制度諸層面. Shijiazhuang: Hebei jiaoyu chubanshe, 1993.

Dien, Albert E. "Instructions for the Grave: The Case of Yan Zhitui." *Cahiers d'Extrême-Asie* 8 (1995): 41–58.

———, ed. *State and Society in Medieval China*. Stanford, CA: Stanford University Press, 1990.

Ding Jianjun 丁建軍 and Jia Yafang 賈亞方. "Jianlun Songdai dingyou zhidu dui guanyuan shitu de yingxiang 简論宋代丁憂制度對官員仕途的影響." *Dalian daxue xuebao* 34, no. 2 (2013): 31–34.

Ding Linghua 丁凌華. *Zhongguo sangfu zhidu shi* 中國喪服制度史. Shanghai: Shanghai renmin chubanshe, 2000.

Ditter, Alexei. "The Commerce of Commemoration: Commissioned *Muzhiming* in the Mid- to Late Tang." *Tang Studies* 32 (2014): 21–46.

Du Juan 杜鵑. "1978 nian yilai *Xiaojing* yangjiu 1978 年以來《孝經》研究." *Zhongguoshi yanjiu dongtai* 3 (2008): 2–7.

Dudbridge, Glen. *The Legend of Miaoshan*, revised edition. Oxford: Oxford University Press, 2004.

Ebrey, Patricia Buckley. *The Aristocratic Families of Early Imperial China: A Case Study of the Po-ling Ts'ui Family*. Cambridge: Cambridge University Press, 1978.

———. *Chu Hsi's Family Rituals: A Twelfth Century Chinese Manual for the Performance of Cappings, Weddings, Funerals, and Ancestral Rites*. Translated with annotations and introduction. Princeton, NJ: Princeton University Press, 1991.

———, trans. *The Classic of Filial Piety*. In Robin Wang, *Images of Women in Chinese Thought and Culture*, 372–380.

———. "Conceptions of the Family in Song Times." *Journal of Asiatic Studies* 43, no. 2 (1984): 219–245.

———. "Concubines in Sung China." *Journal of Family History* 11, no. 1 (1986): 1–24.

———. *Confucianism and Family Rituals in Imperial China: A Social History of Writing about Rites*. Princeton, NJ: Princeton University Press, 1991.

———. "Cremation in Sung China." *American Historical Review* 95, no. 2 (1990): 406–428.

———. "The Dynamics of Elite Domination in Sung China." *Harvard Journal of Asiatic Studies* 48, no. 2 (1988): 493–519.

———. "The Early Stages in the Development of Descent Group Organization." In Ebrey and Watson, *Kinship Organization in Late Imperial China*, James Watson, 16–61.

———. "Education through Ritual: Efforts to Formulate Family Rituals during the Sung Period." In de Bary and Chaffee, *Neo-Confucian Education*, 277–306.

———. *Family and Property in Sung China: Yuan Tsai's Precepts for Social Life*. Princeton, NJ: Princeton University Press, 1984.

———. "Imperial Filial Piety as a Political Problem." In Chan and Tan, *Filial Piety in Chinese Thought and History*, 122–140.

———. *The Inner Quarters, Marriage and the Lives of Chinese Women in the Sung Period*. Berkeley: University of California Press, 1993.

———. "Introduction." In *Marriage and Inequality in Chinese Society*, edited by Ruby Watson and Patricia Ebrey, 1–24. Berkeley: University of California Press, 1991.

———. "Later Han Stone Inscriptions." *Harvard Journal of Asiatic Studies* 40, no. 2 (1980): 325–353.

———. "Liturgies for Ancestral Rites in Successive Versions of the *Family Rituals*." In *Ritual and Scripture in Chinese Popular Religion: Five Studies*, edited by David Johnson, 104–136. Berkeley: Center for Chinese Studies, University of California, 1995.

———. "The Response of the Sung State to Popular Funeral Practices." In Ebrey and Gregory, *Religion and Society in T'ang and Sung China*, 209–239.

———. "Sung Neo-Confucian Views on Geomancy." In Bloom and Fogel, *Meetings of Mind*, 75–107.

———. "The Women in Liu Kezhuang's Family." *Modern China* 10, no. 4 (1984): 415–440.

Ebrey, Patricia, and Peter Gregory, eds. *Religion and Society in T'ang and Sung China.* Honolulu: University of Hawai'i Press, 1993.

Ebrey, Patricia, and Susan Shih-shan Huang, eds. *Visual and Material Cultures in Middle Period China.* Leiden: Brill, 2017.

Ebrey, Patricia, and Paul Smith, eds. *State Power in China, 600–1400.* Seattle: University of Washington Press, 2016.

Ebrey, Patricia, and James L. Watson, eds. *Kinship Organization in Late Imperial China.* Berkeley: University of California Press, 1986.

Ebrey, Patricia, Ping Yao, and Cong Ellen Zhang, eds. *Chinese Funerary Biographies: An Anthology of Remembered Lives.* Seattle: University of Washington Press, 2019.

Egan, Ronald. *The Literary Works of Ou-yang Hsiu (1007–72).* Cambridge: Cambridge University Press, 1984.

———. *The Problem of Beauty: Aesthetic Thought and Pursuits in Northern Song Dynasty China.* Cambridge, MA: Harvard University Asia Center, 2006.

———. "Su Shih's 'Notes' as a Historical and Literary Source." *Harvard Journal of Asiatic Studies* 50, no. 2 (1990): 561–588.

Eicher, Sebastian. "Early Representations of Filial Piety in Dynastic Historiography: Textual History and Content of *Hou Han Shu* Chapter 39." *Journal of Chinese History* 3, no. 1 (2019): 1–33.

Epstein, Maram. "Making a Case: Characterizing the Filial Son." In Hegel and Carlitz, *Writing and Law in late Imperial China*, 27–43. Seattle: University of Washington Press, 2009.

Fang Yan 方燕. "Songdai nuxing gegu liaoqin wenti shixi 宋代女性割股疗親問題試析." *Qiusuo* 11 (2007): 210–212.

Faure, David. *Emperor and Ancestor: State and Lineage in South China.* Stanford, CA: Stanford University Press, 2007.

———. "The Lineage as a Cultural Invention: The Case of the Pearl River Delta." *Modern China* 15, no. 1 (1989): 4–36.

Fei Chengkang 費成康. *Zhongguo de jiafa zugui* 中國的家法族規. Shanghai: Shanghai shehui kexueyuan chubanshe, 2002.

Feng Erkang 馮尔康. *Zhongguo gudai de zongzu yu citing* 中國古代的宗族與祠堂. Beijing: Shangwu yinshuguan, 1996.

Fong, Grace S. "Inscribing a Sense of Self in Mother's Family: Hong Liangji's (1746–1809) Memoir and Poetry of Remembrance." *Chinese Literature: Essays, Articles, Reviews* 27 (2005): 33–58.

Franke, Herbert. "Some Aspects on Chinese Private Historiography in the Thirteenth and Fourteenth Centuries." In *Historians of China and Japan*, edited by W. G. Beasley and E. G. Pulleyblank, 115–135. London: Oxford University Press, 1961.

Freedman, Maurice. *Lineage Organization in Southeastern China.* London: Athlone, 1958.

Fu Hongchu. "The Cultural Fashioning of Filial Piety: A Reading of 'Xiaozhang tu.'" *Journal of Sung-Yuan Studies* 29 (1999): 63–89.

Furth, Charlotte. "The Patriarch's Legacy: Household Instructions and the Transmission of Orthodox Values." In *Orthodoxy in Late Imperial China*, edited by Kwang-ching Liu, 187–211. Berkeley: University of California Press, 1990.

Gan Huaizhen 甘懷真. *Tangdai jiamiao lizhi yanjiu* 唐代家廟禮制研究. Taipei: Taiwan Shangwu yinshuguan, 1991.

Gerritsen, Anne. *Ji'an Literati and the Local in Song-Yuan-Ming China.* Leiden: Brill, 2007.

Gu Donggao 顧棟高. *Wang Jingguo wengong nianpu* 王荊國文公年譜. In *Wang Anshi nianpu sanzhong* 王安石年譜三種. Beijing: Zhonghua shuju, 1994.

Haboush, Jahyun Kim. "Filial Emotions and Filial Values: Changing Patterns in the Discourse of Filiality in Late Chosŏn Korea." *Harvard Journal of Asiatic Studies,* 55, no. 1 (1995): 129–177.

Halperin, Mark Robert. *Out of the Cloister: Literati Perspectives on Buddhism in Sung China, 960–1279.* Cambridge, MA: Harvard University Asia Center, 2006.

Han Guihua 韓桂華. "Muzhiming zhong suojian Songdai guanyuan guizang wenti 墓誌銘中所見宋代官員歸葬問題." *Zhongguo lishi xuehui shixue jikan* 38 (2006): 119–144.

Hansen, Valerie. *Negotiating Daily Life in Traditional China: How Ordinary People Used Contracts, 800–1400.* New Haven: Yale University Press, 1995.

———. "Why Bury Contracts in Tombs?" *Cahiers d'Extrême-Asie* 8 (1995): 59–66.

Hargett, James M. "Song Dynasty Local Gazetteers and Their Place in the History of *Difangzhi* Writing." *Harvard Journal of Asiatic Studies* 56, no. 2 (1996): 405–442.

Hartman, Charles. *Han Yü and the T'ang Search for Unity.* Princeton, NJ: Princeton University Press, 1986.

———. "Poetry and Politics in 1079: The Crow Terrace Poetry Case of Su Shih." *Chinese Literature: Essays, Articles, Reviews* 12 (1990): 15–44.

———. "Sung Government and Politics." In Chaffee and Twitchett, *The Cambridge History of China,* vol. 5, part 2: "Sung China, 907–1279," 19–138.

Hartwell, Robert. "Demographic, Political, and Social Transformations in China, 750–1550." *Harvard Journal of Asiatic Studies* 42, no. 2 (1982): 365–442.

He Shuyi 何淑怡. *Xianghuo: Jiangnan shiren yu Yuan Ming shiqi jizu chuantong de jiangou* 香火: 江南士人與元明時期祭祖傳統的建構. Banqiao: Daoxiang chubanshe, 2009.

He Zhongli 何忠禮. *Keju yu Songdai shehui* 科舉與宋代社會. Beijing: Shangwu yinshuguan, 2006.

Hegel, Robert, and Katherine Carlitz, eds. *Writing and Law in Late Imperial China: Crime, Conflict, and Judgment.* Seattle: University of Washington Press, 2009.

Ho, Clara Wing-chung, ed. *Overt and Covert Treasures: Essays on the Sources for Chinese Women's History.* Hong Kong: Chinese University Press, 2012.

Holzman, Donald. "The Place of Filial Piety in Ancient China." *Journal of the American Oriental Society* 118, no. 2 (1998): 185–199.

Hong, Jeehee. "Changing Roles of the Tomb Portrait: Burial Practices and Ancestral Worship of Non-Literati Elite in North China (1000–1400)." *Journal of Song-Yuan Studies* 44 (2014): 203–264.

———. "Mechanism of Life for the Netherworld: Transformations of *Mingqi* in Middle-Period China." *Journal of Chinese Religions* 43, no. 2 (2015): 161–193.

———. *Theater for the Dead: A Social Turn in Funerary Art, 1000–1400.* Honolulu: University of Hawai'i Press, 2016.

Hu Yunwei 胡雲薇. "Qianli huanyou cheng dishi, meinian fengjing shi taxiang: Shilun Tangdai de huanyou yu jiating 千里宦遊成底事, 每年風景是他鄉: 試論唐代的宦遊與家庭." *Taida lishi xuebao* 41 (2008): 65–107.

Huai Jianli 淮建利. "Beisong Shaanzhou Louzeyuan shibing muzhiwen yanjiu: Yi fanhao muzhiwen wei zhongxin 北宋陝州漏澤園士兵墓誌文研究, 以番號墓誌文爲中心." *Zhongguoshi yanjiu* 2 (2013): 87–108.

Huang Chunyi 黃純怡. "Tang Song shiqi de Fuchou: Yi zhengshi anli weizhu de kaocha 唐宋時期的復讎: 以正史案例為主的考察." *Xingda lishi xuebao* 10 (2000): 1–19.

Huang Kaiguo 黃開國. "Lun Rujia de xiao xueshuo 論儒家的孝學説." In *Zhongghua xiaodao wenhua* 中華孝道文化, edited by Wan Bengen 萬本根 and Chen Deshu 陳德述, 44–61. Chengdu: Bashu shushe, 2001.

Huang Kuanchong 黃寬重. "Muzhi ziliao de shiliao jiazhi yu xianzhi: Yi liangjian Songdau muzhi ziliao weili 墓誌資料的史料價值與限制: 以兩件宋代墓誌資料为例." *Dongwu daxue lishi xuebao* 10 (2003): 19–37.

———. "Renji wangluo, shehui wenhua huodong yu lingxiu diwei de jianli—yi Songdai Siming Wangshi jiazu wei zhongxin de guancha 人際網絡, 社會文化活動與領袖地位的建立—以宋代四明汪氏家族為中心的考察." *Taiwan daxue lishi xuebao* 24 (1999): 225–256.

———. *Songdai de jiazu yu shehui* 宋代的家族與社會. Taipei: Dongda tushu gufen youxian gongsi, 2006.

———. "Songdai Siming shizu renji wangluo yu shehui wenhua huodong—yi Loushi jiazu wei zhongxin de kaocha 宋代四明士族人際網絡與社會文化活動—以樓氏家族為中心的考查." *Zhongyang yanjiuyuan lishi yuyan yanjiusuo jikan* 30, no. 3 (1999): 627–669.

———. "Songshi yanjiu de zhongyao ziliao: Yi dalu diqu chutu Songren muzhi siliao weili 宋史研究的重要史料: 以大陸地區出土宋人墓誌資料為例, *Xin shixue* 9, no. 2 (1998): 143–185.

Huang, Martin W. *Intimate Memory: Gender and Mourning in Late Imperial China.* Albany: State University of New York Press, 2018.

———. *Negotiating Masculinities in Late Imperial China.* Honolulu: University of Hawai'i Press, 2006.

Hymes, Robert. "Marriage, Descent Groups, and the Localist Strategy." In Ebrey and Watson, *Kinship Organization in Late Imperial China*, 95–136.

———. *Statesmen and Gentlemen: The Elite of Fu-Chou, Chiang-hsi in Northern and Southern Sung.* Cambridge: Cambridge University Press, 1986.

———. "Sung Society and Social Change." In Chafee and Twitchett, *The Cambridge History of China*, vol. 5, part 2: "Sung China, 907–1279," 526–664.

Hymes, Robert, and Conrad Schirokauer, eds. *Ordering the World: Approaches to State and Society in Sung Dynasty China.* Berkeley: University of California Press, 1993.

Idema, Wilt, trans. *Filial Piety and Its Divine Rewards: The Legend of Dong Yong and Weaving Maiden, with Related Texts.* Cambridge, MA: Hackett Publishing, 2009.

———, trans. *Personal Salvation and Filial Piety: Two Precious Scroll Narratives of Guanyin and Her Acolytes*. Honolulu: University of Hawai'i Press, 2008.

Ikels, Charlotte, ed. *Filial Piety: Practice and Discourse in Contemporary East Asia*. Stanford, CA: Stanford University Press, 2004.

Ji Naili 季乃禮. *Sangang liuji yu shehui zhenghe, cong Baihutong kan Handai shehui renlun guanxi* 三綱六紀與社會整合: 從白虎通看漢代社會人倫關係. Beijing: Zhongguo renmin daxue chubanshe, 2004.

Ji Xiao-bin. *Politics and Conservatism in Northern Song China: The Career and Thought of Sima Guang*. Hong Kong: Chinese University Press, 2005.

Jia, Jinhua, Xiaofei Kang, and Ping Yao, eds. *Gendering Chinese Religion: Subject, Identity, and Body*. Albany: State University of New York Press, 2014.

Jiang Yuxiang 江玉祥. "Songdai muzang chutu de ershisi xiao tuxiang bushi 宋代墓葬出土的二十四孝圖像補釋." *Sichuan wenwu* 4 (2001): 22–33.

Jin Zhongshu 金中樞. "Songdai jizhong shehui fuli zhidu: Juyang yuan, anji yuan, louzeyuan 宋代幾種社會福利制度: 居養院, 安济坊, 漏泽園." In *Songshi yanjiu ji, di shiba ji* 宋史研究集, 第十八輯, edited by Taiwan Songshi zuotanhui 臺灣宋史座談會, 145–198. Taibei: Guoli bianyiguan, 1987.

———. "Songdai keju zhidu yanjiu 宋代科舉制度研究." In *Songshi yanjiu ji, di shi yi ji* 宋史研究集, 第十一集, vol. 11, edited by Songshi yanjiu hui, 1–71. Taibei: Zhonghua congshu biancuan weiyuanhui, 1979.

———. "Songdai keju zhidu yanjiu 宋代科舉制度研究." In *Songshi yanjiu ji, di shi er ji* 宋史研究集, 第十二集, vol. 12, edited by Songshi yanjiu hui, 31–112. Taibei: Zhonghua congshu biancuan weiyuanhui, 1980.

Johnson, David G. *The Medieval Chinese Oligarchy*. Boulder, CO: Westview Press, 1977.

Kahn, Harold L. "The Politics of Filiality: Justification for Imperial Action in Eighteenth Century China." *Journal of Asian Studies* 26, no. 2 (1967): 197–203.

Kang Xuewei 康學偉. *Xianqin xiaodao yanjiu* 先秦孝道研究. Taipei: Wenjin chubanshe, 1992.

Keightley, David N. "Art, Ancestor, and the Origins of Writing in China." *Representations* 56 (1996): 68–95.

———. "The Making of the Ancestors: Late Shang Religion and Its Legacy." In *Religion and Chinese Society*, vol. 1: *Ancient and Medieval China*, edited by John Lagerwey, 3–63. Hong Kong: Chinese University Press, 2004.

Kieschnick, John. *The Impact of Buddhism on Chinese Material Culture*. Princeton, NJ: Princeton University Press, 2003.

Kindall, Elizabeth. *Geo-Narratives of a Filial Son: The Paintings and Travel Diaries of Huang Xiangjian (1609–1673)*. Cambridge, MA: Harvard University Asia Center, 2017.

———. "The Paintings of Huang Xiangjian's Filial Journey to the Southwest." *Artibus Asiae* 67, no. 2 (2007): 297–357.

Kinney, Anne Behnke, ed. *Chinese Views of Childhood*. Honolulu: University of Hawai'i Press, 1995.

———. "Dyed Silk: Han Notions of the Moral Development of Children." In Kinney, *Chinese Views of Childhood*, 17–56.

——. *Exemplary Women of Early China: The Lienü zhuan of Liu Xiang.* New York: Columbia University Press, 2014.

——. "The Theme of the Precocious Child in Early Chinese Literature." *T'oung Pao*, Second Series, 81, nos. 1–3 (1995): 1–24.

Knapp, Keith N. "Borrowing Legitimacy from the Dead: The Confucianization of Ancestral Worship." In *Early Chinese Religion*, part 2: "The Period of Division (220–589 AD)," edited by John Lagerwey and Lü Pengzhi, 143–192. Leiden: Brill, 2010.

——. "Chinese Filial Cannibalism: A Silk Road Import?" In *China and Beyond in the Mediaeval Period: Cultural Crossings and Inter-Regional Connections*, edited by Dorothy C. Wong and Gustav Heldt, 135–149. Singapore: Institute of Southeast Asian Studies, and Amherst, NY: Cambria Press, 2014.

——. "Creeping Absolutism: Parental Authority in Early Medieval Tales of Filial Offspring." *Confucian Cultures of Authority*, edited by Roger T. Ames and Peter D. Hershock, 65–91. Albany: State University of New York Press, 2006.

——. "Reverent Caring: The Parent-Son Relationship in Early Medieval Tales of Filial Offspring." In Chan and Tan, *Filial Piety in Chinese Thought and History*, Alan K. L. Chan, 44–70.

——. "The *Ru* Reinterpretation of *Xiao.*" *Early China* 20 (1995): 195–222.

——. *Selfless Offspring: Filial Children and the Social Order in Medieval China.* Honolulu: University of Hawai'i Press, 2005.

——. "Sympathy and Severity: The Father-Son Relationship in Early Medieval China." *Extrême-Orient Extrême-Occident Hors-série* (2012): 113–136.

——. "There Are Maggots in My Soup! Medieval Accounts of Unfilial Children." In Rothschild and Wallace, *Behaving Badly in Early and Medieval China*, 19–38.

Kohn, Livia. "Immortal Parents and Universal Kin: Family Values in Medieval Daoism." In Chan and Tan, *Filial Piety in Chinese Thought and History*, 91–109.

Kuhn, Dieter, ed. *Burial in Song China.* Heidelberg: Ed. Forum, 1994.

——. "Decoding Tombs of the Song Elite." In Kuhn, *Burial in Song China*, 11–159.

Kutcher, Norman. *Mourning in Late Imperial China: Filial Piety and the State.* Cambridge: Cambridge University Press, 1999.

Kyan, Winston. "The Body and the Family: Filial Piety and Buddhist Art in Late Medieval China." PhD diss., University of Chicago, 2006.

——. "Family Space: Buddhist Materiality and Ancestral Fashioning in Mogao Cave 231." *Art Bulletin* 92, nos. 1–2 (2010): 61–82.

Lai Guolong. *Excavating the Afterlife: The Archeology of Early Chinese Religion.* Seattle: University of Washington Press, 2015.

Laing, Ellen Johnston. "Auspicious Motifs in Ninth- to Thirteenth-Century Chinese Tombs." *Ars Orientalis* 33 (2003): 32–75.

Lau Nap-yin 柳立言. "Cong Zhao Ding *Jiaxun bilu* kan Nansong Zhedong de yige shidafu jiazu 從趙鼎家訓筆錄看南宋浙東的一個士大夫家族." In *Songshi yanjiu ji, di ershisi ji* 宋史研究集, 第二十四集," edited by Taiwan Songshi zuotanhui 臺灣宋史座談會, 357–436. Taipei: Guoli bianyi guan, 1995.

——. "Hewei Tang Song biange 何謂唐宋變革." *Zhonghua wenshi luncong* 81 (2006): 125–171.

——. *Songdai de jiating he falü* 宋代的家庭和法律. Beijing: Shanghai guji chubanshe, 2008.

——. "Songdai de jiating jiufen yu zhongcai: Zhengcai pian 宋代的家庭糾紛與仲裁: 爭財篇." In *Songshi yanjiu ji, di ershiliu ji* 宋史研究集, 第三十集," 187–265. Taipei: Guoli bianyi guan Zhonghua Congshu Bianshen Weiyuanhui, 2000.

——. "Songdai tongju zhidu xia de suowei gongcai 宋代同居制度下的所谓 '共財'." In *Songshi yanjiu ji, di ershiqi ji* 宋史研究集, 第二十七集," edited by Taiwan Songshi zuotanhui 臺灣宋史座談會, 59–144. Taipei: Guoli bianyi guan Zhonghua, 1997.

——. "Yang'er fanglao: Songdai de falu, jiating yu shehui 养儿防老: 宋代的法律, 家庭與社會." In *Songdai de jiating yu shehui* 宋代的家庭與社會, edited by Lau Nap-yin, 375–407. Shanghai: Shanghai guji chubanshe, 2008.

Lee, Jen-der 李貞德. "Han Tang zhijian jiating zhong de jiankang zhaogu yu xingbie 漢唐之間家庭中的健康照顧與性別." In *Xingbie yu yiliao* 性別與醫療, edited by Huang Kewu 黄克武, 1–49. Taipei: Zhongyang yanjiuyuan jindai lishi yanjiusuo, 2002.

——. "Tangdai de xingbie yu yiliao 唐代的性別與醫療." In *Tangsong nuxing yu shehui* 唐宋女性與社會, edited by Deng Xiaonan 鄧小南, 415–446. Shanghai: Shanghai cishu chubanshe, 2003.

Lee, John. "Recent Studies in English on the Tang-Song Transition: Issues and Trends." *Guoji Zhongguo xue yanjiu* 2 (1999): 365–383.

Lee, Sukhee. *Negotiated Power: The State, Elites, and Local Governance in Twelfth- to Fourteenth-Century China.* Cambridge, MA: Harvard University Asia Center, 2014.

Lee, Thomas H. C. 李弘祺. *Government Education and Examination in Sung China.* Hong Kong: Chinese University Press, 1985.

——. "Songdai guanyuan shu de tongji 宋代官員數的統計." In *Songshi yanjiu ji, di shiba ji* 宋史研究集, 第十八集, edited by Taiwan Songshi zuotanhui 臺灣宋史座談會, 79–104. Taibei: Guoli bianyiguan, 1987.

Levine, Ari. "Che-tsung's Reign (1085–1100) and the Age of Faction." In Twitchett and Smith, *The Cambridge History of China*, vol. 5, part 1: "The Sung Dynasty and Its Precursors, 907–1279," 484–555.

——. *Divided by a Common Language: Factional Conflict in Late Northern Song China* Honolulu: University of Hawai'i Press, 2008.

——. "Faction Theory and the Political Imagination of the Northern Song." *Asia Major*, Third Series, 18, no. 2 (2005): 155–200.

——. "The Reigns of Hui-tsung (1100–1126) and Ch'in-tsung (1126–1127) and the Fall of the Northern Sung." In Twitchett and Smith, *The Cambridge History of China*, vol. 5, part 1: "The Sung Dynasty and Its Precursors, 907–1279," 556–643.

Lewis, Mark. "Mothers and Sons in Early Imperial China." *Extrême-Orient Extrême-Occident Hors-série* (2012): 245–275.

Li Chenyang. "Shifting Perspectives: Filial Morality Revisited." *Philosophy East and West* 47, no. 2 (1997): 211–232.

Li Guilu 李貴录. *Beisong Sanhuai Wangshi jiazu yanjiu* 北宋三槐王氏家族研究. Jinan: Qilu shushe, 2004.

Li Huarui 李華瑞. *Tang Song biange lun de youlai yu fazhan* 唐宋變革論的由來與發展. Tianjin: Tianjin guji chubanshe, 2010.

———. *Wang Anshi bianfa yanjiu shi* 王安石變法研究史. Beijing: Renmin chubanshe, 2004.

Li Shuyuan 李淑媛. *Zhengcai jingchan: Tang Song de jiachan yu falu* 爭財競產: 唐宋的家產与法律. Beijing: Beijing daxue chubanshe, 2007.

Liang Gengyao 梁庚尧. "Jiazu hezuo, shehui shengwang yu difang gongyi: Songyuan Siming qiangqu yitian de yuanqi yu yanbian 家族合作, 社會聲望, 與地方公益: 宋元四明鄉曲義田的源起與演變." In *Songshi yanjiu ji, di san ji* 宋史研究集, 第三十四集," edited by Taiwan Songshi zuotanhui 臺灣宋史座談會, 375–418. Taipei: Guoli bianyi guan Zhonghua Congshu Bianshen Weiyuanhui, 2004.

Liang Hongsheng 梁洪生. "Songdai Jiangxi muzhi jiqi sangqi kao 宋代江西墓志及其喪期考." *Nanfang wenwu* 1 (1989): 88–94.

Liao Hsien-huei 廖咸惠. "Experiencing the 'Lesser Arts': The Mantic Arts and Experts in the Lives of Song Literati." *New History* 20, no. 4 (2009): 1–58.

———. "Exploring Weal and Woe: The Song Elite's Mantic Beliefs and Practices." *T'oung Pao* 91, nos. 4–5 (2005): 347–395.

———. "Geomancy and Burial: The Social Status of the Song Geomancers." *Studies in Urban Cultures* 10 (2008): 96–115.

Liao Yifang 廖宜方. *Tangdai de muzi guanxi* 唐代的母子關係. Taipei: Daoxiang chubanshe, 2009.

Lin Anhong 林安弘. *Rujia xiaodao sixiang yanjiu* 儒家孝道思想研究. Taipei: Wenjin chubanshe, 1992.

Lin, Wei-cheng. "Underground Wooden Architecture in Brick: A Changed Perspective from Life to Death in 10th through 13th Century China." *Archives of Asian Art* 61 (2011): 3–36.

Liu Chengguo 劉成國. "Bei Song dangzheng yu beizhi xiezuo 北宋黨爭與碑志寫作." *Wenxue pinglun* 3 (2008): 35–42.

Liu Houqin 劉厚琴 and Tian Yun 田雲. "Handai buxiao rulü yanjiu 漢代不孝入律研究." *Qilu xuekan* 4 (2009): 39–44.

Liu, James T. C. *Reform in Sung China: Wang An-shi (1021–1086) and His New Policies.* Cambridge, MA: Harvard University Press, 1959.

Liu Jingzhen 劉靜貞. "Beisong qianqi muzhi shuxie chutan 北宋前期墓誌書寫初探." *Dongwu lishi xuebao* 11 (2004): 58–82.

Liu Sha 劉莎. "Handai weixiao qufa xianxiang de fali fenxi 漢代爲孝屈法的法理分析." *Shehui zhong de fali* 1 (2013): 44–60.

Liu Xiangguang 劉祥光. *Songdau richang shenghuo zhong de busuan yu guiguai* 宋代日常生活中的卜算與鬼怪. Taipei: Chengchi daxue chubanshe, 2013.

Lo, Winston W. *An Introduction to the Civil Service of Sung China, with Emphasis on Its Personnel Administration.* Honolulu: University of Hawai'i Press, 1987.

Lo, Yuet Keung. "Filial Devotion for Women: A Buddhist Testimony from Third-Century China." In Chan and Tan, *Filial Piety in Chinese Thought and History*, 71–90.

Lorge, Peter. *The Unification of China: Peace through War under the Song Dynasty.* Cambridge: Cambridge University Press, 2018.

Lü Miaofen (Lü Miaw-fen) 呂妙芬. "Ming Qing Zhongguo wanli xunqin de wenhua shi-jian 明清中國萬里尋親的文化實踐." *Zhongyang yanjiuyuan lishi yuyan yanjiusuo jikan* 78, no. 2 (2007): 359–406.

Lu, Tina. *Accidental Incest, Filial Cannibalism, and Other Peculiar Encounters in Late Imperial Chinese Literature*. Cambridge, MA: Harvard University Asia Center, 2009.

Lu, Weijing. "Personal Writings on Female Relatives in the Qing Collected Works." In Ho, *Overt and Covert Treasures*, 403–426.

_____. *True to Her Word: The Faithful Maiden Cult in Late Imperial China*. Stanford, CA: Stanford University Press, 2008.

Lu Yang 陸揚. "Cong muzhi de shiliao fenxi zouxiang muzhi de shixue fenxi: Yi xinchu Wei Jin Nanbeichao muzhi shuzheng wei zhongxin 從墓誌的史料分析走向墓誌的史學分析: 以《新出魏晉南北朝墓誌疏証》為中心." *Zhonghua wenshi luncong* 84, no. 4 (2006): 96–127.

Lu Yilong 陸益龍. *Zhongguo lidai jiali* 中國歷代家禮. Beijing: Beijing Tushuguan chu-banshe, 1998.

Luo Jiaxiang 羅家詳. *Pengdang zhizheng yu Beisong zhengzhi* 朋黨之爭與北宋政治. Wuhan: Huazhong shida chubanshe, 2002.

Luo, Manling. "Gender, Genre, and Discourse: The Woman Avenger in Medieval Chinese Texts." *Journal of the American Oriental Society* 134, no. 4 (2014): 579–599.

Luo Yinan. "A Study of the Changes in the Tang-Song Transition Model." *Journal of Song-Yuan Studies* 35 (2005): 99–127.

Mann, Susan. *Precious Records: Women in China's Long Eighteenth Century*. Stanford, CA: Stanford University Press, 1997.

Mather, Richard. "Filial Paragons and Spoiled Brats: A Glimpse of Medieval Chinese Children in the *Shishuo xinyu*." In Kinney, *Chinese Views of Childhood*, 111–126.

McDermott, Joseph P. "Family Financial Plans of the Southern Sung." *Asia Major*, third series, 9, no. 2 (1991): 15–52.

——. *The Making of a New Rural Order in South China*, vol. 1: *Village, Land, and Lineage in Huizhou, 900–1600*. Cambridge: Cambridge University Press, 2013.

——. "Women of Property in China, 960–1368: A Survey of the Scholarship." *International Journal of Asian Studies* 1, no. 2 (2004): 201–222.

McGrath, Michael. "The Reigns of Jen-tsung (1022–1063) and Ying-tsung (1063–1067)." In Twitchett and Smith, *The Cambridge of China*, vol. 5, part 1: "The Sung Dynasty and Its Precursors, 907–1279," 279–346.

McKnight, Brian E. *Law and Order in Sung China*. Cambridge: Cambridge University Press, 1992.

——. "Who Gets It When You Go: The Legal Consequences of the Ending of Households." *Journal of the Economic and Social History of the Orient* 43, no. 3 (2000): 314–363.

Miao Chunde 苗春德. *Songdai jiaoyu* 宋代教育. Kaifeng: Henan daxue chubanshe, 1992.

Miao Shumei 苗書梅. "Songdai guanyuan huibi fa shulun宋代官員迴避法述論." *Henan daxue xuebao* 31, no. 1 (1991): 24–30.

———. *Songdai guanyuan xuanren he guanli zhidu* 宋代官員選任和管理制度. Kaifeng: Henan daxue chubanshe, 1996.

Morgan, Carole. "Inscribed Stones: A Note on a Tang and Song Dynasty Burial Rite." *T'oung Pao*, Second Series, 82, nos. 4–5 (1996): 317–348.

Murray, Julia K. "The '*Ladies' Classic of Filial Piety*' and Sung Textual Illustration: Problems of Reconstruction and Artistic Context." *Ars Orientalis* 18 (1988): 95–129

Niu Mingshi 牛銘實. *Zhongguo lidai xiangyue* 中國歷代鄉約. Beijing: Zhongguo shehui chubanshe, 2005.

Nylan, Michael. "Confucian Piety and Individualism in Han China." *Journal of the American Oriental Society* 116, no. 1 (1996): 1–27.

Olberding, Amy. "I Know Not 'Seems': Grief for Parents in *The Analects*." In Olberding and Ivanhoe, *Mortality in Traditional Chinese Thought*, 153–175.

Olberding, Amy, and Philip J. Ivanhoe, eds. *Mortality in Traditional Chinese Thought*. Albany: State University of New York Press, 2011.

Pu Moo-chou 蒲慕洲. "Handai bozang lun de lishi beijing jiqi yiyi 漢代薄葬論的歷史背景及其意義." *Bulletin of the Institute of History and Philology* 61, no. 1 (1990): 533–573.

———. "Ideas Concerning Death and Burial in Pre-Han and Han China." *Asia Major*, third series, 3, no. 2 (1990): 25–62.

———. *In Search of Personal Welfare: A View of Ancient Chinese Religion*. Albany: State University of New York Press, 1998.

———. "Lun Zhongguo gudai muzang xingzhi 論中國古代墓葬形制." *Taiwan daxue wenshi zhexue bao* 37 (1989): 235–279.

———. *Muzang yu shengsi: Zhongguo gudai zongjiao zhi xingsi* 墓葬與生死: 中國古代宗教之省思. Beijing: Zhonghua shuju, 2008.

———. "Preparation for the Afterlife." In Olberding and Ivanhoe, *Mortality in Traditional Chinese Thought*, 13–36.

Puett, Michael. "The Offering of Food and the Creation of Order: The Practice of Sacrifice in Early China." In Sterckx, *Of Tripod and Palate*, 75–95.

Qiu Zhonglin 邱仲麟. "Buxiao zhi xiao: Tang yilai gegu liaoqin xianxiang de shehuishi chutan 不孝之孝: 唐以來割股療親現象的社會史初探." *Xin shixue* 6, no. 1 (1995): 49–92.

Radice, Thomas. "Confucius and Filial Piety." In *A Concise Companion to Confucius*, edited by Paul R. Goldin, 185–207. Hoboken, NJ: Wiley-Blackwell, 2017.

———. "The Ways of Filial Piety in Early China." PhD diss., University of Pennsylvania, 2006.

Raphals, Lisa. "Reflections on Filial Piety, Nature, and Nurture." In Chan and Tan, *Filial Piety in Chinese Thought and History*, 215–225.

Rosemont, Henry, Jr., and Roger Ames, trans. *The Chinese Classic of Family Reverence: A Philosophical Translation of the Xiaojing*. Honolulu: University of Hawai'i Press, 2011.

Rothschild, N. Harry, and Leslie V. Wallace, eds. *Behaving Badly in Early and Medieval China*. Honolulu: University of Hawai'i Press, 2017.

Schottenhammer, Angela. "Characteristics of Song Epitaphs." In Kuhn, *Burial in Song China*, 253–306.

Shaanxi sheng kaogu yanjiuyuan 陝西省考古研究院. "Lüshi jiazu mudi 呂氏家族墓地." *Kaogu* 8 (2010): 46–52.

Shen Qinsong 沈勤松. *Beisong wenren yu dangzheng* 北宋文人與黨爭. Beijing: Renmin chubanshe, 1998.

Shields, Anna. "Grieving for a Married Daughter and a Grandson: 'Entombed Epitaph Inscription for My Daughter the Late Madame Dugu' and 'Entombed Record for My Grandson Who Died Young,' by Quan Deyu (759–818)." In Ebrey, Yao, and Zhang, *Diverse Lives: An Anthology of Chinese Funerary Biographies*, 66–74.

———. *One Who Knows Me: Friendship and Literary Culture in Mid-Tang China*. Cambridge, MA: Harvard University Asia Center, 2015.

Smith, Paul Jakov. "Anatomies of Reform: The Qingli-Era Reforms of Fan Zhongyan and the New Policies of Wang Anshi Compared." In Ebrey and Smith, *State Power in China, 900–1400*, 153–191.

———. "A Crisis in the Literati State: The Sino-Tangut War and the Qingli-Era Reforms of Fan Zhongyan." *Journal of Song Yuan Studies* 45 (2015): 59–138.

———. "Shen-tsung's Reign and the New Policies of Wang An-shih, 1067–1085." In Twitchett and Smith, *The Cambridge History of China*, vol. 5, part 1: "The Sung Dynasty and Its Precursors, 907–1279," 347–483.

———. *Taxing Heaven's Storehouse: Bureaucratic Entrepreneurship and the Sichuan Tea and Horse Trade, 1074–1224*. Cambridge, MA: Harvard University Press, 1991.

Smith, Paul, and Richard von Glahn. "Introduction: Problematizing the Song-Yuan-Ming Transition." In Smith and von Glahn, *The Song-Yuan-Ming Transition in Chinese History*, 1–34.

———, eds. *The Song-Yuan-Ming Transition in Chinese History*. Cambridge, MA: Harvard University Asia Center, 2003.

Stahl, Helga. "Su Shi's Orthodox Burial: Interconnected Double Chamber Tombs in Sichuan." In Kuhn, *Burial in Song China*, 161–214.

Sterckx, Roel, ed. *Of Tripod and Palate: Food, Politics, and Religion in Traditional China*. New York: Palgrave, 2005.

Su Bai 宿白. *Baisha Songmu* 白沙宋墓. Beijing: Wenwu chubanshe, 1957.

Su Pinxiao 粟品孝. "Songdai jiazu yanjiu lunzhu mulu 宋代家族研究論著目錄." *Songdai wenhua yanjiu* 8 (1999): 305–311.

———. "Songdai jiazu yanjiu lunzhu mulu xuyi 宋代家族研究論著目錄續一." *Songdai wenhua yanjiu* 14 (2006): 822–833.

Sugano, Noriko. "State Indoctrination of Filial Piety in Tokogawa Japan: Sons and Daughters in the *Official Record of Filial Piety*." In *Women and Confucian Culture in Premodern China, Korea, and Japan*, edited by Dorothy Ko, Jahyun Kim Haboush, and Joan R. Piggot, 170–189. Berkeley: University of California Press, 2003.

Szonya, Michael. *Practicing Kinship: Lineage and Descent in Late Imperial China*. Stanford, CA: Stanford University Press, 2002.

Tackett, Nicolas. *The Destruction of the Medieval Chinese Aristocracy.* Cambridge, MA: Harvard University Asia Center, 2014.

Tan, Sor-hoon. "Filial Daughters-in-Law: Questioning Confucian Filiality." In Chan and Tan, *Filial Piety in Chinese Thought and History,* 226–240.

Tang Changru 唐長儒. "Du Yanshi jiaxun, houqu pian lun nanbei dishu shenfen de chayi 讀《顏氏家訓後娶篇》論南北嫡庶身份的差異." In Tang, *Tang Changru shehui wenhua shi luncong,* 101–112.

———. *Tang Changru shehui wenhua shi luncong* 唐長儒社會文化史論叢. Wuhan: Wuhan daxue chubanshe, 2001.

———. "Wei Jin Nanchao de junfu xianhou lun 魏晉南朝的君父先後論." In Tang, *Tang Changru shehui wenhua shi luncong,* 86–100.

Tao, Jing-shen 陶晉生. *Beisong shizu: Jiazu, hunyin, shenghuo* 北宋士族: 家族, 婚姻, 生活. Taipei: Zhongyang yanjiuyuan lishi yuyan yanjiusuo, 2001.

Teiser, Stephen. *The Ghost Festival in Medieval China.* Princeton, NJ: Princeton University Press, 1996.

Tian Xin 田欣. *Songdai shangren jiating* 宋代商人家庭. Beijing: Shehui kexue wenxian chubanshe, 2013.

Tillman, Hoyt. *Confucian Discourse and Chu Hsi's Ascendancy.* Honolulu: University of Hawai'i Press, 1992.

———. *Utilitarian Confucianism: Ch'en Liang's Challenge to Chu Hsi.* Cambridge, MA: Harvard University Asia Center, 1982.

Tong Xiangqing 仝相卿. *Beisong muzhi beiming zhuanxie yanjiu* 北宋墓誌碑銘撰寫研究. Beijing: Zhongguo shehui kexue chubanshe, 2019.

Tsao, Hsingyuan. *Differences Preserved: Reconstructed Tombs from the Liao and Song Dynasties.* Seattle: University of Washington Press, 2000.

Twitchett, Denis. "The Fan Clan's Charitable Estate, 1050–1760." In *Confucianism in Action,* edited by David S. Nivison and Arthur F. Wright, 97–133. Stanford, CA: Stanford University Press, 1959.

Twitchett, Denis, and Paul Jakov Smith, eds. *The Cambridge History of China,* vol. 5, part 1: "The Sung Dynasty and Its Precursors, 907–1279." Cambridge: Cambridge University Press, 2009.

Übelhör, Monika. "The Community Compact (*hsiang-yüeh*) of the Sung and Its Educational Significance." In de Bary and Chaffee, *Neo-Confucian Education,* 371–388.

Von Eschenbach, Silvia Freiin Ebner. "Public Graveyards of the Song Dynasty." In Kuhn, *Burial in Song China,* 215–251.

Waltner, Ann. *Getting an Heir: Adoption and the Construction of Kinship in Late Imperial China.* Honolulu: University of Hawai'i Press, 1990.

Walton, Linda. *Academies and Society in Southern Sung China.* Honolulu: University of Hawai'i Press, 1999.

———. "Charitable Estates as an Aspect of Statecraft in the Southern Sung." In Hymes and Schirokauer, *Ordering the World,* 255–278.

Wang Deyi 王德毅. "Songdai de Chengdu Fanshi jiqi shixi 宋代的成都范氏及其世系." In *Songshi yanjiu ji, di ershijiu ji* 宋史研究集, 第二十九集, edited by Taiwan Songshi zuotanhui 臺灣宋史座談會, 513–536. Taipei: Guoli bianyi guan Zhonghua Congshu Bianshen Weiyuanhui, 1999.

———. "Songdai de Henei Xiangshi jiqi zuxi 宋代的河內向氏及其族系." In *Songshi yanjiu ji, di ershiliu ji* 宋史研究集, 第二十六集, edited by Taiwan Songshi zuotanhui 臺灣宋史座談會, 373–398. Taipei: Guoli bianyi guan Zhonghua Congshu Bianshen Weiyuanhui, 1997.

———. "Songdai de Shangcai Zushi jiqi shixi 宋代的上蔡祖氏及其世系." In *Songshi yanjiu ji, di sanshiyi ji* 宋史研究集, 第三十一集, edited by Taiwan Songshi zuotanhui 臺灣宋史座談會, 137–150. Taipei: Lantai chubanshe, 2002.

———. "Songdai de yanglao yu ciyou 宋代的養老與慈幼." *Songshi yanjiu ji, di liu ji* 宋史研究集, 第六集, edited by Taiwan Songshi zuotanhui 臺灣宋史座談會, 399–428. Taipei: Guoli bianyiguan, 1971.

———. "Songren muzhiming de shiliao jiazhi 宋人墓誌銘的史料價值." *Dongwu lishi xuebao* 東吳歷史學報 12 (2004): 1–24.

Wang Lihua 王利華. *Zhongguo jiating shi, Xianqin zhi Nanbeichao shiqi* 中國家庭史, 先秦至南北朝時期. Guangzhou: Guangdong renmin chubanshe, 2007.

Wang, Robin, ed. *Images of Women in Chinese Thought and Culture: Writings from the Pre-Qin Period through the Song Dynasty*. Cambridge, MA: Hackett Publishing, 2003.

Wang Sanqing 王三慶. "*Dunhuang bianwen ji* zhong de *Xiaozi zhuan* xintan 《敦煌變文集》中的《孝子傳》新探." *Dunhuang xue* 14 (1989): 189–220.

Wang Shanjun 王善軍. "Jiafa yu gongcai: Songdai Raoyang Lishi jiazu tanxi 家法與共財: 宋代饒阳李氏家族探析." *Zhongguo shehui lishi pinglun* 9 (2008): 89–102.

———. *Songdai zongzu he zongzu zhidu yanjiu* 宋代宗族和宗族制度研究. Shijiazhuang: Hebei jiayu chubanshe, 2000.

Wei Wenbin 魏文斌, Shi Yanling 師彥靈, and Tang Xiaojun 唐曉軍. "Gansu Songjin mu 'Ershisi xiao' tu yu Dunhuang yishu *Xiaozi zhuan* 甘肅宋金墓二十四孝圖與敦煌遺書《孝子傳》." *Dunhuan yanjiu* 3 (1998): 75–90.

Wolf, Arthur, and Chieh-shan Huang. *Marriage and Adoption in China, 1845–1945*. Stanford, CA: Stanford University Press, 1980.

Wu Chongshu 吳崇恕 and Li Shouyi 李守義. *Xiao wenhua yanjiu* 孝文化研究. Beijing: Zhongguo kexue wenhua chubanshe, 2006.

Wu Fanming 吳凡明. *Cong renlun zhixu dao falu zhixu: Xiaodao yu handai fazhi yanjiu* 從人倫秩序到法律秩序: 孝道與漢代法律研究. Changchun: Jilin renmin chubanshe, 2008.

Wu Hung. *The Art of the Yellow Springs: Understanding Chinese Tombs*. Honolulu: University of Hawai'i Press, 2010.

———. "Private Love and Public Duty: Images of Children in Early Chinese Art." In Kinney, *Chinese Views of Childhood*, 79–110.

———. *The Wu Liang Shrine: The Ideology of Early Chinese Pictorial Art*. Stanford, CA: Stanford University Press, 1992.

Wu, Pei-yi. "Childhood Remembered: Parents and Children in China, 800–1700." In Kinney, *Chinese Views of Childhood*, 129–156.

———. "Education of Children in the Sung." In de Bary and Chaffee, *Neo-Confucian Education*, 307–324.

Wu Songdi 吳松弟. *Zhongguo yimin shi, di san juan, Sui Tang Wudai shiqi* 中國移民史, 第三卷, 隋唐五代時期. Fuzhou: Fujian renmin chubanshe, 1997.

Wu Zongguo 吳宗國. *Tangdai keju zhidu yanjiu* 唐代科舉制度研究. Shenyang: Liaoning daxue chubanshe, 1997.

Wyatt, Don. *The Recluse of Loyang: Shao Yung and the Moral Evolution of Early Sung Thought*. Honolulu: University of Hawai'i Press, 1996.

Xiao Qunzhong 肖群忠. *Xiao yu zhongguo wenhua* 孝與中國文化. Beijing: Renmin chubanshe, 2001.

Xing Tie 邢鐵. *Jiachan jicheng shilun* 家產繼承史論. Kuning: Yunnan daxue chubanshe, 2001.

———. "Songdai de mutian 宋代的墓田." *Hebei shifan daxue xuebao* 32, no. 5 (2009): 120–126.

———. *Songdai jiating yanjiu* 宋代家庭研究. Shanghai: Shanghai renmin chubanshe, 2005.

———. *Zhongguo jiating shi, Song Liao Jin Yuan shiqi* 中國家庭史, 宋遼金元時期. Guangzhou: Guangdong renmin chubanshe, 2007.

Xu Jijun 徐吉軍. *Zhongguo sangzang shi* 中國喪葬史. Nanchang: Jiangxi gaoxiao chubanshe, 1998.

Xu, Man. "Ancestors, Spouses, and Descendants: The Transformation of Epitaph Writing in Song Luzhou." *Journal of Sung Yuan Studies* 46 (2016): 119–168.

———. "China's Local Elites in Transition: Seventh- to Twelfth-Century Epitaphs Excavated in Luzhou. "*Asia Major*, Third Series, 30, no. 1 (2017): 59–107.

———. *Crossing the Gate: Everyday Lives of Women in Song Fujian (960–1279)*. Albany: State University of New York, 2016.

Xu Shaojin 徐少錦 and Chen Yanbin 陳延斌. *Zhongguo jiaxun shi* 中國家訓史. Xi'an: Shaanxi renmin chubanshe, 2003.

Xu Yangjie 徐揚傑. *Song Ming jiazu zhidu shilun* 宋明家族制度史論. Beijing: Zhonghua shuju, 1995.

Yan Jie 嚴傑. *Ouyang Xiu nianpu* 歐陽修年譜. Nanjing: Nanjing chubanshe, 1993.

Yan Zhongqi 顏中其. "Su Song nianbiao 蘇頌年表." In *Su Weigong wenji* 蘇魏公文集. Beijing: Zhonghua shuju, 1988.

Yang Kaidao 楊開道. *Zhongguo xiangyue zhidu* 中国乡约制度. Beijing: Shangwu yinshuguan, 2015.

Yang Shiwen 楊吉文. "Songdai *Xiaojing* xue shulun 宋代孝經學述論." In *Zhonghua xiadao wenhua* 中華孝道文化, edited by Wan Bengen 萬本根 and Chen Deshu 陳德述, 149–169. Chengdu: Bashu shushe, 2001.

Yang Shuda 楊樹達. *Handai hunsang lisu kao* 漢代婚喪禮俗考. Shanghai: Shanghai guji chubanshe, 2000.

Yao Ping. "Good Karmic Connections: Buddhist Mothers and Their Children in Tang China (618–907)." *Nan Nü: Men, Women and Gender in Early and Imperial China* 10, no. 1 (2008): 57–85.

——. "Tang Women in the Transformation of Buddhist Filiality." In Jia, Kang, and Yao, *Gendering Chinese Religion*, 25–46.

——. *Tangdai funü de shengming licheng* 唐代婦女的生命歷程. Shanghai: Shanghai guji chubanshe, 2004.

——. "Women in Portraits: An Overview of Epitaphs from Early and Medieval China." In Ho, *Overt and Covert Treasures*, 157–183.

——. "Women's Epitaphs in Tang China (618–907)." In *Beyond Exemplar Tales: Women's Biography in Chinese History*, edited by Joan Judge and Ying Hu, 139–157. Berkeley: University of California Press, 2011.

Yin, Lee Cheuk. "Emperor Chengzu and Imperial Filial Piety of the Ming Dynasty: From the *Classic of Filial Piety* to the *Biographical Accounts of Filial Piety*. In Chan and Tan, *Filial Piety in Chinese Thought and History*, 141–153.

You Biao 遊彪. "Clan, Ancestral Hall, and Clan Sacrifice in the Song Dynasty." *Frontiers of History in China* 2, no. 2 (2007): 166–180.

Yu Gengzhe 于赓哲. "Gegu fengqin yuanqi de shehui beijing kaocha: Yi Tangdai wei zhongxin 割股奉親緣起的社會背景考查, 以唐代爲中心." *Shixue yuekan* 2 (2006): 87–95.

Yu, Jimmy. *Sanctity and Self-Inflicted Violence in Chinese Religions, 1500–1700*. Oxford: Oxford University Press, 2012.

Yu Xinzhong 余新忠. *Zhongguo jiating shi, Ming Qing shiqi* 中國家庭史, 明清時期. Guangzhou: Guangdong renmin chubanshe, 2007.

Zang Zhifei 臧知非. *Renlun benyuan: "Xiaojing" yu Zhongguo wenhua* 人倫本原: 孝经與中國文化. Kaifeng: Henan daxue chubanshe, 2005.

Zhan Dahe 詹大和. *Wang Jingwengong nianpu* 王荆文公年譜. In *Wang Anshi nianpu sanzhong* 王安石年譜三種, compiled by Zhan Dahe, Gu Donggao 顧棟高 and Cai Shangxiang 蔡上翔; annotated by Beijing: Zhonghua shuju, 1994.

Zhang Bangwei 張邦煒. *Songdai hunyin jiazu shilun* 宋代婚姻家族史論. Beijing: Renmin chubanshe, 2003.

Zhang Bangwei 張邦煒 and Zhang Min 張敏. "Liangsong huozang heyi weiran chengfeng 兩宋火葬何以蔚然成風." *Sichuan daxue xuebao* 22, no. 3 (1995): 97–103.

Zhang Baojian 張保見 and Gao Qingqing 高青青. *Wang Anshi yanjiu lunzhu mulu suoyin* 王安石研究論著目録索引 (1912-2014). Chengdu: Sichuan daxue chubanshe, 2016.

Zhang, Cong Ellen 張聰. "Bureaucratic Politics and Commemorative Biography: The Epitaphs of Fan Zhongyan." In Ebrey and Smith, *State Power in China, 900–1400*, 192–216.

——. "A Friend and Political Ally: 'Funerary Inscription for Mr. Culai' by Ouyang Xiu (1007–1072)." In Ebrey, Yao, and Zhang, *Chinese Funerary Biographies*, 111–121.

——. "A Family of Filial Exemplars: The Baos of Luzhou." *Journal of Chinese Literature and Culture* 4, no. 2 (2017): 360–382.

——. "How Long Did It Take to Plan a Funeral?: Liu Kai's (947–1000) Experience Burying His Parents." *Frontier of History in China* 13, no. 4 (2018): 508–530.

——. "Negative Role Models: Unfilial Stories in Song *Biji* (Miscellaneous Writing)."

In Rothschild and Wallace, *Behaving Badly in Early and Medieval China*, 39–55.

———. "Of Revelers and Witty Conversationalists: Song (960–1279) *Biji* (Miscellaneous Writing) as Literature of Leisure." *Chinese Historical Review* 23, no. 2 (2016): 130–146.

———. "Preserving a Father's Memory: 'Funerary Inscription for Chao Juncheng' by Huang Tingjian (1045–1105)." In Ebrey, Yao, and Zhang, *Chinese Funerary Biographies*, 122–129.

———. "The Rise and Fall of a Northern Song Family: The Baos of Luzhou." *Chinese Historical Review* 20, no. 2 (2013): 138–158.

———. "Things Heard in the Past, Material for Future Use: A Study of Song (960–1279) *Biji* Prefaces." *East Asian Publishing and Culture* 6, no. 1 (2016): 22–53.

———. "To Be 'Erudite in Miscellaneous Knowledge': A Study of Song (960–1279) *Biji* Writing." *Asia Major*, third series, 25, no. 2 (2012): 43–77.

———. *Transformative Journeys: Travel and Culture in Song China*. Honolulu: University of Hawai'i Press, 2011.

Zhang Guogang 張國剛. *Jiating shi yanjiu de xin shiye* 家庭史研究的新視野. Beijing: Sanlian shudian, 2004.

———. *Zhongguo jiating shi, Sui Tang Wudai shiqi* 中國家庭史, 隋唐五代時期. Guangzhou: Guangdong renmin chubanshe, 2007.

Zhang Jingming 章景明. *Xianqin sangfu zhidu kao* 先秦喪服制度考. Taipei: Zhonghua shuju, 1971.

Zhao Chao 趙超. *Gudai muzhi tonglun* 古代墓誌通論. Beijing: Zijincheng chubanshe, 2003.

———. "Stone Inscriptions of the Wei Jin Nanbeichao Period." *Early Medieval China* 1 (1994): 84–96.

Zhao, Dingxin. "The Han Bureaucracy: Its Origin, Nature, and Development." In *State Power in Ancient China and Rome*, edited by Walter Scheidel, 56–89. Oxford: Oxford University Press, 2015.

Zhao Xiaohua 趙小華. "Tangren de xiaoqin guannian yu xiaoqin shi 唐人的孝親观念與孝親詩." *Huanan shifan daxue xuebao* 4 (2006): 45–52.

Zheng Yan 鄭巖. *Weijin Nanbeichao bihuamu yanjiu* 魏晉南北朝壁畫墓研究. Beijing: Wenwu chubanshe, 2002.

Zheng Yaru 鄭雅如. *Qin'en nanbao: Tangdai shiren de xiaodao shijian jiqi tizhihua* 親恩難報：唐代士人的孝道實踐及其體制化. Taipei: Taida chuban zhongxin, 2014.

———. *Qinggan yu zhidu: Weijin shidai de muzi guanxi* 情感與制度：魏晉時代的母子關係. Taipei: Guoli Taiwan daxue chuban weiyuanhui, 2001.

Zhou Mi 周密, *Songdai xingfa shi* 宋代刑法史. Beijing: Falu chubanshe, 2002.

Zhou, Yiqun. "The Child in Confucianism." In *Children and Childhood in World Religions: Primary Sources and Texts*, edited by Marcia Bunge and Don S. Browning, 337–392. New Brunswick, NJ: Rutgers University Press, 2009.

———. "The Status of Mothers in the Early Chinese Mourning System." *T'oung Pao* 99, nos. 1–3 (2013): 1–52.

Zhu Hai 朱海. "Tang Xuanzong yuzhu *Xiaojing* fawei 唐玄宗御注孝經發微." *Weijin Nanbeichao Suitang shi ziliao* 19 (2002): 99–108.

———. "Tang Xuanzong yuzhu *Xiaojing* kao 唐玄宗御注孝經." *Weijin Nanbeichao Suitang shi ziliao* 20 (2003): 124–135.

Zhu Lan 朱嵐. *Zhongguo chuantong xiaodao de lishi kaocha* 中國傳統孝道的歷史考察. Taipei: Lantai chubanshe, 2003.

———. *Zhongguo chuantong xiaodao sixiang fazhanshi* 中國傳統孝道思想發展史. Beijing: Guojia xingzheng xueyuan chubanshe, 2011.

Zhu, Rui. "What If the Father Commits a Crime?" *Journal of the History of Ideas* 63, no. 1 (2002): 1–17.

Zhu Ruixi 朱瑞熙. *Songdai shehui yanjiu* 宋代社會研究. Zhengzhou: Zhongzhou shuhuashe, 1983.

Zhu Shangshu 祝尚書. "Chuan Shiqian zhi fengshen, neng chushen er ruhua: Lun Ouyang Xiu beizhiwen de wenxue chengjiu 傳史遷之風神, 能出神而入化: 論歐陽修碑誌文的文學成就." In *Songdai wenhua yanjiu* 宋代文化研究, 第八輯, edited by Sichuan daxue guji zhengli Yanjiusuo and Sichuan daxue Songdai wenhua yanjiu zhongxin, 79–94. Chengdu: Bashu shushe, 1999.

Zhu Xiaoli 朱曉麗. *Chuannan Songmu shike tushi fenxi ji shuzi tapian yanjiu* 川南宋墓石刻圖式分析及數字拓片研究. Beijing: Renmin chubanshe, 2018.

Zou Qingquan 鄒清泉. *Beiwei xiaozi huaxiang yanjiu* 北魏孝子画像研究. Beijing: Wenhua yishu chubanshe, 2006.

Zu Hui 祖慧. "Songdai rongli yiyuan wenti yanjiu 宋代冗吏溢員問題研究." *Zhongguo shi yanjiu* 4 (1998): 92–100.

Zuo, Ya. "It's OK to Cry: Male Tears in Song China." Unpublished manuscript.

GLOSSARY-INDEX

ABOUT THE AUTHOR

Cong Ellen Zhang, associate professor of history at the University of Virginia, specializes in the social and cultural history of the Song dynasty (960–1279). Her major publications include *Transformative Journeys: Travel and Culture in Song China*; *Record of the Listener: Selected Stories from Hong Mai's* Yijian zhi (translator); and *Chinese Funerary Biographies: An Anthology of Remembered Lives* (coedited with Patricia Ebrey and Ping Yao).